MW00330138

ALISON SINGH GEE is an award-winning international journalist whose work has been translated into eight languages and has appeared in *People, Vanity Fair, In Style, Marie Claire, International Herald Tribune, The Wall Street Journal* and *Los Angeles Times*. For eight years, she was a staff features writer/correspondent for *People* magazine. She won the 1997 Amnesty International Award for Feature Writing for her Asiaweek cover story about child prostitution in Southeast Asia. Alison lives in Los Angeles with her husband and daughter

Praise for *Where the Peacocks Sing*

"Like *Eat, Pray, Love* but with more heart... [*Where the Peacocks Sing* is] a unique and uplifting read that's as much about traveling to India as it is about finding happiness."
—*Library Journal*

"Alison Singh Gee achieves that rare distinction of making her story—as fabled and surprising as it is—entirely relatable. Gorgeously written and filled with poignant moments and characters who deserve their own stories, her book brings a crumbling Indian palace and its neighboring terrain to vivid life..."
—Kavita Daswani, author of *For Matrimonial Purposes*, *Kingpin*, and *Lovetorn*

"With its blend of humor, sincerity and seriousness, Gee's story easily could be *Eat, Pray, Love*'s down-to-earth cousin, offering a unique twist on the typical tale of Westerners traveling to India to find themselves."
—*LA Weekly*

"[A] compelling, moving, and often hilarious account of self-discovery. A journey from the world of Hong Kong bling, to the gentrified ways of old India, [*Where the Peacocks Sing* is] a story that stays with you, revealing its magic a little at a time."
—Tahir Shah, author of *The Caliph's House*

"A raconteur with deadpan humor and a shining purpose. We gladly enter her ever-changing adventure in India—a glorious life of former expectations freed by the unexpected."
—Amy Tan, *New York Times* bestselling author of *The Joy Luck Club*

"While its settings are exotic, Singh Gee's experiences of finding one's place within the family and the world at large are near-universal. Where the Peacocks Sing is a charming memoir with cross-genre appeal to fans of multicultural literature and women's fiction."
—Shelf Awareness

"Finally, a book that tells you what happens after you marry the Prince (and fail to appreciate his mother's cooking). Alison Singh Gee's moving, amusing memoir is a true-life, all-too-modern retelling of the classic children's fairytale..."
—Eleni Gage, author of *North of Ithaka* and *Other Waters*

"Descriptive, wild, and adventurous, *Where the Peacocks Sing* is a global serenade to modern India, to love, and to figuring out who you are and what matters—in the most surprising ways and places."
—Rachel DeWoskin, author of *Foreign Babes in Beijing*

"Singh Gee raises fascinating questions about our relationships with property and how our dreams can shape and even sabotage our happiness... I got a far more interesting picture of modern rural India than can usually be gleaned through the media. Most importantly [this book] made me think hard about what the word Home actually means."
—JoJo Moyes, author of *The Last Letter from Your Lover: A Novel*

Where *the* Peacocks Sing

A Palace, a Prince,
and the Search
for Home

ALISON
SINGH GEE

SPEAKING
TIGER

SPEAKING TIGER PUBLISHING PVT. LTD
4381/4, Ansari Road, Daryaganj
New Delhi 110002

Copyright © Alison Singh Gee 2014

First published by St. Martin's Griffin 2014
First published in India by Speaking Tiger 2018

ISBN: 978-93-88070-35-5
eISBN: 978-93-88070-18-8

10 9 8 7 6 5 4 3 2 1

For sale in South Asia only

The moral rights of the author have been asserted

Printed at Shree Maitrey Printech Pvt. Ltd., Noida

All rights reserved.
No part of this publication may be reproduced,
transmitted, or stored in a retrieval system, in any form or
by any means, electronic, mechanical, photocopying,
recording or otherwise, without the
prior permission of the publisher.

This book is sold subject to the condition that it shall not,
by way of trade or otherwise, be lent, resold,
hired out, or otherwise circulated, without
the publisher's prior consent, in any form
of binding or cover other than that in
which it is published.

To my family:
the Gees of Los Angeles,
the Singhs of Old Delhi,
and Ajay and Anais of Mokimpur and Atwater Village

Every day is a journey, and the journey itself is home.
—Matsuo Bashō

Prologue

I often wonder when India and its fabled palaces first seized hold of my imagination. But I remember when I was about eight, or maybe nine, I saw my first such royal residence. Not in the flesh (or stone, as it were) but in a book at the library. I still remember lifting the heavy cover of a big picture book, flipping the thick pages, catching sight of a dome here, a tiled courtyard there, archways and fountains, an orchard of swaying palms, and then suddenly floating into this alternate universe.

These sprawling homes lay in the desert like heavy, jeweled necklaces scattered along the sand, and they shimmered under a bright, never-setting sun. "India, Land of a Thousand Palaces," the caption read. Just for a moment, I allowed myself to wonder what it would be like in those great rooms and quiet hallways—the tiled passages, the chandeliers casting off light like diamonds flung into the air, the scent of potted lilies and gardenias wafting from the courtyard, and the kitchen smells of fresh ginger, coriander, and white pepper filling a dining room so big it echoed when you spoke. Just for a moment I lived there.

But my mental escape into those images didn't last for long. I remember being called away from the book by one of my siblings. I took one last glance at the cover—a maharaja and his maharani standing in front of their sprawling pink palace—and then gently closed the cover of the tome.

It was time to go home. Home to our yellow stucco house with the berry bushes lining the front and the unruly hedge along the steep, cracked driveway. Back to the blare of the living room television and six brothers and sisters squabbling over eight pieces of pizza. Back to tin TV trays and a threadbare embroidered-silk sofa and the encyclopedias and worn toys and boxes of navel oranges stuffed randomly into every corner. Back to a life I never quite felt I belonged to and yet was so deeply formed by.

What I realize now is that while I walked away from that book, and that well-born Indian couple and their refined home, the power of that image never really left me. It stayed deep somewhere in the folds of my brain, guiding my choices, forcing me off certain paths and down other roads. One glance at the glossy photographs in a library book and I was led down cool stone floors, through halls redolent of jasmine and cardamom, and into a secret room, a palace, a destiny. And just like that a whole life begins.

✴

It would be years and years from that moment before I would truly learn about these grand houses of Northern India, beyond merely giving them an admiring look. For two centuries, from the late 1700s to the mid-1950s, graceful homes known as havelis lined the streets of Delhi. They ranged in size from impressive manors to mini palaces, depending on how many stacks of rupees one's family had stashed in its vaults. At first, havelis were reserved for Indian aristocrats or British dignitaries. But before long even those who had no title but who ran flourishing businesses—trading rubies and sapphires, for example—or those who wielded political influence built status-boosting havelis for themselves.

These houses had deities, peacocks, and lotus flowers carved into their wooden doors. They had scalloped window frames, gold-leafed ceilings, multiple kitchens, ballrooms that echoed when the servants swept and wiped the marble floors. They had waterways that snaked like the Venetian canals through the property to cool and beautify the gardens. And like a feudal manor, each haveli had its own distinct society, housing not only an entire family but also servants, artisans, musicians, vendors, and priests who devoted their lives to running the house.

The owners of these palaces envisioned their grounds as walled utopias. There were tropical courtyards fragrant with blossoms, private orchards of jamun, chiku, and mango trees, and kitchen gardens swelling with eggplant, bitter gourd, and honeydew; there were marble fountains and stone benches, horse stables and goat sheds. Family cows and buffalo provided fresh milk; hens offered still-warm brown eggs for spicy midday curries. Cultured families hosted evenings of music, inviting Delhi's most celebrated *qawalli*, or ballad, singers to croon into the hot night as tabla players pounded out heartbeats and sitar virtuosos sent their ethereal strains into the sky.

Just outside the haveli gates churned the chaos of urban Indian life: rows of beggars, their hands outstretched, homeless children nursing on the breasts of beleaguered mothers, Hindu devotees chanting prayers, marketplace vendors hawking onions and eggplant and garlic, sacred cows and stray dogs feeding from overturned trash baskets.

For the fortunate few, the haveli was a refuge from a world gone mad.

With the late-twentieth-century push to modernize Indian cities, most havelis have fallen victim to the wrecking ball. Others have been subdivided into tiny graceless flats. Today, if you walk the teeming, hot streets of Old Delhi, past once-pristine havelis, you can still catch a flash of their fallen grandeur—an arched window; a peeling, faded ceiling mural; the silhouette of a regal elephant carved in marble above a gated doorway; a toppled stone fountain in the middle of a weed-wild garden.

If you mention these old manors, many Indians will recite an old proverb: "Havelis are such a rare private world that even a nightingale cannot enter one."

Yet somehow I did.

One day, after I had been engaged to my Indian-born fiancé for nearly a year, he revealed to me that he had grown up in one of these manor-palaces on the outskirts of Old Delhi and that his family still spent most winters and weekends there. As a boy, he was tended to by a family of servants, played cricket along a half-mile-long driveway, and chased rabbits through acres and acres of family farmland.

His clan still owned the palace, but no longer the fortune. In fact, they were nearly broke. Still, Ajay and his family continued to cling to the memory of what the palace once was and the lofty status it had brought to the family.

Now the two of us, Ajay and I, stood heir to the oldest, grandest wing of the haveli, this great white elephant of a home, and virtually no money. With this revelation, my life suddenly became more complicated, more fascinating, more fraught, and more luminous than I could ever have imagined.

Part I

≺+ 1 ⊁

Fear of Flying

I never knew peacocks could fly.

I never knew they could do much of anything. As a child growing up in Northeast Los Angeles, I only ever saw them at the botanical gardens in Pasadena or roaming the zoo. They were stunning birds, with their built-in tiaras and show-off coloring. But let's face it: They seemed pretty useless. Waddling across manicured lawns, admiring flowers, plopping their fat stomachs onto grassy patches in the shade, these pampered birds only broke a sweat when the garden groundskeeper rang the dinner bell. Peacocks were charming but relatively pointless, flashing their plumage like a socialite working her best fur and jewels, and that's all.

Or so I thought.

My understanding of peacocks was about to take a quantum leap.

I was sitting on the terrace of a palace in India. This was not some trussed-up five-star hotel in a commercialized Indian city, lousy with Patagonia-clad tourists. This was the ancestral home that had belonged to my fiancé Ajay's family for the past century, and it was the kind of regal spread you'd find in a Merchant Ivory film—huge, awe-inspiring, and vibrating with legacy. The house stood like a porcelain deity in the middle of a lush and flowering village called Mokimpur, which is also the name the Singh family gave the house. Ajay had spent much of his childhood at this magnificent residence, playing hide-and-seek in its hundred rooms, racing his village friends along the river, and jumping into the deep, cool reservoir when the summer heat became unbearable.

With its fragrant mango groves, silent skies, and choruses of songbirds and screeching parrots, Mokimpur was about as different from my hometown as the moon. Later, when I looked at a globe and placed my finger on Northern India, I realized that Ajay's tiny village sat almost literally on the opposite side of the sphere from where I grew up. But it's not like I needed a map to tell me what I already knew in my heart.

As an American journalist based in Hong Kong, my life was anything but placid, predictable, or comforting. My cell phone buzzed every two minutes; I had a half-dozen deadlines to meet every day, and a whirling social world that included lots of good friends (most of whose last names I somehow never quite learned). Hong Kong, the futuristic gateway to the East, had skyscrapers instead of trees, subway platforms instead of terraces, daredevil taxis instead of slow-moving yaks. Lunch was often a bowl of noodles eaten standing up; dinner, cocktail party hors d'oeuvres and a lethal gin and tonic. (Breakfast wasn't actually in my vocabulary—I usually jumped out of bed at the blast of the alarm clock, wriggled into a dress, strapped on some heels, and dashed out the door.) In this insanely built-up, inhumanly crowded place, where apartment towers seemingly sprang up overnight like bamboo, the locals liked to say that the national bird was the jackhammer.

Not so in Mokimpur.

It was my first week in India. Ajay and I were idling over steaming cups of chai and plates heaped with mouthwatering veg *pakora*, deep-fried cauliflower, onions, potatoes, and carrots with a spiced, crispy coating. Three servants dressed in kurtas and loose cotton pants ferried about filling teacups and delivering fresh chutney and hot *samosas*. As Ajay and I lounged on the veranda, I watched dozens of wild peacocks, shrieking with glee as they glided from mango tree to neem tree, streaking the sky with their over-the-top rainbow colors.

Peacocks, not jackhammers, are the national bird of India. Here they were almost unrecognizable to me, not at all like their L.A. cousins. Indian peacocks were tenacious and fierce, agile and vocal. Roaming wild in the villages, these birds were just like the people—warriors in the primordial battle for survival. I watched them in the middle distance and shook my head. "All this time I thought they were ground dwellers," I said to Ajay. "Who knew these humongous things could jet through the trees like that?"

"This is India," Ajay said. "We do whatever we need to do to survive—if that means flying, we fly." He took a sip of his chai and tilted his head. "An Indian peacock can kill a baby cobra in thirty seconds flat. Their beaks are laser sharp. Before the snake knows what's happened, it's been sliced into a pile of sashimi." He looked dashing in his white kurta pajama suit, and worlds apart from any man I'd ever dated.

Suddenly, we heard a great flapping of wings and a thud so

loud it caused us to turn in our chairs. Two peahens and a peacock had landed on the veranda ledge, a few feet from where we sat. They jumped down and, like plump gymnasts, bounded over and pranced around us. Their giant bodies wobbled on sinewy legs that looked like they'd done their share of kicking other pheasant ass. The birds turned their faces to the sky and let out a series of shrieks. I covered my ears and winced.

"What in God's name are they doing?" I asked.

"They're dancing in the sun to keep themselves warm," Ajay explained, wrapping a shatoosh around his neck. "They move around all day in packs foraging for seeds in the fields, searching for rain."

"But why are they crying like that?" I asked.

"They're not crying," Ajay said. "They're singing. They're excited because they think they hear thunder, and thunder means rain. You should hear them go at it when a jet flies overhead. They scream as if an apocalypse has come to the village."

I couldn't help but feel sorry for the poor birds, because the modern world had confused their primal instincts so much. It wasn't rain that was coming whenever they heard a boom in the sky; it was just another planeload of tourists, hoping to find cheap handicrafts and an unspoiled stretch of beach on the Subcontinent. I also felt a little disheartened at my own warped intuition: What sounded to me like cries of sadness were actually shrieks of glee. Maybe modern life in the big city had confused me, too. In Hong Kong, some nights I lay awake wondering if there was any escape in the world from flashing neon signs and construction rubble.

Just as quickly as they had landed, the peacocks took off into the sky, rising swiftly above the trees, over the palace wall and into the farmland beyond. I sprang up to watch them as they flapped out of sight. Indian peacocks did not just fly. They soared.

All my life, I had been a bona fide city girl, a creature of the first world at its commercial finest. After college in California, I had gone to graduate school in London, and now I lived in Hong Kong, the Orient's Manhattan, only four times as fast. I worked as a journalist for Time Inc., jetting throughout Asia on assignment. My days began with *The New York Times* and a latte from the Pacific Coffee Company in Wanchai, and often ended at a crowded cocktail party in the city or at a catered dinner fete on a Chinese junk, cruising Victoria Harbour.

India was never part of my life plan. After all, it sat on the other side of the world, some nine thousand miles from Los Angeles—the chaotic, dusty, and painfully poor side, I was sure. But since I'd met Ajay, everything in my life had changed. He not only loved his native land, he belonged to it. He had an almost primal attachment to his home village and the family palace that rose from the wheat fields.

"No matter where I go, where I live, or what I become, when I come back to Mokimpur, it's home like no other place," he explained to me. "I get an inexplicable feeling of peace here. If I ever reached a breaking point in our life in Hong Kong or America I know I could return to Mokimpur and recover. I wouldn't need to do anything or talk to anyone. I would just need to stay here and reestablish my connection with the land."

I had never felt that way about any place before. Home for

me was always a backdrop for chaos and pain. A place to run from, not to. Part of me admired, or maybe I should say envied, Ajay's unshakable attachment to his village. Another part of me lusted after the palace's hundred rooms and the fabulous make-over I knew I could give it. And the deepest part of me wondered if this could be my home, too.

In the days to come, I would learn that life here was about hours of silence, sipping chai and contemplating the clouds. The main events of the day were family meals, three-hour lunches that broke up only when it was time for tea. We would take afternoon ambles along the village river and eat our dinners by kerosene lamp. While the servants tidied up the kitchen, we were free to sit around talking with the family for hours or read stacks of books by candlelight, stretched out in the big four-poster wooden bed that once belonged to Ajay's great-grandfather.

While all this might sound idyllic, I truly did not know if this was what I wanted, if this could ever be what I wanted. Life here was just so drastically different from the overscheduled, underexamined existence I had gotten accustomed to living. In Mokimpur, my motor shifted to idle. In my normal life my brain threatened to explode with ideas and details and the more-than-occasional anxiety attack; here it seemed to go on strike. Now on my fourth cup of chai, I took in the scene in the fields—a row of villagers sheathed in saffron- and ruby-colored saris plucking mangoes from a shady grove. Then I turned and suddenly caught sight of my image in one of the haveli windows. Mokimpur's all-day dress code was homespun cotton kurta pajamas, but I had put on a Diane von Furstenberg wrap dress, suede platforms, and Kate Spade sunglasses. I laughed at my reflection. I looked like a wannabe starlet cast in the wrong destiny. My mind knew me as corporate girl, first-world chick, habitué of Philippe Starck–designed bars.

But my soul seemed to be opening itself up to some other identity. "Holy cow," I whispered to myself. My heart raced. I took off my shades and ran my hands through my shoulder-length hair.

If I were Alice falling through the looking glass, Mokimpur is where I would land. A frisson of panic coursed through me. "What exactly am I doing in this Indian village?" I muttered to Ajay.

He laughed and reached for my hand. "You're here to learn to milk cows and collect eggs from underneath hens in the coop. To wake to the chatter of wild parrots, not CNN. To taste a mango plucked straight from the tree. To learn that real meals take hours to make, not thirty seconds in the microwave." He was on a roll and he knew it. "You're here to forget about your cell phone and your Mac laptop," he continued. "Maybe you're here to learn the real rhythm of the earth. It's not staying out dancing until five in the morning, you know. That's actually when most of the villagers get up." Right on cue, a peacock landed on the terrace, shook his feathers, lifted his head, and shrieked, as if echoing Ajay's soliloquy.

I looked at Ajay quizzically, but he hadn't even registered the bird. His face was as calm and content as I'd ever seen it. So I allowed myself to wonder what Mokimpur could mean to me.

My heart told me I had arrived here for a reason. Maybe I could bring new life to the palace. And I had the feeling that Mokimpur could offer me something essential and precious in exchange. An escape from the twenty-first century? A place to call home? Or maybe the palace could send earthbound me into flight.

⤙ 2 ⤚

Searching

I didn't even know I was searching for anyone or anything when I found Ajay. Or at least I never admitted that much to myself. During my first few years in Hong Kong, I didn't have a lot to complain about. I had a great job, an eccentric, well-heeled boyfriend, and an East-West mien that got me into every club in town. "Live it up" was practically my personal mantra. I socialized with other privileged expatriates, held court over scones and jasmine tea at the Mandarin Oriental Hotel, and could count on one hand the number of times I had cooked myself a meal at my little flat. I was out almost every night, tottering about town on four-inch heels, fabulizing until I had to hail a cab home and flop into bed.

As a popular columnist and features writer for the Sunday magazine of the *South China Morning Post,* Hong Kong's big English-language newspaper, I juggled a full roster of sometimes adventurous, sometimes worthy, often shamelessly glamorous stories. One day I might be interviewing Gong Li on the set of her latest Beijing film or hanging out with Jackie Chan at the

Peninsula Hotel. On another day, I might be following a prominent politician back to her Sichuan family village.

More relevantly, I was dating Nigel, a British fund manager who lived in a rambling flat with a view of the South China Sea. Nigel was perfect on paper: dashing, Oxford educated, and a finance whiz on his way up. He lavished me with Hermès scarves and weekends in Bali. In other words, I was set. Or so I thought.

Once the six o'clock bell rang at work, Nigel and I moved through Hong Kong as if we were living on a cruise ship, supping nightly at Felix or the China Club, or sailing on a moonlit Victoria Harbour on his firm's boat. When we met at his home after work, his Thai amah whipped up pad thai and crab curry. If it was too humid to play outside, I rollerbladed around the flat's expansive living room instead.

My closet was jam-packed with little black dresses and beaded purses. My bathroom drawers overflowed with NARS lipstick, Vamp nail polish, and hangover cures. Indeed, practically every cent I made as a journalist fueled my wardrobe and personal maintenance fund. I'm embarrassed to admit this now, but I left it to Nigel to pick up the tab for the rest of our life.

And yet I just wasn't happy.

On the rare occasion when I sat still for longer than a minute, my heart would tell me something was truly not right. Something was missing from my all too spectacular life. Something profound.

Something I could not figure out. All my life I had gotten the message that "making it" meant being rich, pampered, and beautiful—wasn't that what the pages of *Vogue* were all about? Oh sure, there were other images between the glossy covers, but the photographs of the enchanting, chic, and materially blessed were the ones that spoke to me. So many of the young women I knew in Hong Kong and Los Angeles basically followed the same credo, so how far wrong could I have gotten it? And yes, nights out with Nigel in this exotic city were dazzling, and I took it as an affirmation of just how successful I had become that *le tout* Hong Kong wanted us over for dinner or out on their Sunday junk trip.

We were rarely alone, and that was by design—both of ours, I now see. I realized that Nigel often clung to me most when his old school friends salivated over my latest Armani minidress or my Phuket Yacht Club tan. And no matter how grand a time we had had at the latest expat fete, we couldn't often share a party postmortem on the way home in the cab. By the end of the night, Nigel was often in a fog, having had his fill of the expat revelry that followed his twelve-hour workdays. We never woke before 11 A.M. on Sunday, unless, of course, there was another party to go to. Once, the "orgasm parrots"—wild cockatiels whose screams were so loud they could be heard a mile away—dared to begin their chant in the early hours. Nigel often joked that he'd send the amah outside to throw rocks at them in the trees.

It wasn't just the noisy birds that Nigel loathed. If I ever turned up to an event or dinner party looking anything less than stunning, he thought little of shooting a verbal barb my way. "You've been looking rather shabby lately, my dear," he said one night as he gave my thrown-together outfit and last year's heels a once-over. I could feel the chilly disapproval emanating from his stare. "Look at Helen," he said, as his eyes glided over to a friend of mine, turned out beautifully in a Vivienne Tam sheath and Prada heels. "Now, that's a good woman."

"How dare you," I hissed as I pushed past him and ran off. I spent the next hour in the powder room—thirty minutes bawling and then another thirty trying to repair the damage to my eye makeup. That night, I went back to my own small flat in the Chinese part of town—alone.

What can I say? Nigel and I enjoyed gossiping about other expats in our circle—who had a mistress in Shenzhen, who got the unceremonious boot from the Deacons firm, who got a botched nose job in Seoul, who picked up syphilis in Bangkok—but we never once mused about the children we would have, the home we would build, how we would look when our hair had turned gray and our magnificence had faded. At least not together.

A lasting revelation came one day after I returned home from the HMV Megastore in Central, the business district. I had picked up a Chieftains CD and stuck it in the stereo. Nigel loved the Irish band—he said their Celtic tunes transported him to the U.K. The next day, he ran down to HMV and bought his own copy. After he had gone to bed, I thought about that small act of retail glee and realized something essential. Nigel needed his own copy because, clearly, our record collections were never going to join together in holy matrimony. And neither were we.

That's not to say that he didn't love having me, magazine columnist and girl-about-town, on his arm. He did. For my part, I loved the feeling of being adored, protected, and paid for—and I guess I realized that I would have a bloody hard time replicating this level of existence on my own.

In so many ways, I was living the life I had always fantasized about. Yet if I ever dared turn down the soundtrack of our life—disco beats pounding from the nightclubs, the noisy excitement of helicopter rides above the colony, the false mirth of mindless dinner party chatter—I heard an echoing. It was coming from my soul.

It is 1946, and my mother, then a sixteen-year-old girl dressed in a homemade frock, her hair bouncy from a do-it-yourself permanent wave and held in place by a silver barrette, boards a train from Sacramento to Los Angeles, with her father. The week before, her parents had received a telegram from another Chinese family living in California. The Gees were looking for a suitable wife for their youngest son, Peter, twenty-three. Unlike my mother's family—her father is a former soldier who now runs a small poultry business—the Gees are rich. They own a thriving import-export business in L.A.'s Chinatown and several buildings that line Chung King Road and Hill Street. Their family is the only clan in all of Chinatown to have a car. After dinner, my mother's parents reread the telegram together in the kitchen. That night, as my mother sleeps, her parents pack her suitcases and arrange for train tickets.

The families make plans to meet at Fong's Café in Chinatown. There, my mother sits in a red leather booth with her eyes shyly cast downward, every few minutes sneaking glimpses of the man who might soon be her husband. He wears a plaid shirt like a cowboy and black leather shoes that must have cost a fortune. He is almost six feet tall, with a thick mane of black hair and a large, well-shaped nose like a movie star's. He paces the aisles of the restaurant and whistles loudly until his father barks at him to stop. He asks her one question: "Do you like onions?" She looks up at him and sees a young man of dazzling good looks and a nervous energy that compels him to shake his leg, even when he is standing.

"Yes." She nods. "I like onions."

"Well, I don't like onions," he growls, throwing his hands up in defeat.

The two families gather my mother's suitcases and walk to the Gees' main business, a Hill Street general store lined with penny candy, canned foods, tobacco, and baskets of bok choy and ginger. At least fifteen customers and their children wait in line to buy their weekly supplies. My mother's father and my father's dad shake hands.

A month later, Peter drives the family car up to Sacramento to pick up his new bride-to-be. On her first night in Los Angeles, my mother gazes out the windows of the Gee family home, perched above the Hill Street store, and stares at the city. A stoplight flashes green, yellow, and red all night, and happy drunks, full on chow mein and Chinese whisky, stagger down the street. It's so very different from the scene she views from her Sacramento bedroom—the chickens scratching for worms in the backyard, the fruit trees, branches heavy with kumquats and guavas.

She thinks of her mother and father and her little brother, Jimmy, some four hundred miles away. She begins to cry, quiet sobs at first. Once she realizes that she is not going back, that she is never going back to her little pink house in Sacramento, the sobs bloom into full-on howls. My father opens the door to her bedroom and finds her blowing her nose into a tissue, her shoulders shaking with sadness.

"What are you crying about?" he roars, having no vocabulary to comfort her. My mother stifles her sobs, silently changes into her night-gown, and slips into bed. Little does she realize then that over the course of her fifty-year marriage, these are but the first of many, many tears.

A few weeks after my father dies, I sit with my mother as she sifts *through his closets. We stuff his suits and ties and old books into garbage bags. She will call Goodwill to take them in the morning. I finally ask her the question I've wanted to ask her for so many years. "So why did you marry him, Mom?" I say, as gently as I can. "Did you feel like you had to? Like you just had no choice?" My mother puts down the plastic bag, clears off a space on my father's bed, and sits down. She blinks her eyes thoughtfully and says, "Well, nobody make me marry him. I could say no if I wanted to. But when I went to their store and look around, everything look good. So I say yes."*

⭑

There were many times throughout my life when I wished that my mother had never made that trip down the California coast to Fong's Café (regardless of what that would have meant for my own existence). I have always remembered that Tolstoy quotation: "Happy families are all alike; every unhappy family is unhappy in its own way." It may sound contradictory, but both parts of that statement describe what it was like growing up with my clan. At our happiest, we were mounds of presents stacked up around a fragrant Christmas tree. We were station-wagon road trips to Yosemite singing "Ninety-nine Bottles of Beer." We were summer tents in the backyard sleeping under the stars.

But when we were unhappy, that house seemed to hold no hope. We six siblings were often devastated, made so by a father who could cuddle us on his lap at one moment and then send us reeling across the room with a slap on the face in another.

⭑

Searching

"Ali-ah!"

The summons across the house fills me with a heavy black dread. I slowly put my comic book down on my bed and make my way through the dining room and living room, all the while flinching at the midday shadows coming off the lamps, the chairs, the upright piano. My father is sitting there, in his bedroom, in his favorite chair, the black tufted leatherette throne with the matching ottoman. It is Sunday, and he is reading the paper in his pajamas while the football game blares from the television.

"Here," he says, holding up a black-and-white "Doonesbury" strip. "I like this cartoon. Can you cut it out for me?"

I take the page and walk out of his room, holding the open paper in my hands as reverentially as someone might hold a Bible. I am seven, maybe eight, but already I know not to take lightly a request from my father.

"Do you have scissors?" I ask my sister.

"No," she says, not even looking up. "Ask Mom."

I wander into the kitchen, which is always dark and cold even in the middle of the day. "Mom, do you have any scissors?" She is holding her worn brown purse in her hand and heading out the back door. "Ah . . . I don't know. Look around. They're here somewhere. I have to go to the market."

I survey the kitchen. Pots and pans clutter the counters; a burlap sack of rice sits on the floor. I pull open a kitchen drawer and run my hands over the contents—chopsticks, rubber bands, a hammer, a rusted can opener. No scissors.

"Oh, well," I say to myself, pushing aside dishes and cans left on the breakfast nook table and laying the newspaper out. I fold the paper so that I can crease the edges and tear out the cartoon. Then I gently pull away one side, two sides, three, and then four and hold

23

the liberated strip up in front of me. The edges are uneven, and one side of the cartoon is slightly ripped, but other than that it looks good. I run over to my father's room, holding the piece of paper in my hand.

"Here, Ba," I say, laying it out on his metal TV tray and running into the living room.

It takes only a moment for the fallout to hit.

"What is this?" My father's voice booms from his room. "What is this?"

I look around the living room for someplace to hide. He appears at the door, a hulking shadow silhouetted by the sun. Too late! My heart begins to pound.

"I told you to cut this out for me and you ruined it!" he shouts, holding up the cartoon. "Come here!" I shuffle over to him, practically whimpering. "I told you to cut this out for me! This is what you do?" He crumples the cartoon and throws it at my feet. I look up. His forehead and cheeks have turned a deep red. His breathing comes heavily, like snorts, through his nose. He takes off his glasses and wipes the rage from his eyes. Then he raises his hand and slaps my face.

The sting spreads across my cheek, and I shake my head in disbelief. My sister drops her book and looks at me, her silence a cloak of invisibility shielding her. It is no use calling for my mother—she is gone. Even if she had been there, would she have done anything to protect me? My father, satisfied, stomps back into his room.

I run across the house and into my bedroom and quietly shut the door. Then the tears pour out. I stare at my red face in the mirror over the old oak dresser and wipe my eyes with my baby blanket. Then I do what I often do when my father is home and my mother is out at the store: I crawl into my hiding place—between the dresser and the wall—and I stay there until the sunlight outside the Sunday afternoon window disappears, wishing that my father would die.

So many times during the decades that follow, I think about that slap, and what my father is seeing as his hand collides with that small, tender face—my face. Is it the visage of a child who simply wants to please her father? Or perhaps he is seeing the face of his sister, to whom I bear an uncanny resemblance, the older sibling from whom he has been estranged for so many years, so much so that as a grown man, he rarely sees her, even though they live a ten-minute drive from each other, she on the wealthy side of the hill. Or maybe he sees in that face everybody and nobody—his mother, his boss, the man at the bank who has slighted him.

He never hits me again, but that one slap, coupled with the verbal smacks that he so often and easily doles out to me and everyone else in the family, is enough to send me running away as soon as I am able, over oceans and continents. Without ever wanting to glance back.

My father grew up in a Chinese family in which a lot of money was at stake. Brother and sister and brother battled each other, and my father, the youngest and emotionally the weakest, lost every war. We grew up hearing stories about how he had been cheated—out of money, out of reputation, out of a grander fate. We had lost everything, he'd wail, and that was despite the fact that we had each other.

Houses, jewelry, and debt aren't the only things children inherit from their parents. They also inherit a view of the world. Anyone, it seemed, could cheat you out of what was yours. Under my parents' roof, I always felt as though the floor were forever shifting under my feet. I could be sitting in the living room watching my favorite television show when suddenly the whole house erupted into an argument, sending tremors of fear through my bones. The walls could crack and disintegrate at any moment, just as the ground around us had during a big Southern California earthquake when I was in elementary school.

I still recall my mother taking us back to my school, once the tremors had ended. We pressed our noses against the chain-link fence that now surrounded the campus and stared at the once-beautiful brick building, the second story toppled to the ground. Only a week before the quake my mother had sent me to class with a rare present, a hand-sewn apron for art class, with my name embroidered across the top. When she asked the post-earthquake crew to recover it for me, they reported back that nothing was there. Everything had been destroyed.

"They stole it, I know they did," my father said. How could anyone be so mean, I wondered. How could anyone steal a little girl's apron? I held on to his bitterness and fear, constantly anxious about when the next upheaval of nature—or of fate—would strike. We were forever one earthquake away from losing it all.

By the time my teenage years rolled around, the family was in shambles. My fragile adolescence had been blown to pieces with the discovery that my father was spiraling into mental illness. He refused to see a doctor, insisting that the problem lay with everyone else—my mother, his siblings, the neighbors, his kids. My father had always been emotionally distant; now he was also delusional. Unable to deal with his incessant career failures, he believed he owned stately houses all over California; he owned whole neighborhoods, part of Disneyland, even Baja, Mexico.

Yet I continued to believe that if I achieved enough and made him proud, maybe that would chase the delusions away. But nothing I did was ever enough. When at twenty-two I told him I had been accepted to graduate school in London, he laughed and shook his head. "I know my children. And you—especially you—you don't have the capacity to live abroad by yourself." Even dressed in his worn striped pajamas and plastic slippers at two in the afternoon, my father had the easy ability to crush me. All it took was a few carefully chosen words—and those came seamlessly to him.

It was during those years that I discovered that loving him was like sticking a blade into my own heart. It got me nowhere, except awake in the middle of the night, recalling the years when my father was the strongest, the smartest, the funniest, and I lay curled in my bed, wondering why I had been cheated out of a father who loved me, and one I could love in return.

✦

Ultimately, I knew I could not blame Nigel for my discontent with life in Hong Kong. The problems lay deeper than that. I had a posse of so-called friends who could get past any velvet rope in town but who would also hiss secrets I confided as soon as I left the room. Who could you trust in a world like this?

I had let petty grudges wear away my ties to my brothers and sisters, and I had no idea how to get my family back. My Los Angeles–based younger brother, Brian, and I had once shared a whole secret universe of teddy bears and hiding places. Recently, though, we had fallen out. It was ridiculous, really. During a visit to his house, I had telephoned Nigel several times and stuck

Brian with the bill. I had meant to leave a check but forgot, hopping back onto a Cathay Pacific flight without a second thought. In hindsight I don't blame him for getting angry and feeling hurt. After the bill—over a hundred dollars—arrived at his house, he called me in Hong Kong, racking up yet more overseas phone charges, and said something nasty. I hung up, paced the flat, and fumed.

Until then, I had thought of his house as my home in the States, and that was even though I told him his neighborhood, a 1970s planned community that seemed perfectly content with its Benihana steak houses, Home Depots, and Chuck E. Cheeses, "wouldn't work" for me, his hipper-than-thou sister.

After our blowup, Brian and I didn't talk to each other for about a year. I told myself that I lived seven thousand miles away in a fabulous city; maybe he no longer mattered. But the fact is I questioned how swiftly he seemed to have escaped our tumultuous past and settled into suburban life, while I was still on the lam. I longed for a home, and he had one. I didn't even know Brian was expecting his first baby until his wife was nine months pregnant.

I had not reached out to my mother for so long that when I finally telephoned her one Christmas morning, I discovered her area code had changed. "Ba is sick, he's lost thirty pounds," she told me almost as soon as she answered the phone. Her voice was riddled with worry. She didn't say it, but I knew instinctively that my father would soon die. "When are you coming home?" she asked. "Soon," I told her simply and untruthfully and hung up the phone. A few minutes later, I grabbed my purse and jumped into a cab headed for Lan Kwai Fong, where sushi and sake and neon lights awaited me, no awkward questions asked.

.✦.

"*Why did I move to* Hong Kong? Oh, that's easy—to get away from Chinese people." I always began my conversations with new acquaintances with this signature joke, earning myself a few laughs in every crowded bar, as my latest band of friends and I held aloft shockingly expensive cocktails while the beautiful crowds from Shanghai, Beijing, and Taiwan paraded past us. But I was only half joking. I really did leave Los Angeles to sever my daily ties from Chinese people—namely, the ones I was related to.

It wasn't that I didn't care about my parents or my three sisters and two brothers—quite the opposite. They were everything to me—every iconic childhood memory, the source of my self-esteem and my self-hatred, my joy and my black emptiness. But I had had enough of the pain that came with being part of that volatile and passionate clan—at least for now.

So in Hong Kong, I tried hard not to care, especially about my father, and I tried hard not to waver from that. I had chosen to leave, and live alone in a foreign country. And in fleeing thousands of miles across the Pacific, I chose myself, and a chance at a different future.

I know now that I could have chosen other roads, but this seemed the clearest path out of a life I no longer wanted. I would be losing myself (and the turmoil of my childhood) and, I desperately hoped, finding myself all in this one major odyssey.

⤙ 3 ⤚

Meeting Ajay

Four years after I moved to Hong Kong, I signed on as an editor with Time Inc.'s Asia-based magazine *Asiaweek*. It was often called the *Newsweek* of Asia, and the work brought a big change from the frothy stories I often wrote at the *South China Morning Post*. At *Asiaweek*, the incessant deadlines and way-past-midnight closings were grueling, but the subject matter—the imminent flooding of the Three Gorges in China, strange and exorbitantly expensive beauty rituals in Japan, the rampant kidnapping of upper-class housewives in the Philippines—kept me riveted. I was still covering Chinese cinema, but I was now also expanding my area of expertise to more substantive issues—politics, women's issues, economics—and this gave my life a new and welcome gravitas. When I won Amnesty International's Magazine Feature Writing Award for my cover story about child prostitution in Southeast Asia—a story I had worked on for months—I knew my life was moving along a new path.

A few months after I joined the *Asiaweek* staff, our editor decided we needed a company-wide powwow. She summoned all our far-flung correspondents for a weeklong meeting at our Hong Kong headquarters in Causeway Bay. I had met most of the other foreign-based reporters—a motley crew that included a height-challenged Pakistani who was too clever for his own good, an earnest former professor from Beijing, and a scrappy former backpacker who had bought a manual typewriter and set up shop in Bangkok—and I can't say I was too excited about seeing any of them again.

But on the first day of the corporate summit, Joel, a friend at the magazine, called me into his office. "Hey, Alison," he said, "meet Ajay, from India."

In my quest to become a more serious journalist, I had begun to oversee culture and human-interest stories from all over Asia. One of the writers I often worked with was *Asiaweek's* India correspondent, Ajay Singh. Based in New Delhi, Ajay was an expert in Indian politics and culture, and he often had tea with the likes of the Dalai Lama, the Indian president, and Bollywood movie stars. We hadn't had the opportunity to meet in person, but I thought Ajay was a skilled and meticulous reporter—and yes, I did notice that he sounded sweet over the phone. Frankly, though, I was too busy jetting off to Malaysia with Nigel and fending off advances from a number of Chinese film directors and producers to pay any mind to a journalist in faraway India.

Now suddenly fate had thrown us into the same room.

Much to my surprise, Ajay Singh, the guy I only thought of when I needed a story about Bombay pollution or a bizarre outbreak of the plague on the Subcontinent—yes, *that* Ajay Singh—was a six-foot tall, film-star-handsome Indian man with chai-colored skin, almond-shaped brown eyes, and impeccable manners.

"Hello," I said, extending my hand and standing up straight, my eyes brightening. I remember trying to put on graceful airs— "Be swanlike!" my head commanded—but then I burst into an uncontrollable smile. The anxieties sprinted through my brain. Had the morning rain left my hair matted against my forehead? Had my lipstick survived my commute across town? Did last night's jaunt in Lan Kwai Fong show under my eyes? Did my dress, already a few months old, look dated and shabby?

None of this seemed to matter to Ajay. His eyes lit up when he gazed at my face. I stared back at him with something that, I realize now, was close to cellular recognition. In one glance, he recalled my father, my first boyfriend, my college love, my future. It was a jarring juxtaposition. This was Ajay Singh, our India correspondent. This was Ajay Singh, the person I had been waiting for.

How did I know? Who can explain such a phenomenon? In that first moment of meeting, I sensed that Ajay had the kindness and the depth I had been searching for throughout the years and across all those oceans and continents. By aligning with him and joining our life stories, I would somehow find my way.

"Lovely to meet you, Alison," Ajay said. His voice was warmed by a British accent. "It was good fun working with you on that Delhi art scene story." He smiled sweetly, his eyes shining. I beamed back at him, while thinking, "It would have been even more fun if I had known you looked like this!"

It soon became clear that Ajay had felt a connection, too. He sought me out at every business function during that week. I, career girl who had resolved never to date anyone in the workplace, found myself swept up in a major conference room crush. Over the next few days, we looked for each other at every opportunity and engaged in a few gaze-filled conversations, smiling shyly across oval conference tables. During our rubber-chicken corporate lunches (rubber tofu in Ajay's vegetarian case), he charmed me by recounting his checkered work history: manager of a tea plantation, gentleman chicken breeder, apple orchardist, failed eucalyptus-tree farmer, and—finally, success!—journalist for the *Wall Street Journal Asia*. Every day he wore a different linen coat with a Nehru collar—a style that felt so charming, so idiosyncratic, especially compared to the pinstripes and wool that usually surrounded me.

There was not much of an opportunity to explore a budding romance while our boss droned on about focus groups and more effective ways of covering the Indonesian riots. Still, at the end of the conference, before saying good-bye, we managed to touch hands for a brief moment (while the boss was turned the other way, I recall). For the plane ride home, I gave him a favorite book of short stories, *A Good Scent from a Strange Mountain*. And with that, I cast my fate to the summer wind.

The next week I received an e-mail from Ajay, who was back in New Delhi, thanking me for the book. We started writing letters to each other—first one page, then three, then five. He wrote to me about the curry-colored hills in India and his travels to the notorious "rat temple" in Rajasthan. I told him my tales of backpacking through China and about the week I had spent with the last generation of bound-foot women in a tiny village in Sichuan Province. He wrote back about the summer he had gone "undercover" as a curry chef in Tokyo, where, as he chopped onions, he surreptitiously interviewed other illegal workers from India. We shared news from our daily lives, three thousand miles apart. Ajay especially loved my epistle about my crusade to liberate three small turtles from their oppressive home—a plastic bucket under a friend's bathroom sink. I ultimately set them free in the beautiful pond in Hong Kong Park, shouting *"Liberación!"* in a spontaneously channeled Spanish accent while holding one fist in the air. (Ajay especially applauded that final verbal gesture.)

One day a heavy rectangular package wrapped in brown paper and twine appeared at my office. I tore it open and found an unbound manuscript of Ajay's comic novel, *Give 'Em Hell, Hari*. He had made the cover by pasting a computer-generated image of the Taj Mahal on a sheet of white paper.

I stared at the manuscript on my desk all day. Truth be told, I was nervous about reading it. The pages would tell me so much about who Ajay was, how much talent he actually had, and—let's face it—what sort of future he might be able to offer me. What if the story was hackneyed, the writing riddled with clichés, the book a waste of effort, of life? That night, I carried it into bed with me and turned to page one.

Give 'Em Hell, Hari is the story of a young Indian man who has always dreamed of seeing his words in print, so he begins to write impassioned, opinionated letters to the Indian newspapers. His missives reflect a talent so promising that an editor offers him the position of newsboy at an international news bureau. Written as an epistolary novel, the book showcases many vivid, original characters, some of them Western and others Indian from all castes—a microcosm of Subcontinental urban life.

I read the entire manuscript in two sittings. As I finished the last page and closed the book, I whispered to myself, "This is completely brilliant." I could not wait to e-mail Ajay the next morning. "This book must be published," I wrote once the sun had come up. "I am in love with it." And possibly with you, too, was the postscript I wanted to add, but didn't. Not yet.

I understand now that what I was doing was truly unfair to Nigel. Throughout this whole chapter of our life together, he never suspected a serious emotional defection on my part—although it was becoming increasingly clear to both of us that we would never stand together in the front of a church. A few months before I'd met Ajay I even dared to ask Nigel, "What do you think? Are we getting married?" He blushed crimson, shrugged, and answered, "I don't know." Then, even more cryptically, he added, "Sadly, I just don't want to join any club that would have me as a member." He would tell me months later that he knew we were growing apart but simply didn't know how to pull things together again. Nigel seemed to accept the distance. But I, a romantic idealist beneath the shiny frocks, would never endure such a chasm between my partner and me. Nor would I forgive the unwillingness to struggle. We had reached the end, and that much some part of me tacitly acknowledged.

Voracious reader that he was, Nigel even pored through Ajay's manuscript, which he appropriated from my bedside table. "Bloody good book, even though it falls apart in the middle," he remarked. "Tell your India correspondent that I said well done." I justified my interaction with Ajay with the fiction that I was simply getting to know another human being. After all, Ajay and I had never physically been alone together for longer than five minutes, and throughout our correspondence, I never once mentioned romance.

Looking back now, however, I see our e-mail exchange for what it was: an old-fashioned courtship through letters. An epistolary romance.

Three months into our increasingly intense communication, Ajay's morning e-mail came with an unusual subject line: "Please Sit Down As You Read This." I leapt up to shut my office door, sat back down, and rolled my chair to my computer. "There is something I need to tell you," the message said. "We've gotten to know each other so well through our letters. Each one has been more vivid and passionate than the last. I'm writing to tell you I've fallen in love with you. I'm coming to Hong Kong to be with you."

I sat in my office for the next hour and did nothing but think. Ajay wrote that he had fallen in love with me. I had to admit that I felt the same way. The situation was romantic and thrilling—and profoundly messy. Yet somehow I knew I had found the relationship that would take me to the next plane. I owed it to myself to explore this path and follow it wherever it led me.

A few days later, I called Nigel at work, and we decided to meet in Lan Kwai Fong for a sushi dinner. Our last, as it turned out. "Nigel, you know, I'm really sorry about this," I said, blinking back tears, "but it's over." I knew that I needed to have this conversation, to cut these ties, to choose another fate, but that didn't make it any easier. I slipped his house key off the Tiffany silver chain he had given me and slid it across the table, our fingers touching for the last time.

He was dressed in a double-breasted suit, his striped Hermès tie still tightly knotted around his neck. "I had a feeling you were going to do something like this," he hissed, stabbing a piece of tuna sashimi with his chopstick, and draining his sake glass.

✦

The next weekend, I returned to Nigel's flat during the workday, ringing the bell for his Thai maid to open the door. "Why you leave?" Matina asked, grabbing hold of my arms and searching my eyes for answers. She told me that Ethel, the Garuda Air stewardess girlfriend of Nigel's insufferable accountant flatmate, Benjamin, was still living there. "Ethel smart, Ethel want baby, Ethel want a good life. So Ethel stay. Where you go? To Sai Ying Poon, la? That small flat near fish store? So small, so dark. My sister live around the corner. Life no good. You come back to us. Nigel take you back. Really, he's sad all the time. He take you back, I know it. Tell him you make a mistake." Had I? I took one last glance at Nigel's living room, with its porcelain lamps arranged in easy, tasteful symmetry and its beautiful but bland Asian paintings. The sunlight winked off the harbor in the middle distance. I sighed and turned to go.

I hired a local moving man who silently loaded my five suitcases, a small armoire, my CD collection, three boxes of books, a computer, and some Ming-style chairs into his beat-up old van. "Chu lai," he called to me, wiping the lines of sweat rolling down his cheek with a crumpled Kleenex and motioning to the passenger seat. *Come on.* I jumped into the van, glad not to have to pay for a taxi ride across town. As he drove, I rode in silence, watching my Hong Kong life pass before me. We lurched down Conduit Road, and in my mind I said good-bye to the pristine high rises, the startling panorama of the harbor, the parade of gleaming Mercedeses whizzing up the hill, the lively expat pubs, with their Ralph Lauren–clad crowds noisily spilling out onto the curb. Then we descended into the flats of Hong Kong, where gas fumes choked the air. Discarded wooden crates sat in anarchic piles on the corner. The fluorescently lit shops sold dried stingrays, ginseng root, and lotus soup.

After the moving man dumped my things into my tiny, laughably bare apartment in Sai Ying Poon, I plopped onto the couch and cried. Dabbing at my eyes with toilet paper, I looked around the flat. I had rented it several months before, but given my open invitation to stay at Nigel's luxurious digs, I hadn't spent more than a few nights there—and it showed. The two or three framed photographs on the wall hung askew. The walls were streaked with water stains and smelled of mildew. Boxes filled with my winter sweaters and old books sat in a stack in one corner of the living room.

"My new home," I snorted. "Welcome to the height of luxury." Through the window came the aroma of my neighbor's dinner as it sizzled in a wok—fermented bean curd. Gone, of course, was the Thai maid; my flat had a galley-sized kitchen with an archaic refrigerator. The view? My bedroom window faced a fish store. And forget about space to rollerblade. My living room was barely large enough to fit a love seat and one chair.

I thought back to the Christmas holidays I had spent at Nigel's family home in England, near the Scottish border. Even if I never truly loved Nigel, I had fallen passionately in love with his house. A graceful 1920s estate set on lush rolling lawns, the Carter family home looked like a *Home & Garden U.K.* photo spread waiting to happen. At holiday time, the living room was dressed up with an eight-foot spruce that smelled of Scottish forests. Jewel-like heirloom baubles hung from every branch. We ate dinner around a hundred-year-old oak table in the kitchen, warming our hands above the Aga when the winter chill of the English countryside became too much to bear. In the afternoons, Nigel and I pulled on Wellingtons and bundled up in voluminous hunter green down coats and Burberry scarves and braved the two-mile hike across fields of horses, cows, and sheep to a neighborhood pub. There, pints of local ale and plates heaped with shepherd's pie awaited us. (Nigel refused to walk anywhere unless food and drink lay at the end of the trail.) I would never have described Nigel as a happy person—he always seemed profoundly conflicted about what was important in life—but when he returned to his family home in that verdant, peaceful English village, he seemed uncharacteristically relaxed and, well, almost content. *Almost.* Recalling those days together, I allowed myself to think fondly of him for a few moments.

Then my elderly neighbor switched on his transistor radio and the scratchy strains of Cantonese opera jarred me out of my reverie. I returned from the graces of upper-middle-class England to the lower-middle-class confines of Hong Kong—and my cramped flat. Was my childhood replaying itself in this never-ending cycle of moving from low to middle to high to low again? My eyes settled on a stack of letters and cards that Ajay had written me during these past few months. One of them featured a photo of an Alaskan husky with the words "Peace on Earth" written across it. Ajay had sent it in August, not realizing it was a Christmas card. I had to ask myself, how well—really—did I know this person? We hadn't so much as gone on a date; never had we even kissed. I couldn't even remember how tall he was.

I tried to imagine Ajay in India, to conjure up a scene from his life there. Of course, I knew of the Indian palaces and pampered lives of the maharajas, but Ajay lived in the city. I didn't know much about India's urban centers, but what I did know concerned me. I had seen international news footage of India—beggars crowding the street corners, shoeless children in tattered clothing, city slums teeming with filth and disease. I could only envision something like this: Ajay in a white Indian pajama suit sitting on the floor of a small third-story apartment, with a half-dozen family members surrounding him. I saw an aged grandfather reading the *Times of India*, two small cousins spinning a wooden top in a corner, a spinster aunt ironing the family's mounds of cotton clothing, Ajay's mother chopping onions and potatoes in a windowless kitchen, and Ajay, propped in front of a laptop computer, trying to write his latest *Asiaweek* story, amid all this domestic chaos. Of course, I realize now how narrow my view of Indian life was and almost laugh aloud. But at the time this was the modest scenario that I believed awaited in my future.

I gasped and rubbed my temples. "What if this is all a crazy fantasy?" I asked myself. "What if Ajay is not the one for me, and I've just broken up with someone who would have always taken care of me?" I thought suddenly of the intricate Tibetan rug Nigel had given me for Christmas and the glamorous birthday party he hosted for me at the China Club, all of us sheathed in silk and diamonds. I picked up Ajay's letters, postmarked in Hindi, and fanned myself with them. It was so much hotter, so much stickier, in Sai Ying Poon than it was in the Mid-Levels, where Nigel lived. "I can't believe I traded a flesh-and-blood man for this ridiculous stack of promises," I muttered, shaking my head.

Early the next morning, I was jolted awake by the sound of the fishermen unloading their trucks filled with half-dead grouper and catfish. They cursed each other—"Aiya! Aiya! Siu-sum-ah!" *For God's sake, watch out!*—and blasted Cantonese pop music as if nobody in the city could possibly be asleep. Clang! Bang! Screech! This was the soundtrack of my new life. "Yama goucho-ah!" one fisherman cried, as he started up his truck and roared off. *You've got to be kidding.*

One month later, I met Ajay at Kai Tak Airport. I caught sight of him walking through the terminal, wearing a white collarless shirt, jeans, and leather sandals. Striding amid the frantic, noisy crowds of Cantonese travelers, he practically glowed, as if he were a young deity. He carried with him a duffel bag crammed with treasures for me from India: sapphire earrings, embroidered coasters, a painting by a young Delhi artist, a tiny wrought-iron sculpture of a woman reading a book, an Indian cotton comforter cut from a hand-blocked paisley fabric. They were all stunning, thoughtful gifts. Then he brought out a stack of the letters we had written to each other by e-mail. He had printed each one, meticulously arranging them according to date. As a crowning touch, he had tied a raffia string around the pile. When I showed him the identical collection of our missives that I had printed and placed lovingly on my dressing table, we burst into laughter and held each other. Perhaps this is my destiny, I thought to myself. To live in this tiny, unremarkable flat with a kind, handsome, soulful man I could love forever. Ajay and I said nothing, but we both sensed a profound force taking control of our lives. We had both found home.

A week after landing in Hong Kong, Ajay proposed.

And I said yes.

⤞ 4 ⤝

Good-bye High Life, Hello New Life

Ajay moved his bags in and never moved out. He managed a transfer to our Hong Kong office, and we began our new life together. Our first few weeks together left me feeling certain about Ajay's sweetness, but not so sure about the 180-degree turn my life was suddenly making.

Over the next few months, we allowed our lives to unfold and intertwine. Ajay easily bonded with our mutual *Asiaweek* buddies over noisy Sunday dim sum lunches in our 'hood. We spent weekends hiking up tropical trails on the nearby islands and hanging out at the HMV, listening to the latest CDs. On occasion, we talked about all the children we would one day have.

At midday, Ajay popped down to my office and we strolled to Victoria Park to the outdoor *dai pai dong,* a Chinese café. We lunched on spring rolls and noodles as the cockatiels screeched in the trees. More than once during our lunch hour, we spread out a bamboo mat and napped in a shady patch of the park. Evenings, we walked along the harbor, stopping to sit on a stoop and share an ice cream cone or to roam the aisles of our favorite used bookstore. The Filipina amahs walking to church, chatting noisily in Tagalog—that was a parade for us. The old men dressed in their singlets, listening to Cantonese opera and showing off their dogs in the park to each other—well, that was a celebration.

After three months of life together, we went on our first holiday. Boarding a tiny skiff in Phuket, Thailand, we crossed the Andaman Sea until we reached the shores of Railay Beach, a serene stretch of sand untouched by the Ritz-Carlton. Our dimly lit hostel room cost about twenty dollars a night—forget about room service, our quarters didn't even have hot water. But somehow that was okay. We spent most of the day stretched out under leafy banana trees, reading George Orwell and Arundhati Roy and staring out at the waveless lagoon. As we sat at the beachfront cafés in the late afternoon and raised our fifty-cent piña coladas to each other, I could not help but think how stunning the sunset looked—even more beautiful than it did from the terrace of the private villa I shared with Nigel during a trip to Bali, not so long ago. Most of the time, Nigel and I would not even be able to glimpse the sun's descent; he was always having one more puffed-up conversation with his mates before we ventured out into the evening air. By then, the sunset had disappeared into the ocean, a glow of blazing pink along the horizon, the sun already sunk behind an oil rig, a mocking suggestion of what could have been.

✦

And yet life with Ajay was certainly not perfect. How could it be? Perfection? Happiness? They were a state of mind, not an objective reality—that much I realized. Most people can't just change overnight, and I know I certainly didn't. I had just made a radical 180-degree turn, and that brought with it a whole new set of concerns. I'd spent years reveling at the height of society, and part of me adored the view from the Peak, Hong Kong's highest point—both physically and metaphorically. Now, even with this fascinating man sharing my breakfasts, lunches, and dinners, I found walking through Central Hong Kong to be a melancholic journey.

My old life beckoned to me whenever I passed a gleaming store window. But I could barely afford to dry-clean the dresses I already owned, let alone buy anything new. I loathed waiting in the queue for minibuses and felt mocked by the Chanel-suited *tai tais*, those wealthy Hong Kong housewives lunching at chic hotel cafés, picking at HK$240 bowls of designer noodles and HK$300 chopped salads with their gleaming silver chopsticks. In this city of buffets heaped with oysters on the half shell, I was quickly growing tired of having tofu, wok-fried at home, yet again.

I spent the long journeys across town on the bus staring out the window and contemplating the upheaval of my former life. What I wondered: Could I ever really be satisfied with more depth, more connection, but no luxury? All the while, Nigel was still calling, leaving me messages, each more grasping than the last. "Joyce Flowers just opened in the lobby of my building," he said on my voice mail. "I thought about how much you loved getting those delectable blooms. You do love displaying them in your office, don't you? How about we meet at your favorite little sushi place in Lan Kwai Fong?" I won't lie. The promise of that swish, fragrant existence did beckon to me. Especially since my new life with Ajay was less about gazing at city lights from the top-floor restaurant at the Peninsula, and more about drawing up our oh-so-tight budget on the first of every month as the lights from the fish market blared through our terrace windows.

We declined most dinner invitations and suggested meeting friends for harborside walks or coffee instead. I even hesitated before indulging in a freshly baked croissant in the window at the Mandarin Oriental bakery, reasoning that rice crackers from the corner Park 'n' Shop would satisfy my hunger just as quickly. I was fully aware of the irony of my present situation. So many years ago, as I had boarded a flight out of L.A., I thought I had escaped the middle-class subsistence I dreaded, with its Sunday coupon clipping, utilitarian underwear, and make-do spirit. Yet here I was, so-called glamorous magazine columnist, right back where I started.

Yes, we enjoyed simple moments together, but daily life with Ajay brought about cultural clashes, some of them less endearing than others. Ajay's lack of pretension could be charming, but it was also sometimes, well, embarrassing. Expat Hong Kong was a whirl of formal balls, dinner parties, and black tie weddings, but Ajay hadn't considered that when he packed. He did not bring a single suit with him when he first moved. Two weeks after he landed, I was invited to an ex-flame's wedding at the American Club. I donned my most beautiful gown, a floor-length crimson slip dress, and exotic diamond earrings. Ajay dressed in the best clothes in his suitcase: a linen shirt, plaid trousers, and leather moccasins. He looked handsome as always to me, but clearly not up to colony standards. Let's just say le tout Hong Kong sat up and took notice.

"I see you found a new man," said Charles, the groom, an ironic smile pasted on his handsome face. Charles still asked me out for after-work drinks, even though his engagement band shone from his ring finger. He was flawlessly turned out in an Armani tux, his black hair slicked back, Prada glasses perched on his nose. "You've been hiding him from us, haven't you?" he said. I tried to play it cool, but what I was thinking was, poor Ajay. I knew he felt the judgment of three hundred society wags burning into his jacketless back. I did, too. As the crowds glanced at me, and then gave Ajay the once-over, I could practically read the mocking captions floating from their well-coiffed heads: Oh, how the mighty have fallen.

How could they possibly see what I saw in Ajay? Well, they couldn't. Or more likely, they refused to. So many Hong Kong residents were immigrants from the mainland, either peasants who had radically reinvented themselves or city elite from Beijing and Shanghai who, throughout the tumult of the twentieth century, were forced to leave everything behind when they had fled China for their lives. Most of Hong Kong's privileged class had clawed their way to the top; because of this, outward symbols of success meant everything. Whatever you might possess on the inside hardly seemed to rate. When they looked at Ajay they didn't see a soulful, gentle writer who brought grace and calm when he walked into a room. What they saw was an outsider who couldn't afford a tux.

At awkward moments like that, truthfully, I found myself asking what exactly it was that I saw in him.

✦

After the wedding dinner ended, and most of the partiers sped off in their Benzes and Rollses, Ajay and I strolled around the moonlit grounds of the American Club, stopping to toss a ten-pence coin into a gurgling fountain.

"What did you wish for?" I asked.

"I can't tell you exactly, or it won't come true," Ajay said. "But my vision had you and a room full of beautiful children in it, that's for sure." I stared out into the harbor and smiled. The evening might have been a sartorial disaster, but we were still having a magical night together. I thought back to a Robbie Burns dinner I'd attended with Nigel the past winter. By the time the last reel had been danced, Nigel was already floating into his mind bubble, and I was dreading the long, silent ride home.

✦

My circle of Hong Kong friends were both amused and appalled by my new fiscal constraints. Arabella, a well-heeled London-born girl, was by far the most vociferous—and the least humored—by my fall from riches, my self-inflicted exile from the smart set. Recently engaged to Piers, a wealthy barrister (and one of Nigel's best friends), Arabella waved her almost comically big diamond engagement ring back and forth as she cautioned me, like Jane Austen's Emma, about my prospects. "I mean, Ajay is divine in many ways, but it can't be fun taking the minibus everywhere, can it? You know, all those contagious local people coughing at the fumes all the time. Think about it, darling."

Arabella spoke from experience. Before she had reeled in Piers, she was your classic failed Londoner, having come to Hong Kong with little more than two suitcases full of Marks & Spencer rags and a little black book filled with a few choice phone numbers. Back then, she was known to walk three kilometers in the soul-oppressing subtropic humidity just to save HK$3 on minibus fare. Her first few months in Hong Kong were spent crashing on the couches of accommodating London friends of friends as she pounded the pavement for work as a publicist. When she turned her nose up at my new circumstances, I wondered—almost aloud—about her failed memory. "Too many gin and tonics at the China Club cause a brain freeze, darling?" I wanted to ask her but didn't. I might have moved to a flat well below the Peak, but I still believed in taking the high road.

A week after my tête-à-tête with Arabella, my good friend Charla asked me out for lunch. It was a mild joke among our crowd that Charla had married smartly, that she had done things the "right way." Her husband worked in finance (although nobody had a clue what he actually did), and they lived the classic expat existence—four-bedroom flat, view of the harbor, live-in maid, and holiday trips to any country that had a Four Seasons. Charla always patiently listened to me when I used to complain about Nigel. I admired her beauty, her tasteful flat, her vision of life, her standards. Being wealthy and pampered didn't keep her from developing her heart or brain. I loved her and she loved me. That day, after we supped on gourmet Thai food—her treat— she grabbed my hand. "You know, I can't really imagine you not shopping for the rest of your life," she said, peering into my eyes. "Ajay is from India. You're from Los Angeles. Do you really think you can live out the future his way?"

Such words stung. But my friends certainly got me thinking. And worrying. While I thought I had finally found the path to my destiny, these buddies thought I had simply taken a wrong turn on the highway to the future, a bad-luck detour into an unpleasant lifestyle slum. Were they right? Had I lost my way?

✦

I see now that these friends were acting out of genuine concern, not snobbery. It didn't make sense to them: How could I move from the Mid-Levels to the flats and expect to be happy?

A few days after we'd returned from Railay Beach, Ajay got an official-looking letter from London. "I'm pleased to inform you," began the missive from Ajay's U.K.-based agent, "that *Give 'Em Hell, Hari* has been accepted for publication." Included in the envelope: a contract offering 750 pounds sterling (about US$1,200) for the book. That night we celebrated with a special dinner on the terrace. "Maybe with that money we could plan a return trip to Thailand," Ajay said as he lifted his glass of Portuguese rosé.

The next morning, we idled in bed a little longer than usual. Finally, there was some surplus money in the bank, and we both realized that if we needed to, we could catch a cab to work and forego the dismal minibus ride. I was rinsing the breakfast dishes in our tiny galley kitchen as Ajay brushed his teeth in the bathroom when suddenly I heard him cry out.

"Oh no! My toof! My toof!" I ran into the bathroom. Ajay was clutching his mouth and staring into the sink. "My cap! It fell into the think and went down the drain," Ajay lisped. He lowered his hand and showed me the black gap where his tooth had been. Ajay called the office. He'd be late, he explained, and ran off to find an emergency dentist. When he finally came into the office that afternoon, his temporary cap was in place, but his face was ashen. "What's the matter?" I asked.

"You're not going to like this," he said slowly. "The cap cost me a lot of money."

"How much?"

He paused. "My book money is gone."

I steadied myself on the side of my desk.

"I'm sorry," Ajay said quietly.

I took a deep breath. "It's not your fault," I said, blinking back tears. "How could it be? "The important thing is that your tooth is fixed."

There would be no return trip to Railay Beach, and it was back to the minibus and soy-based dinners for us.

Surely, having Ajay in my life was worth the trade, wasn't it? He was one of the kindest, most thoughtful people I had ever met. If I fell sick, he dropped everything to make me fresh *khichry* (an Indian rice porridge) and bring me a stack of good books to read. He sat by my bedside reading funny quotes from the newspaper as I blew my nose for the ninety-ninth time.

Whenever we were apart, even if we were reading in different rooms in the apartment, my heart cried out for him. Maybe some part of me sensed that with Ajay now in my life, my view of the world was shifting, and he was an inextricable part of that. Once when he was more than two hours late for dinner, I became practically nauseated with worry. Pacing from the living room to the patio, I stood out on the terrace and peered into the busy street below. No sign of Ajay. I repeated this hunt about ten times over the next hour. What if he'd gotten lost and couldn't find his way home through these Chinese streets? He had no cell phone, so calling him wasn't an option. Instead, I telephoned the local police headquarters and explained that my boyfriend was extremely late and that I was deeply concerned. I could hear the officer on the other end of the line suppressing a laugh.

"Officer, you don't understand," I protested. "He doesn't know his way around. He's not from Hong Kong. He's from India." First there was silence, and then the officer said, "Your boyfriend is from India? Oh, madam, relax. He is just out having a few drinks with some friends." I was about to start shouting down the line when I heard the doorknob turning. It was Ajay. Finally.

"Where have you been?" I cried. "I've been worried sick over you." The explanation: He had decided to walk home through Wan Chai to get some fresh air and passed the harbor. Once there, he suddenly felt compelled to witness the sun sink into the horizon, its fuschia and purple streaks reflecting off the skyscrapers. "I'm sorry," he said, head bowed, as I stood with my arms akimbo, fuming. "I should have called. The sunset reminded me of a trip to Bombay I'd taken with my parents when I was nine. I just wanted to enjoy the sky."

*

There was clearly something much stronger than simple attraction and a common love of sunsets drawing us together. I didn't realize this when I first met Ajay, not even as I got to know him through our letters, but ultimately it dawned on me: Since I opened that first book in the library so many decades ago, a certain India had always called to me—the India I had seen in that book of palaces and maharanis.

I had long held on to an idea—at least somewhere deep in my subconscious—of India as a land of sitar concerts under a balmy evening sky, camel rides across the desert, and aromatic feasts spread across long wooden tables. Of lovely people in stunning, jewel-bedecked saris and pajama suits. Of searchers who meditated for days on end in the hope of arriving at a greater truth. Of the keepers of some secret life wisdom passed down through the generations. This sublime side of India was, of course, in distinct contrast to the land of beggars, disease, and poverty that I had feared. In essence, I had two fantasies of India—one opulent to an extreme, the other destitute and desperate to the opposite extreme.

The few Indian people I had known in my life had etched themselves into my memory in vivid ways. Most Indians in the West spoke English fluently (middle- and upper-class students learned the tongue of their British colonizers from an early age), so it was easy to engage in deep conversation. But Indians rarely said the expected; they might speak English as well as the rest of us, but they were not Americans. For example, when I once casually asked an Indian acquaintance if she had fun showing her family around at Disneyland, she practically scowled at me and said, "It was so frivolous. If all those people there spent half their ticket money on relieving poverty we'd live in a much different world." Their perspectives were formed on the other side of the globe, in a society that had some Western infrastructure but that was essentially Indian—and that brought a certain poetry, richness, and knowledge, and a vastly different political outlook, to the conversation.

In London, in graduate school, I met Sonia, an Indian born in Trinidad. She had a diamond nose ring and cropped hair that she'd dyed shocking pink. When I first glanced at her, she scared me a bit, just like those punks with stiff Mohawks cruising

King's Road did. I found her oddly alluring. She lived in a sleek flat in Hampstead with an emotionally stunted British boy from a prominent family. Sonia refused to wear clothes in any other colors but black and white, and that was so she'd match the all-gray walls of the house. We spent that whole magical year in London sharing the stories of our decades across the pond from each other, both of us being Asian women living in Western societies, and over lamb curries and plowman's lunches, we talked about our families and growing up. Conversations with Sonia were rarely warm and fuzzy—she challenged me to think deeply about racism, class, and solipsistic Western perspectives. She pushed me to think about my life in different ways.

Then there was Omari, a college student who worked in the lobby kiosk of the building where I was once employed. As his kindly parents arranged boxes of Tic Tacs and manned the till, Omari served the yuppies in the skyscraper their morning coffee and cinnamon buns. I often caught him staring, like an awkward teenager with a crush, and sometimes he would giggle because he was nervous. A few times he slipped me a cup of homemade chai and a muffin. Another time he carried a stack of my magazines up to my office for me. After a while, I looked forward to visiting the kiosk every morning, if only to say hello to Omari and to witness the gentle dynamics of his family behind the counter, so different from my parents' own unpredictable relationship.

I still vividly remember my first visit to an Indian restaurant. I was in college, and my mother and I had driven up to Northern California to visit Peter, my artist brother, living in Berkeley. He offered to take us out to lunch at what must have been the cheapest place in town. "It's called Mezhban, on Telegraph Avenue. It's Indian food—have you ever tried it?" he asked us. My mom and I looked at each other dubiously. "You won't believe the buffet," he said. "It'll revolutionize your life."

"Can't we just go to someplace normal?" I asked, feeling my irritation rise at his insistence. I had grown up enamored of Indian palaces but refused to try a single curry. "Indian restaurants always seem a little weird." I still remember reluctantly pulling open the restaurant door and seeing the waiters with their white Nehru-collared shirts. I recall smelling the pungent spices—cumin, coriander, *garam masala*. It was so overwhelming, as if all my senses were suddenly engaged, as if I were coming to life again—more than I bargained for at an Indian dive. I can still envision my brother sitting at the table with a heaped plate, devouring lentils with this beatific look on his face. At first, I picked at the Chicken Korma and Aloo Gobi and the strange rice with the peas thrown into it. But before long I was eating like a normal person, and then really digging in. I headed back to the buffet for seconds, and then thirds. By the end of the meal, I was hooked.

Could I have known then that India would become such a major part of my life? There was just no way, at least not consciously. For while my first impressions of India were of pink palaces and bejeweled royalty, as I grew older I also learned about the country's underbelly. In high school I'd seen the *National Geographic* photo essays of impoverished Indian families begging on the street, and the deformed men afflicted with elephantitis. I saw pictures of village huts made of cow dung and sprawling shantytowns in Bombay—I would wrinkle my nose as I looked at them, practically smelling the stench rising from such photographs. I'd heard that even tourists who stayed in five-star hotels could fall ill with terrible diseases such as dengue fever, malaria, and parasitic infections and end up sweating it out in local hospitals like the poor colonial victims in a Rudyard Kipling fable. A current events class taught me that even if you were middle-class, you probably shared a tiny flat with a dozen family members and rode to work or school on a public bus so jam-packed you had to gasp for air.

So while my fantasies of magical, mystical India may have conjured up the Beatles bedecked in marigolds, blissing out to the trills of a wooden flute and meditating next to a shaded lotus pond, my rational mind knew that India was one of the most desperate countries on earth, a place where the average person earned about a hundred dollars monthly. And I didn't want to be aligned with India because I didn't want to be poor. I wanted to be rich—just as my father had taught me. My fantasies of the country were one thing, reality quite another.

Yet here I was a decade after college, in love with a man from India. The country's economic status had risen in the 1990s, creating a cushy urban middle class. But Ajay's stories about urban life conveyed to me that the majority of the country was still very much impoverished and in the throes of development. One such tale came out during one of our first nights out in Hong Kong. As we were headed to a publicity event on the second floor of a restaurant in a swanky skyscraper, Ajay stopped at the foot of an escalator.

"What's the matter?" I asked.

"I'm still not used to such things," he said. I looked at him, puzzled.

"What things? It's an escalator . . . what's the problem?"

He told me that most Indians had never ridden one, as they were a rare, costly luxury installed only in swanky commercial buildings. He himself had first encountered one a couple of years ago in Japan, when he had left his country for the first time for a business trip to Tokyo. The escalator had gotten a bad rap in India. More than one woman had braved a ride only to get her trailing sari caught in the moving stairs, resulting in much bedlam and wailing in the echoing marble-lined lobbies of Delhi's and Bombay's five-star hotels.

Even though he didn't make a huge amount of money by Western standards, Ajay had been the third-highest-paid Indian journalist in Northern India. There he, too, had gotten used to living in the top echelon of society and buying whatever little treats caught his eye—an antique saxophone, a new set of dishware for his mother, rare books from the local antiquarian. Now, together in Hong Kong, we were both suddenly Have-Nots.

One night we were walking past the neon-lit shops in Causeway Bay when Ajay stopped in front of a store window. "That's a smart shirt," Ajay said, pointing to a pinstriped button-down. We ducked in and looked at the price tag: HK$700, about US$90.

I grimaced. "That's our grocery money for a week." He hung his head and walked out the door. He was dealing with Hong Kong prices now, and we were lucky if we could treat ourselves to a nice meal out once a month. At those moments, when we had to pass by a sushi restaurant, with its beckoning aroma of fresh miso soup, or listen to wealthy expat friends gurgle on about their next Mandarin Oriental adventure to the Philippines, things could get pretty tense between us.

One night after drinks at Arabella and Piers's house on the Peak, we walked down to the moonlit main road and waited for the minibus. One of Arabella's friends drove by in her Mercedes and then slowly backed up to where we stood. She rolled down her window and cooed, "Did you two need a ride into Central? I'm not sure the minibus is running at this hour."

"Thanks, but we've already called a cab," I swiftly lied and turned the other way before she saw my face glow red. Later, in the minibus headed down the hill, I sat next to Ajay with my arms crossed, my anger practically blowing out of my nose.

"We need to make more money," I said. "How can you stand to see me live like this?"

Ajay lowered his head, the lights of Central flashing neon colors onto his face. He said nothing for a while. Finally, in bed later that night, he cleared his throat and broke his silence. "In India, we have a saying: 'Always look down, never look up,'" he said. "When you are trying to determine where you stand in life, don't look upward at the rich people, the people with everything. Look downward at the people who have nothing, those begging on the street, those living in the slums. There's no end to looking up and feeling badly. And if you try to spit upward it only falls down upon your own face. Only by looking downward can you understand your dharma."

I wanted to scream. I wanted Ajay to offer me some promises, not proverbs. But for once, I held my tongue. I allowed his words to rattle around in my head.

In the days that followed, I tried to follow Ajay's example and console myself with loftier thoughts. Standing on the terrace, I gazed over the side to the street below. A woman dressed in a man's old plaid shirt and baggy jeans walked in sync with her young daughter, stopping to search trash cans for plastic bottles and aluminum cans. "Kan kan, Mama," the girl said, holding a handful of treasures. *Look, Mom, look at what I have.* The woman smiled and opened up her sack. The little girl smiled back. I imagined they shared a cramped flat with three other families in government housing across town. I knew that in Hong Kong, the poorest of the poor rented six-by-four wire cages stacked five high. That's where they would keep their few possessions—a change of clothes, a few pieces of dishware, a pack of cigarettes— and sleep at night. I'd seen whole families living on a single sampan bobbing on the harbor, the faces of the children already leathery from the relentless sun.

I sighed and shook my head. I had looked down and seen my dharma. So I'd never have a palace. At least I'd have Ajay. At least I'd have love.

There's a picture of my five siblings and me sitting in our den, a room we call the "new heng," a Chinglish way of saying new living room. In the photo, we're all dressed up for Halloween—I'm a cowboy in a black hat and red plaid shirt; my little brother Brian is also a cowboy in a gingham shirt. Our faces glow with delight. Many of my favorite family photos are snapped in that den. For us, the new heng is a place of beauty and order set amidst our unruly home, a palace rising from within a shantytown.

We children are not often allowed in there, and never do we spread out our toys there to play. Walking through the door we instinctively lower our voices and keep our movements measured—nobody wants to disturb the sanctity of the new heng. A ten-foot sectional couch cut from textured teal-blue silk curves around two sides of the room. Along another wall is a black lacquered shrine. Matching chairs made luxurious with plump red silk cushions anchor the other side. Embroidered scenes of China—a pagoda rising from a serene lake, an Asian owl perched on a cherry tree branch—grace another wall. In the middle of the room sits a red carpet, which has the characters for Double Happiness embossed along its perimeter. Years later, Mom will tell me that my father's father, Yeh Yeh, had custom ordered all the furniture as a housewarming present. The couch itself had cost five thousand dollars, the rug three thousand—and this was back in the 1950s.

I stretch out on the red carpet and trace the Double Happiness characters with my fingers, believing it will bring us luck. In that room I always feel pampered and protected, not hassled and trapped like I do in the rest of the house. My mother catches sight of me daydreaming on the rug and says, "Once you've walked on red carpet, you can never go back to concrete." I'm a kid and I have no idea what she means by that. So I laugh. She sounds likes she's channeling a fortune cookie prophecy. But her words stay with me.

✦

One evening, Ajay and I rode the minibus home during a driving Hong Kong rainstorm. Since the Sai Ying Poon bus stop was several blocks from our apartment, we had to walk the distance in the downpour. By the time we arrived in our building we were soaked, our hair matted to our heads and our light wool suits sopping with water. We got to our door, our path marked by a trail of puddles, and Ajay punched the code into the lock.

"What's that?" I said, pointing to liquid that was seeping out from our apartment into the hall.

Ajay's eyes flashed alarm and he pushed the front door open. Water poured out of our living room.

"Oh my God," Ajay shouted. "The rain. It must have flooded the terrace and seeped into our apartment! Quick, grab a bucket."

We spent the next few hours bailing out the rainwater, throwing it over the terrace walls and onto the street. Then we grabbed my Ralph Lauren bath towels and wiped down the furniture and mopped up the floor. My beautiful Tibetan rug, a gift from Nigel for my thirtieth birthday, was thoroughly soaked, its vibrant blues and reds now blurring into each other.

"It's ruined, completely ruined," I said as I slumped onto the couch.

Ajay sat down next to me and put his arm around my shoulders. "We'll buy another one. One of these days, we will. I promise."

For the next few days, every time I crossed the living room I thought of my devastated carpet, now draped over the terrace wall in a futile attempt to dry it out. As I walked across our living room floor, I no longer had this thing of great beauty to comfort my steps. Gone was this luxurious vestige of my former life. My melancholy lingered for weeks, and my mood was as black as the clouds that now hung above us. It was typhoon season.

I knew, given our financial status, that we would not be

replacing that Tibetan carpet anytime soon. I glanced over at Ajay quietly reading a book. It never seemed to matter to him what we had or what we didn't have. He was happy, it seemed, just to be here with me. For now, I reasoned, concrete would have to do.

5

Rebirth

That sodden evening in our apartment marked a turning point. Losing my treasured carpet to the storm shook me, that's for sure. But strangely enough, I realized, it didn't kill me. Could I actually learn to live with the bare floors? As if trying to find an answer, I broke out the Rollerblades and did a two-second loop through our microscopic living room. It was fun, but I admit that all the while I silently prayed I would not be carpetless forever.

"And why would I have to be?" I asked myself one afternoon as I walked along Queen's Road in Central. I was smart. I was capable. I could do this, I said almost aloud, as if reciting a mantra. I waited at a red light to cross the throbbing intersection at Queen's Road and Pedder Street and looked at the sea of shiny black heads in front of me and took in the swell of sound—horns blaring, Cantonese opera screeching from transistor radios, raucous conversations about the stock market, idle chatter about the local pop stars. There were way too many people in this insane city. I watched for the light to flash green and then braced myself and took a step, forcing my way against the human tide that pushed against me, moving in the opposite direction—forever moving in the opposite direction. I staggered through the crowd, finally managing to reach the other side of the street. Free from the throng, I ducked down a quiet alley, dropped my hefty tote on a pile of crates, and rubbed my pounding temples. Life in Hong Kong was always a test. On some level, I reminded myself, I was making the grade. I had relocated halfway around the world, clutching little more than a suitcase and a passport. And I had done it alone.

"Sometimes I wonder what possessed me to move here in the first place," I told Ajay that evening on the couch. My bones ached, my head throbbed. I wanted nothing to do with the cacophony of city lights and construction booming and banging outside our four walls.

We stared at the ceiling for a few moments, and then Ajay cleared his throat. "From all you've told me, I think you came here to be reborn."

Reborn?

I let the images float through my head—a diapered baby spiraling through space and time, landing in Hong Kong and suddenly sprouting into a grown young woman with flowing black hair, Lancôme lip gloss, and a DKNY frock. I laughed at the thought. In my five years in Hong Kong, I certainly had transformed myself from a headstrong and flighty whippet of a girl trying to escape the damage of her childhood to a worldly, polished, and forever-in-motion young woman whose career was finally taking off.

Since I'd stepped off that American Airlines flight from L.A. and waltzed into my first high-society Hong Kong dinner party,

Rebirth

I had often thought about the many lives we live within one existence on earth, the myriad personas we try on in our quest to find one that truly fits. If I was looking for a personal revolution, I had come to the right place. Hong Kong was a boomtown, a magnet for people who wanted to start over, a gleaming Emerald City for those whose lives were small but whose dreams were colossal. So many refugees from the mainland had washed up on these golden shores yearning to become someone else. Dirt-poor peasants, the politically damned, the socially oppressed, and those simply ravenous for something bigger.

It wasn't just the Chinese who came to find a new life or reinvent themselves. The British, who until 1997 could seamlessly turn up in Hong Kong and live and work in the colony with the wave of a passport—they routinely fled to Hong Kong, too. Thousands of U.K. citizens each year came here to outpace a collapsed career or a broken heart, to search for adventure or just to lay claim to a falsely elevated class background. The upscale Seibu food courts were filled with Brits whose less-than-posh accents revealed rough beginnings. Workers from lower-class families relocated to Hong Kong on cushy expat packages to do the labor that few others wanted to do—building the new airport from the ground up, for one—and they were handsomely compensated for the sacrifice.

These provincial wannabes suddenly found themselves hobnobbing with the smart set at the Jockey Club or on corporate junk trips slicing through the South China Sea, and commanding a staff of Filipina maids—a world they could never have stepped foot in if they hadn't ventured out of England, Scotland, or Ireland. Indeed, the fact that Hong Kong was brimming with U.K. losers and misfits had even spurred a widely used label,

"Failed in London, Try Hong Kong," and its all too appropriate acronym, FILTH.

Nigel was forever turning up his nose at a certain posse of hypergroomed girls from London trying to pass themselves off as well-bred fillies. Once while dining at the China Club, he pointed out a lovely girl with aristocratic good looks and a measured élan straight out of a Somerset Maugham novel. "That Caroline is an absolute fraud," Nigel sniffed. "Grew up in Essex, went to some third-rate university, works in PR. And now she acts as if she's landed here straight from Princess Diana's inner circle. Such an imposter."

Even the hugely successful, Oxford-educated businessman David Tang had rebirthed himself in Hong Kong. His family had originally come from the southern farming region of Guangzhou, but when push came to shove, he named his chic lifestyle company Shanghai Tang, after the famously cosmopolitan city in the north. Let's face it: Guangzhou Tang simply didn't emanate the same rarefied appeal.

I knew the truth: I wasn't so much different from all these other pretenders to the throne. When I left Los Angeles so many years ago and turned up here, I, too, was seeking a radical break from my past and the ephemeral Hollywood universe I was writing about.

There was so much more I wanted to escape. My parents and their complicated relationship with money—and each other. My siblings and their constant battle to establish a hierarchy. It was almost as if we had a caste system within one family, and who was a Brahmin or an Untouchable seemed to change day to day, depending on what we had achieved that week. Bring home the As, the classroom accolades, and the sports awards and you got invited to watch TV in my father's room, cradling a bowl of ice cream in your lap. Anything less and you were faceless, nameless. Even worse, you were a nuisance, a disgrace. I wanted to escape all of this, myself, and the conflicting perspectives I had developed on money, love, and security.

We have each other but it isn't enough.

I needed to sort it all out. And what better place to do that than an island seven thousand miles from home?

So I quit my job, packed up my apartment, broke it off with my postcollegiate boyfriend, said hasta la vista to my family, and took off to Hong Kong for a simple reason: I wanted my life to change.

"You know, I think you're right in a way," I said to Ajay, sitting upright on the couch. "I came here because I wanted to be reborn. It's not like my life in L.A. was awful. I mean, I think lots of young girls dream of having what I had—a great job at a magazine, a cool producer boyfriend who loved me, invitations to amazing parties. I came here because I wanted to shed my old skin and become someone different. I think somewhere deep in my brain I was desperate to figure out a different way to live. But then I just fell into a lot more of the same. Well, that is, until I met you."

Ajay sat up and put his arm around me. "Well, rebirth, reshaping yourself—that can be a good thing," he said, nodding his head. "We Hindus highly recommend it, you know."

Ajay was only half joking. He'd been raised in a Hindu so-ciety, so reincarnation wasn't just a spooky theme for the latest blockbuster film, as it was for me. Rebirth was a fact of life. In India, people from all castes and classes commonly believe that the soul has multiple lives and the form you take reflects your karma from your previous life. If you were born into a Brahmin or princely family, it was probably because of your good deeds in past births. By the same logic, to be born an Untouchable is the result of bad deeds in previous lives. In fact, just to be born hu-man is a big deal in Hinduism. "It takes 640,000 births through the animal world to become a human," Ajay told me. Evidently, it's an excruciating process. As Ajay put it: "You start out as a cockroach and make your way up the food chain." Where do you end, I asked? "As a cow," he replied.

"A cow!"

"Yes, but an Indian cow—not one of your beefsteaks."

"But I've heard that cows in India are miserable, that they have to scavenge food from trash cans and live on the streets."

"Not all cows. Some have it really cushy. I once saw a cow in Bihar that lived in an air-conditioned barn and listened to piped music all day. It even had a mirror to admire itself in."

"I don't believe it."

"What don't you believe—the pampering of the cow or the possibility that she had it so good because of her karma?"

"Both."

A few weeks earlier, apropos of not much, Ajay had told me about a bizarre encounter he had during his twenties. He was living full-time in his family's ancestral village, a place he de-scribed to me as dusty and desolate. He was in between jobs and decided to give farming eucalyptus trees a try. As he walked through his village one day, he was stopped by one of the towns-people he knew.

"Good day, Mr. Singh," the man said. "May I call on your help? Something very strange has happened. My young son is just now remembering his last life—he believes he was part of a landown-ing family in Bulandshahr and would like to see them again. Sir, could you drive us to meet his family?"

Ajay explained to me that, every once in a while, children who have just begun to talk suddenly speak enthusiastically about the man or woman they previously were. In the case of the villagers, the Sohan Singh family, their three-year-old son, Rajinder, had swiftly been flooded by memories of his life as Anil, a man who owned a brick-making kiln in Garh, a bustling town thirty miles northeast of Mokimpur. The little boy recalled that he had a wife named Janaki and two children and said he had died sud-denly after a celebration in his village. When he passed away, he was lying in a hammock in the backyard. He remembered that when his wife found his body—his arms splayed, his tongue protruding from his mouth—she screamed.

Relatives of the village boy wanted to track down this past-life family. They asked around and discovered that there was a Bulandshahr brick factory owned by a businessman named Na-resh Jindal. Yes, he had a brother named Anil, who died about four years ago, from having gorged himself on sweets at a Diwali party. He was a diabetic, and the syrup from the mountain of *jalebi* he had devoured had sent his blood sugar to fatal levels.

As it turned out, Ajay couldn't take the villager and his son to Bulandshahr. His parents had driven the family car back to Delhi the week before, and he was getting around by foot and on horseback. So the man caught a ride with another villager. A few weeks after the encounter, he ran into Ajay again and told him of the peculiar reunion between his toddler and the family he had "left behind."

The Sohan Singhs brought Rajinder to the Jindal family home. Without prompting, the boy instantly recognized his so-called former wife and daughters, calling them by their pet names, Dimple, Allo, and Burfi. "I am here again—the same person," he explained to his past-life family when they looked at him in disbelief, sizing up his tiny form. "Only now I have returned in a small body."

When Ajay told me this story, I stared at him, amazed. "Weren't you freaked out?" I asked, slowly shaking my head.

"No, not at all," Ajay said. "Hindus believe that the human soul lives on long after the body has withered. It simply inhabits another body, whether that be human, animal, or insect. It's God's version of recycling. Where else would a soul go but into another body?" He shrugged his shoulders and held out his hands. His question hung in the air as I gazed out the window at an infinite sky. I didn't have an answer. But I was certainly interested in searching for one.

Forcing a rebirth upon one's self only goes so far. Like the little boy in the village, I had reached a point at which my soul started calling me home. So, after Ajay and I had been living together for six months, we decided to head to Los Angeles to spend time with my family. I hadn't seen my parents or my brothers and sisters for two years. During this time, my whole life had evolved—and some in my former Hong Kong circle might say it had devolved.

The last time I blew into L.A., Nigel and I descended from our business-class flight like boom-era gods, my carry-on loaded with gleaming goodies from Shanghai Tang. Rather than bunk with my parents in an unhip part of town, we lodged at the Shangri-La in Santa Monica and strolled along the boardwalk to a seaside restaurant every night.

During this visit with Ajay, we'd be riding coach across the Pacific and relying on the kindness of family and friends to put us up. Absent would be lavish gifts from the East—jewelry boxes, silk ties, cashmere scarves—and my hot-off-the-runway frocks. I wondered if the financial wear of the past few months would show. Would my family take one head-to-toe glance and wonder what great tragedy (or failure of judgment) had befallen me?

A few nights before our trip, as I arranged my sundresses and flip-flops in my suitcase on the living room floor, I turned to Ajay and said, "I'm scared."

"Why?" he said, concern shining in his eyes. "What are you scared of? We're just going home to see your parents, your brothers and sisters. Your family will always be your family." He sat down on the floor next to me. "I sometimes think the sadness I see in you is from your broken ties," he said. "Only by going home can you make yourself whole again. My mother used to tell me this old Indian saying when I was a boy: 'I have searched from the village to the city to the banks of the Ganges, but I found what I was looking for only when I went home.'"

I reached for Ajay's hand, brought it to my lips, and kissed it. It smelled of lavender and mango, the fragrant notes in his village-made ayurvedic lotion. He was right. Maybe what I was most afraid of was confronting my past, dealing with the silence and unresolved feelings I had allowed to echo in the thousands and thousands of miles that separated my family and me.

Still, fear or no fear, there was no stopping this desperate longing to go home. It was time for my new self to meet my old self.

And it was time for my new love to meet the people who have always sustained me—even if I hadn't admitted as much to myself in several years. They say you can never go home, but I was determined to make it most of the way there. When we decided that on our budget we couldn't afford a hotel and needed to find one of my siblings to stay with, I picked up the phone. I dialed a series of numbers by heart, surprised by how easily they came back to me.

"Brian, it's Ali," I said, blinking back tears. "I'm landing in L.A. on Tuesday." It's a reassuring aspect of human nature that no matter what has passed between two people, once close, they seem always to search for a way to reconnect.

When Brian heard my voice on the phone, he laughed. "Grace," he said, calling to his wife. "Bring the baby over here. Ali's on the phone!" He informed me that not only were we welcome to stay at his house, but he also expected me to do babysitting duty during our trip.

"Congratulations on finding Ajay," he said. "Can't wait to meet the dude. And don't even try to make any long distance calls from my telephone this time. I'm blocking the international service before you get here." I couldn't stop myself from laughing. We were on our way back.

We certainly weren't able to treat everyone to dinner at the Ivy—even if Nigel had—but everyone expected Ajay to reach them through their stomach anyway.

"Okay, the maharaja scores double points if he cooks," my sister Ann said on the phone before we left Hong Kong. "Can he make lamb *vindaloo?*" So there Ajay was the night before our long journey, pouring cumin and mango powder into Ziploc bags and tucking the packages into a suitcase, next to ten gleaming Asian eggplants.

"You might not believe this," I said to Ajay, eyeing his stash, "but you can actually buy eggplants in America at a place called Ralphs. And what's with all the spices—they look like illegal substances! You are so going to be strip-searched by customs."

"I'll take my chances," Ajay said, his eyes shining with the zeal of the perfectionist that he is. As if to make a point, he tossed a fresh young coconut into the bag and zipped it up. "If I'm cooking for your family, they are going to taste India, not some pathetic American facsimile. Your Ralph can keep his eggplants."

We called all the Gees to Brian's house for a noon lunch one Sunday, but at 2 P.M. that fateful day Ajay was still frantically grating fresh ginger and chopping tomatoes. The night before, he'd spent five hours making homemade cheese (and a royal mess of gallon containers of milk and half-squeezed limes).

"What are you going to do, stand there cooking all day?" my father barked, shaking his leg up and down as he sat on the couch.

"I could have ordered takeout from a stand in Bombay and had it delivered to L.A. faster than this," Ann growled sotto voce to me. She reached for another piece of *naan* and poured herself another full glass of Shiraz.

But when Ajay's meal—*baigan bharta, mattar paneer,* and *chunnas*—finally graced the table, it was clear: The effort was worth it. "I am floating over the Taj on a magic carpet," Brian said as he spooned steaming hot *mattar paneer* into his mouth. "There are like twelve subtle layers of flavor in every single bite. Incredible!"

Later that afternoon, Brian took me aside. "Gotta tell you, Ali, I like this guy," he said. "Better set the wedding date now before he figures you out."

Before she left for home, my older sister kissed Ajay on both cheeks. She stood back for a moment to take in his handsome visage and regal carriage. "I'm going to tell all my friends that my little sister is marrying an Indian prince."

Little did any of us know how right she was.

While the sibs loved Ajay, they still questioned the choice I was making. "Don't take this the wrong way," Brian whispered one afternoon, as he caught me flipping through the *L.A. Times* real estate section and gazing wistfully at a picture of a whitewashed two-story Santa Monica hacienda. He glanced back into the kitchen, where Ajay was whistling an Indian folk tune while he made chai for all of us. "But you're gonna have to wait till your next life for a house like that. I mean, maybe if you married Nigel, or that other guy you were dating—what's-his-face, that Morgan Stanley preppy—you'd stand a chance at a pad like that.

But Ajay? He's a journalist who's probably from a modest background in India. Are you sure you know what you're doing?"

At a pool party she held in our honor, my older sister pulled me aside. "You know, if you had just married Andrew . . ." She was referring to my postcollege boyfriend, a rich kid who was now producing movies and living in a ranch house in Malibu. "If you had, you wouldn't ever have to worry."

"But he wasn't right for me," I protested. "He treated me like an afterthought, not like 'happily ever after.' Did I tell you that one year he even blew off my birthday party so he could work late on a stupid alien film?"

"Yeah, well, at least you would have gotten something." She sighed and shook her head. Her diamond wedding ring flashed a million points of light around the pool patio. "This way, you're going to be stuck in some apartment all your life."

In one pivotal moment, her position "my little sister's marrying a prince of a man" had morphed into "but he's got zero net worth, and my little sister's a fool."

My head spun at these about-face comments. My family said they loved Ajay, but they didn't like his bank account. Nor did they like his third-world background. It was the same mixed message I'd gotten all my life: *We have each other but it isn't enough.*

I understood where my family was coming from. I was their glamorous, gifted, fearless sister who could snag a big fish if she'd just set her mind to it. We had all grown up wanting more—more attention, more love, more pizza, more peace—and we all spent our lives working hard for that. Despite our decidedly middle-class, sometimes traumatic beginnings, we were, each of us, a big success, if not financially then at least career-wise. Brian was a labor lawyer, Ann a respected social worker. Terry was a paleobotanist living in Germany, Peter was an accomplished artist, and my eldest sister had run her own business and raised brilliant children. Although none of us had achieved this, at our core, we believed that living in unequivocal comfort—a beach-side mansion, first-class flights, nannies to deal with the diapers, wash dishes, and do all the heavy lifting—that level of material compensation would go a long way to make up for any lack we had suffered as children.

But would it? I knew my siblings wanted the best for me, but with their designer SUVs, living rooms lined with too many over-priced tchotchkes, and requisite summer holidays in Oahu and Spain—the trappings of the upwardly mobile that they were—I wondered if they even knew what that was. What did you marry for, anyway: love or money?

I had clipped the *L.A. Times* photo of the hacienda to take back to Hong Kong—a memento of this poignant homecoming, a lifelong dream, a wish for the future. I took it out of my diary and threw it in the trash.

A few days later, Ajay and I were having lunch with my mom at a Pasadena restaurant. Ajay told my mother that they were born on the same day, August 15, twenty-five years apart. I could tell the pair—twin Leos, as I started to call them—felt an easy kinship. My mother's hand was placed on Ajay's arm as they wordlessly sat on the restaurant patio, soaking up the mild winter sun.

"Okay, you lovebirds, I'm going to check out the card shop," I said. "Back in a few." They didn't even flinch when I got up. As I began to walk away, I heard my mother say, "So, what is India like?"

When I returned about thirty minutes later, the pair was talking animatedly. Ajay was gesticulating, his hands out to his side, as if describing the size of something. My mother was blinking her eyes in what looked like disbelief. As I moved within earshot, I heard her say, "One hundred rooms? That's a very big house!"

"What's a big house?" I dropped my bags on a chair.

"Oh, you know, our family home in the village," Ajay said. "The one I told you about . . ."

"You told me about your village where you used to go hunting, the dusty one with the storks and snakes and no electricity." My face grew dark with confusion. "I've never heard anything about one hundred rooms before."

Ajay cleared his throat. He looked down into his coffee. "Our family home is a haveli, an Indian manor. I guess you could call it a small palace. My great-grandfather built it at the turn of the twentieth century. We call the house Mokimpur, after the village that surrounds it."

"A palace? Your family owns a *palace*? What's it like?"

"It's very nice."

"How nice?"

"It's beautiful," Ajay said. "There's not another house like it for miles around. I used to spend all my school breaks there with my family—all my uncles, aunts, and cousins. We have mango groves, a family temple, fields where the villagers grow sugarcane, wheat, and papaya. There are wild peacocks by the dozen and orchards full of other birds, too. I still know all their whistles by heart. There are cousins living in the other wings, but in the years to come, we'll share the main house with Karan, my younger brother."

"What? We're really going to live in an Indian palace? Are you joking?"

"Why would I be joking?"

"Why didn't you ever tell me this before?" I plopped into a chair, feeling dazed.

"Oh, I don't know. I just didn't think it was that important."

I glanced at my mother. Her grin stretched across her face. Her eyes were mere slits of glee. She nodded her head in self-congratulation, as if to say, yes, yes, yes, we did it! I silently prayed she wouldn't start pumping a fist into the air. It was fair to say that Ajay's disclosure had sent her into a state of bliss.

I wasn't far behind her. A tsunami of happiness—or was it validation?—slammed against me and rushed into my pores. My whole body was swelling with emotion, as if it were just coming to life. My mind went on a galloping camel ride to my future, straight to the triple-height foyer of an Indian palace— *my* Indian palace! At Mokimpur—my house even had a name— men floated through labyrinthine halls in silk turbans and gold sashes; women swanned around terraces in jewel-toned saris. Servants stood in each corner, waving giant peacock-feather fans. In my reverie, I glimpsed rooms lined with gilt-framed por-traits of maharajas and maharanis supine on velvet daybeds. I saw patios lit by hundreds of votive candles and heard sitar players strumming sultry tunes under a full moon. My mind snapped back into focus. My mother and Ajay were staring at me from across the table, and all I could do was shake my head in disbelief. Ajay didn't think that growing up in a palace was an important detail to mention to me? He clearly didn't know whom he was talking to.

Click-click. Click-click. Click-click. Click-click. The hazard lights are flashing in our light blue station wagon, the beat-up boat on wheels that we call "the Whale." My father has double-parked in China-town as he runs into a small restaurant that sells Peking Duck. I glance at the restaurant window and see the roasted birds hanging, brown and stiff, their necks twisted onto large steel hooks. And I know instantly where we're going: to that rich family's house, the big white gated mansion high on a hill above the ocean.

I don't know much about these people other than that my dad has spent a lot of time lately with the man who lives there, a slick blond guy with black-framed glasses, black slacks, and a big watch. He likes Peking Duck and so Ba brings him one each time we visit, even though my father complains and complains about the cost. The man always smells like cologne and cigarettes, and when he opens his double front door, his two children, one boy and one girl, rush out to greet Brian and me and pull us into their playroom.

"Come on!" the girl cries. "Let's go play." The playroom is lined with a half-dozen huge pinball machines, a simulated driving game, even a full-size Pac-Man game. Everywhere I look there are giant candy-colored rubber balls, roller skates, skateboards, surfboards, hula hoops, even a massive glass jawbreaker dispenser. When we tire of fiddling with one game, we move on to the next and the next, our tongues and lips bright blue and pink and yellow from sucking on the massive spheres of candy.

"Let's go swimming," the girl says to me, and we change into our

suits and head outside. The pool stretches out like an ocean. The family's surname and a dancing leprechaun in a green and black suit and top hat are painted at the bottom, and I remember staring through the chlorinated water at that montage, that tableau of fresh wealth, and wondering if I could ever swim fast enough to the pool's depths and touch it before my lungs ran out of air.

When it is time to leave, my father sprints out to the car and then bounds back into the house. "Here, I got something for you." He hands the man the Peking Duck, and I see the man and his wife exchange glances and smile. "Hey, thanks, Pete," the man says, accepting the foil bag and placing it on his kitchen counter.

The little girl grabs my hand and pulls me around the corner. "My dad doesn't like those ducks," she whispers. "He gives them to his friend."

My face twitches in confusion. "Why not?"

"He says they taste funny and he doesn't know where they're from."

We're wheeling down the winding driveway now, the four of us in the Whale, and my father idles the car for a moment. He glances back up the hill, at the big white mansion, as the black wrought-iron gates slowly clang shut. My mother and Brian and I turn around in our seats and gaze with him.

"Maybe not this year," my father says, "but someday, kids. Someday." I know he's talking about the mansion and the big pool with the leprechaun and the family's last name. And I know that we'll have our own big pool with a big GEE painted in bright red at the bottom and a playroom lined with toys and candy someday. And I know

he's talking about us striking it rich, richer than any of his siblings someday.

And I know that my father is telling the truth.

When we returned to Hong Kong, I decided to invite a dozen friends over to our flat for a terrace dinner. After such a costly trip to the States, we had no business throwing a big party, but I was in the mood to celebrate. So I set the outdoor table with sprays of bougainvillea, champagne flutes, and chilled bottles of prosecco, and my friends filed in, each carrying a bottle of Portuguese rosé or a box of egg tarts or a bouquet of supermarket flowers.

All around us, hurricane lamps cast a rich light onto our faces, transforming our small world into a bubble of good cheer. Ajay had spent the day cooking *daal* and *aloo gobi*—a simple but delectable spread of spiced lentils and potatoes and cauliflower—and we set out *naan* and *samosas* from an Indian cafe at Chungking Mansions. After so many weeks away in Los Angeles, I was thrilled to see my good friends Susan and Lisa from *Asiaweek*, and we sat next to the koi pond, catching up on Hong Kong news.

Just as we sat down for dinner, Arabella turned up. She was wearing a red dress and a short fur coat, even though it was a balmy 76 degrees. I air-kissed her cheeks, poured her a glass of bubbly. I looked down at my simple floral shift and ducked back inside our flat. I quickly shed the dress and wrapped myself into an embroidered silk sari, the color of ripe pomegranate seeds, slipped on some metallic heels, and headed back out to the party.

"So, how was that long journey home?" Arabella asked, raising one eyebrow. I knew she was alluding to our coach-class flight. I let the remark pass. She raised her eyebrow again. "Did the parentals approve of your latest?"

"They did, indeed," I said, forcing a smile. I looked at Arabella, wondering when exactly she had become such a bore. "I would say they're looking forward to his contribution to the Gee gene pool. Oh, and we got some interesting news about Ajay's family in India."

"Oh, really?" Arabella lifted her champagne flute and took a long, cool sip, all the while keeping her gaze fixed on my face.

"Yes, it turns out Ajay has quite a fascinating history. He grew up in a turn-of-the-century palace."

Arabella's mouthful of prosecco sprayed across the table. The party chatter stopped. Everyone turned to stare. "Oh, my God!" she cried out, grabbing a napkin and furiously dabbing at her face. "What! He grew up in a palace? Did his parents tend the grounds or something?"

"No," I said, calmly wiping the spew off my right hand. "It's his family home, built by his great-grandfather. One hundred rooms spread across twenty-six acres."

"But . . . but . . . how can that be?" Her eyes darted back and forth.

"Can't explain it. It just is. I guess it's the universe conspiring to give me everything I ever dreamed of." I shrugged. My Inner Princess beamed a dazzling smile.

Gracious in victory, I handed her a stack of Park 'n' Shop napkins. "Here, Arabella. There's prosecco all over your lovely fur. You might want to clean yourself up." Then I got up and crossed the terrace into the house, the golden embroidered border of my ruby-red sari bouncing moonlight all over my night of triumph.

During the next few years, Arabella and I would play social chess many more times. But when she confided about her divorce from Piers, only four years after their lavish wedding, the game stopped being amusing. "I have to look for a job, and I'm not exactly thrilled about that," she told me in an e-mail from London, the hometown to which she had returned. "And I'm in my late thirties and a single mom. Who in his right mind would want *me?*" I could have felt smug and victorious. Instead all I felt was heartbroken.

◄◄ 6 ►►

Castles in the Sky and Other Useless Places

When I was a little girl, I always believed I'd live in a château in some sweeping valley in France or in a Spanish-style mansion dotted with swaying palms and wild geese cavorting in the garden. Even though my mother sometimes wrung her hands over paying our mortgage, I was convinced my own house would be magnificent.

Such convictions of grandeur were something I must have inherited. My father also dreamed of rambling mansions with endless grounds, and he spent his entire working life, first as an engineer and then, to his embarrassment, as a bank appraiser, grasping at the sky. But how he'd make those dreams a reality, none of us knew.

In the 1960s, he began his Department of Water and Power job filled with promise, but a few years into his career, he fell into a thirty-foot ditch and broke his neck. I still remember staring out the picture window of our house as an ambulance returned him to us, transporting him into his bedroom on a gurney. After two months in traction, he went back to his office, wearing his short-sleeved dress shirt and a neck brace. His bosses didn't exactly greet him with open arms and bear hugs. My father wasn't the easiest person to get along with—my mom always grumbled about him "shooting off his mouth." His bosses refrained from sending him out on jobs—the clean desk treatment. After seven months, Ba couldn't stand going in anymore and left—an early retirement. One of his next employers, the City of Beverly Hills land surveyors, made his path clearer. When my father's employment contract expired, they simply shook his hand and said good-bye.

Still, on his earnings, my father managed to save enough to buy plots of land all over California, albeit in only useless places. When I was a child, seven or eight years old, my family spent our weekends visiting these "rectangles of heaven," as he called them.

Before our trips, my mother got up before the sun rose to pack enough sustenance for eight hungry mouths. We then trundled into our wood-paneled station wagon, our walking shoes neatly laced, and sped toward our future. My mother's foot space in the front seat was jammed with shopping bags brimming with our lunch—ham sandwiches wrapped in wax paper, potato chips, bottled drinks, and a roll of paper towels.

After a couple of hours we arrived at our destiny: a vacant lot. The doors flew open and my five siblings and I spilled out. As my mother spread out the picnic, I tossed a beach ball to my younger brother; the others played tag around the property. It hardly mattered that our promised land was covered in weeds and empty soda cans and nothing else.

Halfway home my dad would pull into a Denny's for dinner, and we'd gobble up burgers, fries, and Cokes. Afterward, we climbed back into the car for the long drive home in the dark.

Such joy. I learned early that these were the kinds of pleasures that real estate could bring you.

✦

Yes, my father chased after castles in the sky, but I think he believed that owning a grand house was his birthright. His father was an import-export tycoon and the mayor of L.A.'s Chinatown. My dad grew up above the family's general store on Hill Street. I still remember the steep dark staircase that led up to the four-bedroom apartment and the lanterns that hung in the living room, their tassels tickling the tops of my head with a swish of silk. From that vantage point, my father spent hours gazing out the windows at the downtown skyline—the kitschy, colorful pagodas and palaces of Chinatown, the parade of gleaming cars driven by excited tourists, and the skyscrapers of central L.A., which I imagine my father as a young child might have thought of as urban castles.

We spent our childhoods driving from our home near Pasadena down the Arroyo Seco freeway to Hill Street, and then tumbling out of the car to wander the Chinatown courtyards, pitching pennies into the fading wishing wells and dreaming of the lives that lay ahead for us. For me, those visions were almost always about the whole family moving into a majestic new house, with a tiled pool, walk-in closets, and a fancy intercom system. All of us, together.

Every month or so, my sisters and I put on our mod floral dresses and my brothers their vests and white shirts, and along with our wealthy cousins, we supped at the sprawling Chinese banquets my grandfather hosted. "Only peasants eat rice," my aunt would caution if we dared ask for a bowl. "Save your hunger for the abalone and the oysters." As if on cue, a line of waiters in white jackets and black bow ties would emerge from the kitchen, brandishing silver platters heaped with Chinese delicacies.

In the front of the restaurant my grandfather, Yeh Yeh, sat, looking like a benevolent emperor. He only spoke Cantonese, which I didn't yet understand, so it's not as though we ever had a meaningful conversation. But I was always captivated by his kind mien and his hands mottled with sunspots. I can still see his face, the way he smiled and patted the back of my hand and slipped me red envelopes stuffed with gold coins. When he died in the early 1970s, the family split apart, having fought over my grandfather's fortune and property. My dad's brothers took the bulk of the estate—they had spent many decades building up the family business, I understand now. After the funeral and the reading of the will, we saw our cousins maybe once a year; my parents could never quite transcend the belief that we had lost out on a more luxurious future. My relatives retreated to their gracious homes in the manicured suburbs; we, clearly the losers in the inheritance battle, tended to our wounds, pulling closed the doors of our little house in L.A.

My father sometimes told me of the home his family left behind in China, a two-story courtyard house. Indeed, it still stands in Guangzhou Province, our ancestral portraits hanging crooked from the walls, my grandmother and grandfather staring out from those framed photos at the few clan members who look after the place. Throughout my childhood I hungered to see that house, to touch imagined carved rosewood chests and run my fingers along silk bedding. I wondered if our cousins ever thought twice about that broken-down clan house. Why should

87

they, when they had their own palaces in America? But for me, the loss of this big house was cause for mourning, even when I was a child. That house was a piece of myself that we had left behind, an amputated limb or an excised organ, waiting to be reclaimed and returned to the very center of my body.

✦

My dad's dreams of vast acreage and castles in the sky didn't come without a plan. He was determined to build a fantasy cabin on our Cedar Pines mountain property in San Bernardino. One day he gathered all the kids into his office. "See these glass jars?" he asked, pointing to a row of empty jam vessels set atop his filing cabinet. "Every time you have an extra quarter, a dime that's just sitting in your pocket, toss it into one of these. In no time we'll have enough money for our mountain cabin." When I was older, I once poured out all the coins in our "dream cabin collection" onto the dining room table and counted. The grand total: $58.75.

My father did not disappoint completely when it came to real estate. In the 1980s he bought us a second home: a classic ranch house in a pristine San Fernando Valley tract community. We kids stayed in Los Angeles while my parents escaped there on the weekends.

This wasn't exactly a luxury for my mother. We children were her laughter and comfort, and leaving us was like cleaving her soul away. But my father needed to escape the city and our unruly family life, and so my mother dutifully packed their bags every weekend. "It's for his health, so his brain can rest," she said.

She would toss two crumpled twenty-dollar bills on the dishwasher to pay for our weekend food as if that would make everything all right. I think I was fourteen at the time; I needed my mother to guide me through the mean girls and Clearasil. But at that point our Friday afternoons no longer meant weekend road trips, kids and parents jammed in the car, the oldies channel turned up loud; it meant a silent, empty kitchen and McDonald's dinners. I had no idea why my dad's brain needed a rest—not yet, anyway. All I knew was that his tirades were happening more and more often and I was figuring out better places to hide, niches that could accommodate my growing limbs. I still remember coming home from school and finding nothing but a hastily scrawled note and a thin stack of money to greet me.

My father said he planned for us all to move into the new house as soon as the three youngest Gee children finished high school. That promise eased the pain of parentless weekends a little. On our first visit to the ranch house, Peter, Brian, and I raced upstairs to choose a room. Armed with No. 2 pencils, we excitedly wrote our names in the closets, claiming one bedroom each. I sometimes wonder if our childhood names—Boo, Bing, and Ali—are still scribbled on those closet walls.

My father never bothered to furnish the place. He seemed happy just to eat his meals on a metal TV tray, sitting on a lawn chair in the dining room. When he tired of being indoors, he dragged the chair to the driveway and sat in the sun with his flannel pajamas on. During those moments, his leg no longer shook up and down as if manifesting his jumbled mind. He stopped pacing through the house. This, finally, was the dream house he had been working toward. Happiness for him wasn't in the trappings of Wickes leather couches, Levitz floor lamps, and Lladro tchotchkes. Rapture came in staking claim to land of one's own. Bliss was in finally having found home.

Two years after he bought the house, my father began summoning us at 2 A.M. for emergency family meetings. The shoreline in Baja was being invaded by Guatemalans, he ranted. Who could protect our property—thirty-six miles of pristine beach? We glanced at each other, confusion on our faces. We had never even been to Baja.

A chemical imbalance—in retrospect we think he had bipolar disorder—was the cause of his delusions. All his fantasies revolved around owning other magnificent pieces of property: He was the CEO of a factory in Sri Lanka; he was the president of Disneyland; he owned the entire street on which my sister had just bought a cottage. One day, he decided to stop working as a bank appraiser. He dragged the expensive black lacquer furniture that his father had bought him in the 1950s down to the curb and telephoned Goodwill to cart it away. Another afternoon, my sister came home to find flames shooting out of the trash can. My father had taken our beautiful Chinese rug with the Double Happiness characters woven into it, doused it with gasoline, and set it on fire.

At the time, my mother could barely write full sentences in English. She'd been married at eighteen; by thirty-one, she'd had six kids. She had little hope of holding down much of a job in America. One year after my father had given up work, Mom called another kind of family meeting. She told us that she had no choice but to sell the ranch house. "Who wants a big house like that anyway," she said, shrugging her shoulders. "All the way out in the Valley, so hot out there, so far from the city." But

I remember that when she signed the transfer-of-deed papers she sobbed until her face was swollen and red.

Even now, when I drive past Lindero Canyon Circle Drive on the 101, the exit we took to the ranch house, a big part of me still shrieks and withers. If only I had been old enough, strong enough, capable enough to pay the mortgage, to save the house, to spare my family such dishonor. But I was only fifteen when we lost our home. Still, I felt more shamefaced than my mother did as we packed up my father's possessions—his TV trays, his scratched-up pots and pans, his stacks of old library books—and handed the keys over to the real estate agent.

I have no doubt this is why the very idea of Mokimpur—a real palace—meant so much to me. I learned from Ajay that nearly a century ago his great-grandfather envisioned a rambling manor rising from fields of wheat. Ignoring the doubts of men with lesser vision, he ordered it built and watched it take shape over a decade at the turn of the twentieth century. He constructed it with his children, his grandchildren, and their children in mind. He must have known Mokimpur would be a legacy that would last as long as stone.

A few weeks after I first learned about Ajay's family palace, I plotted my maiden voyage to India. I had to see for myself that this great family palace was for real . . . and not just my dream.

Part II

⊰⊹ 7 ⊹⊱

The Journey Begins

It was our first December together, and Ajay and I sat on an Air India flight bound for New Delhi. Seven months had passed since he'd moved into my flat in Hong Kong and proposed, and one month since I'd found out about the Singh family haveli. Now we were on our way to see a palace somewhere in the wheat fields of India. To say that I was excited about visiting my fiancé's palace was like saying the Taj Mahal was a nice little shack. I was in awe of the cosmos for having answered my subconscious desires, I was stunned whenever I thought about how lucky I'd struck it, and, well, I was apoplectic with excitement. Not only was I marrying a man who had the kindness and bearing of a royal, I was now on my way to see his grand hundred-room home.

Our plane, a 1970s 737, idled on the runway of Kai Tak Airport for what must have been an hour. Even still parked on Hong Kong ground, I felt an unambiguous shift from British sensibility to Indian worldview. Indeed, I could smell it. Within the plane's confines, the air had suddenly become redolent of cumin and coriander. The aroma wafted from the huddles of families unpacking their steel tiffins—those stacked circular tins that will forever remind me of Indian domestic life—to reveal full Indian meals, replete with *daal, aloo gobi,* and *roti,* all strangely (and suspiciously) piping hot. To my eyes, the Indian mother was clearly a hyperprepared professional nurturer, and all of these women seemed to have their meal plans down. So efficient and practiced were they that I half-expected a couple of them to break out folding tables and paisley cloths from their jam-packed carry-ons. "Chalo, khana kao," cooed a father, holding out a piece of chutney-doused *naan* (it looked as though it had come straight from the tandoor) to his toddler daughter. *Come on, let's eat.*

In the rows before me, turbans in many colors—pink, lilac, beige, white—wobbled as their occupants engaged in spirited conversation. A young boy tripped on the turquoise-colored scarf of a female passenger and darted back to his mother. The female flight attendants, draped in bright blue saris, passed out small cartons of Frooti, a mango-flavored punch, and foil bags of "time-pass," spicy crackers that help snackers "pass the time."

"Bloody addictive," I whispered to Ajay as I dumped another package of time-pass into my palm and then into my mouth. "Well, don't get too carried away with that stuff," he said, as he confiscated four foil bags from my tray. "Otherwise you'll end up like Mrs. Mansha Malwani over there." I glanced to my far right and caught sight of a 250-pound woman wrapped in a saffron-colored paisley sari, her bare stomach bulging from the naked space between her tight blouse and her skirt, like a sausage—or more aptly, a *seekh kabab*—bursting out of its casing. She popped *ladoos,* tennis-ball-sized sweets, into her mouth, then followed that binge by shoveling handfuls of time-pass into the waiting cavern. Ajay laughed silently until tears ran down his face.

"Control yourself," I hissed in mock anger, glancing at the woman to make sure she wasn't taking in my fiancé's unruly behavior. Uh-oh, too late, I thought, surveying the cracker crumbs and brown sugar sprinkled like so much glitter down her front. "Mrs. Mansha Malwani" caught my gaze. She sent a searing look our way, opened her mouth, and burped. Ajay exploded with mirth and, much to my horror, so did I.

I thought for a moment about my first flight to Asia—from Los Angeles to Hong Kong—so many years ago. The Rotary Fellowship I had won set me up for a year's study of Mandarin and creative writing at the University of Hong Kong, an incredibly lucky twist of fate. But it also took me seven thousand miles away from home. Apart from a few acquaintances from college and graduate school, I hadn't known a soul in the region. Even so, I had stuffed all of my clothes, books, and courage into a couple of suitcases to travel across the Pacific to an uncertain future. There had been one thing about which I'd been absolutely clear: I had made the journey because I wanted my life to change.

The adventure I was starting today—Hong Kong to India, my life to Ajay's—echoed that pivotal transpacific voyage for me. I had to wonder just where this flight to New Delhi was leading me.

I felt Ajay's gaze on me, and I looked up at him. "A rupee for your thoughts, madam," he said, his face alive with pleasure. He was going home.

"Just wondering about the future, and what your world in India is going to be like. I mean, you had a whole life in this alternate universe before you met me. Tell me what to expect."

"Hmmm, that's kind of like asking me to explain what life on Venus is like if you've been living on Mars," he said, running his hand through his hair. "Let's see, what can I tell you?" He sat silently, in deep thought, for a few minutes. Then he rose in his seat and said, "Did I ever tell you about the time I found a monkey raiding our refrigerator?"

I smiled and kissed his cheek. "I've heard that one," I said, unintentionally stepping on his "a-ha!" moment. The story was one of my favorites. Ajay had come home after school to find a monkey standing in front of the refrigerator with a chicken drumstick in one hand and a can of beer in the other.

"I guess I've told you that one a few times. Okay, did I ever tell you about the time I became a vegetarian?"

"Well, you've told me that you and other Hindus believe it's not right to eat other animals," I answered, folding up the *Times of India* and placing it on my lap. "But no, you never told me the precise incident that transformed you into a cow hugger." I opened my eyes wide, anticipating the tale.

Ajay's family is from the Jat caste, a martial social order, and his background has affected him in, shall we say, curious ways. For one, he and his entire clan seem to share a genetically programmed obsession for guns and hunting. That's what Jats do, Ajay told me, they shoot things and they eat them. So every evening at Mokimpur, he and his cousins would go for walks in the fields, shotguns slung over their shoulders, to search for game. If they managed to bring back a couple of black partridges they would be rewarded with a special dinner curry. Brown partridges rated second best, a plump hare a distant third.

One evening when Ajay was twenty-two, he and his cousin Vivek set out, determined to bring something special back for the kitchen. They walked for close to four hours without seeing so much as a pigeon. "Let's turn back," Ajay said, his brow dotted with sweat. "We can just have lentils tonight." His stomach let out an angry growl as he searched the horizon for the way home.

"We can't give up yet," Vivek said, adjusting his gun on his shoulder and taking a swig of water from his canteen.

Suddenly, the cousins heard a noise in the sky. "Look!" cried Vivek. "Storks! Shoot!" Both boys lifted their shotguns and fired, sending dozens of pellets into the air. Partridges, sparrows, and doves flew out of the brush around them. A half-dozen white rabbits hopped in panic through the fields. Ajay staggered slightly from the recoil of the gun and looked up. One stork spiraled silently through the hot sky, a fifteen-pound lifeless mass descending to earth. The cousins ran through the fields to retrieve it, the barrels of their guns still warm. When they came upon the fallen bird, lying on its side, Vivek lifted his hands in the air and cried, "Aju, there's enough meat for two pressure cookers! Even the servants will eat like maharajas tonight!"

The boys brought their feathered prize to the kitchen, where Hoti Lal, the family's head servant, stood in the doorway. "What have you got?" he asked. He glanced down at their bloodied hands and laughed. "Start cutting the onions!" he told his daughter, Mala.

That night the stork reappeared as gamey chunks in a brown curry. It smelled delicious. But the dish proved a bitter meal for Ajay.

His grandmother refused to touch the stork curry. "I'll stick to lentils and bread." She pushed aside her plate and waved to Hoti Lal for a fresh setting. "It's not good to kill a stork," she said, wagging her finger.

"Why?" Ajay's eyes grew wide.

"Because they mate for life, don't you know? The surviving

partner will not eat a single morsel. He'll commit suicide by starving to death."

"Granny, that's not true," Ajay protested. "That's just an old wives' tale." He looked down into his plate and tried to eat another forkful. But already his stork curry had grown cold and sour.

The next evening Ajay went out into the fields, this time without his gun. He walked in silence for three miles until he reached the area where he had felled the stork. The daylight was fading, and the crickets struck up their twilight song. In the distance, against a background of green rice fields, stood a lone white figure. It was the dead stork's mate.

"My grandmother's story started to make sense," he said, his brown eyes shining earnestly. "The stork looked so sad. I vowed never to kill again."

"Wow, what a story," I said, wondering what other life lessons might be learned from those fields surrounding the palace. "Tell me another. Tell me about the haveli."

A flight attendant breezed by, glancing at our waists. "Do buckle up," she said, gathering up our empty Frooti boxes. "We'll be taking off in three minutes."

I strapped on my seat belt, put my hand into Ajay's, and prepared for the ascent. Then, with a rattle and a roar, our plane took off into a flawless sky.

◂◂ 8 ▸▸

Delhi Earth

"Chai, madam?"

It was my first morning in Delhi, at Mrs. Singh's family home, and a twelve-year-old girl with a diamond nose ring and no shoes was standing beside my bed, holding a silver tray with a white ceramic teapot, a tiny teacup, and a pile of shortbread biscuits on a chipped plate. I quickly brushed my hair out of my face and took a close look at her. She, a creature with zero body fat and about twenty metal bangles dangling from a birdlike wrist, was standing there, staring at me with as much curiosity as I had for her. Every time she moved, her bracelets chimed together, sending a little musical spell into the air. Was she a servant girl or a deeply tanned fairy?

"Chai, madam?" She smiled. Her teeth were a brilliant white.

"Yes, yes, please." I cleared my throat, sat up, and pulled an Indian quilt up to my chest. It wasn't a dream. We had landed in India.

Our plane had pulled into the Indira Gandhi International Airport the night before at 4 A.M. I exited the plane half-asleep, wearing four-inch heels and pulling a jam-packed carry-on through the grim-looking halls. Thank God Ajay was there to lead me through the fluorescently lit corridors and huddles of zombie-eyed families. As we approached the immigration check-in, hundreds of women in saris and men in kurta pajama suits mobbed the counters, like an angry amoeba, shapeless but insistent.

Ajay saw my eyes suddenly widen. "Don't worry," he said, laughing. "Indians never queue. Lines haven't yet been invented on the Subcontinent." Indeed, the crowds stood in defiantly amorphous clumps, roughly facing the exit. Families began pulling their homemade snacks—*parathas* and *samosas*—out of their bags once more. A boy took a soccer ball out of his duffel and kicked it across the hall to his sister, who then kicked it back, thumping it on the shins of those unlucky enough to be in the way. A group of teenage girls produced a boom box and began practicing a Bollywood dance. A half-dozen men, standing next to a NO SMOKING sign, lit up their cigarettes. Every five minutes or so, we inched forward, ever so slightly.

Just as we were making headway in the line, a woman in a salwar kameez, a flowing collarless top over loose pants, pushed in front of us. She was towing a small army of toddlers.

"Excuse me," Ajay said. "We were in the line ahead of you."

"I didn't see you," she said, shooting him a withering look. "Next time stand where people can notice you. Besides, I have four young ones who need to get home. If you know the Vedas, which you probably don't, you would know that Sita waited fourteen years for Ram to return to her village. Surely you can wait five more minutes in line."

"See what I mean?" Ajay said, holding his hands up in resignation and then waving the unruly family in front of him. "Queuing up is a Western concept."

Fans whirred throughout the cavernous room. The rows of fluorescent rods flickered overhead. A toddler pushed and pushed his mother's face as she held him and then let out a four-alarm wail that sent us covering our ears. Suddenly, the whole room went dark. "Power cut," Ajay said, pulling his linen handkerchief from his pocket and wiping his eyes, which were red-rimmed with exhaustion. I heard men's voices shouting back and forth, and then, just as quickly as the room had gone dark, the emergency electrical system clicked on, sending the lights and the fans sputtering back to life. Ajay smiled wearily. "Welcome to India."

"I guess what I've heard about India all these years is true." I snuggled next to him and wrapped his hand in mind, feeling something—Was it fear? Excitement? A sense of renewal?— thanks to the delightful bedlam. "Chaos *is* the national sport."

"Why not?" Ajay shrugged. Two portly men passed by and tossed their red-hot cigarette butts at our feet. "*Vive le chaos!*" Ajay said, holding one hand up at them in a phony thank-you and stomping the small fire out.

As if on cue, the immigration officer waved us forward. Grabbing our passports, he looked at Ajay and then looked at me. "Who is this?" he asked in Hindi, gesturing at me.

"She is my future wife." Ajay spoke in English, as if choosing sides.

The officer looked me up and down and nodded. Was that an official nod or an approving one? I wondered. Then he stamped my passport with a loud thud. "Welcome to India, madam."

Stepping into the greeting hall, I was once again over-whelmed by the crowds, the sheer swell of chattering, disor-dered humanity. How would we ever find the Singhs? I scanned the expanses for anyone roughly resembling Indian landed gen-try. I mean, what did almost-royals look like here? I had seen an old family portrait, snapped when Ajay was eight, back in the late 1960s. Mr. Singh looked like a pleasant if conventional sort of chap; Mrs. Singh, sheathed in a stylish gingham sari, her almond-shaped eyes fringed with long eyelashes, was quite the beauty. I imagined Ajay's dad, thirty years on, to be a distinguished, graying-at-the-temples man in an embroidered Nehru-collared coat, and his mother an elegant woman in a flowing sari.

"Aju, Aju!" a woman called out. A frail-looking man in a loden coat and a sturdy woman with a no-nonsense gray-streaked bob stepped forward, holding out woven shawls. Ajay rushed forward and hugged his parents. I reached out with both hands, put on a smile, and said, "It's so good to finally meet you, Mr. and Mrs. Singh. You must be exhausted. Thank you so much for coming to meet us at such an appalling hour."

Mrs. Singh looked at me and said something in Hindi to Ajay. "What? What?" I asked. It was something I would be ut-tering on a regular basis during visits with the Singhs. "What did your mom say?"

Ajay looked at me and shrugged. "She said she can't under-stand your American accent."

In the morning, after chai in bed (or as Indians call it, "bed tea"), I got up and tiptoed into the hall. Rather than drive five hours straight to Mokimpur, we had gone from the airport to Mrs. Singh's family home in Roop Nagar, a stately four-storied 1960s house near the University of Delhi. Mr. and Mrs. Singh resided here whenever they needed an infusion of city life. I searched for the bathroom I had ducked into last night. In my sleep-deprived haze, it had struck me as basic but functional. In the light of the winter morning, I scanned the cold, tiled room and sighed. Unless I was missing something, there was no bathtub and no shower. All I saw by way of bathing implement was a bucket with a plastic mug hanging from the side—no instructions, either.

I turned on the sink's tap and put my hand under it. "Oh. My. God!" I cried. It was ice-cold from the Delhi winter chill. "Oh-kaaay," I said, placing my toiletry bag on a worn wooden stool. "I guess I won't be taking a bath this morning." Instead, I quickly splashed myself with water—shivering profusely—dashed on some makeup, and pulled on a navy blue sweater dress and my favorite black suede platform shoes. I couldn't help but wonder if there was a master bathroom with plush carpeting, central heat, and a rainfall showerhead around the hall somewhere. I took one last look around the spartan room, damp with mold, a bare bulb perched above the sink, and cringed.

Outside, I heard the singsong rhythms of Hindi floating down the hall. I followed the voices, hoping they'd lead me to Ajay—and breakfast. "There you are," he called from the dining room. He was reading the *Times of India* and nursing a steaming cup of chai. Mrs. Singh stood in the kitchen, rolling balls of gold-hued dough on a round wooden chopping board, flattening them with the palm of her hand, and then placing them onto a steaming griddle. She wore a mod green-and-white floral salwar kameez and silk slippers but no expression. Somehow she managed to look graceful and humorless at the same time. The room smelled of warm cooking oil and some savory spice—was it cumin?

I cleared my throat and said, "Good moh-nin', Mrs. Singh." I spoke with a put-on British accent, thinking that this would ease our East-West communication issues. After all, Britain had colonized India for over three hundred years, so if I spoke with a U.K. lilt Mrs. Singh might be able to decipher my speech. But in my nervousness, I wound up sounding less like Princess Diana and more like Dick Van Dyke in *Mary Poppins*.

"Good morning, Alison," she said, glancing at me. She took another peek, this time looking me over, up and down. Was it the phony accent, I wondered? Shaking her head, she said something to Ajay in Hindi. He nodded. "Haan, haan, Mama." *Okay, Mom.*

"What? What?" I asked Ajay. I suddenly became painfully aware that, standing there in the kitchen doorway in my four-inch platforms, I towered over Mrs. Singh. Indeed, I simply dwarfed her. It was as if I were a comic strip giant, some symbolic rendering of a looming American Imperialism, with she, as India, cowering at the fear of spiritual—and, well, sartorial—contamination.

"What? What?" I held out my hands. "What did she say?" Ajay cleared his throat. "My mother says those shoes won't get you very far in the village."

Indians believe you can taste a family's entire legacy in one *paratha*, a savory wheat pancake often eaten for breakfast. That much Ajay told me just before we left for India. Every Indian woman spices her *parathas* in a way that is special only to her, he said. "And her skillets carry the scent of generations of cooking." Indeed, I once read an article that explained that the thickness, texture, and width of each *paratha* is also distinct to each cook, depending on the size of her palms, the shape of her fingers, and the strength with which she kneads her dough. "When a mother is handing you her homemade *paratha*," Ajay added, "she is handing you a piece of her soul."

I knew all of this, and yet I still did the unthinkable. I refused to eat Mrs. Singh's *parathas*. By the time she had handed me a stack of her house specialty, I had lost my appetite. Oh sure, I picked at what was on my plate, but not more than that. To this day, I'm not sure why I chose that very moment to not be hungry. It was rude, hurtful, and, worst of all, unforgiveable. If I had that moment to live again, I would have gobbled up a dozen *parathas*.

Because that's when the real trouble began.

When Ajay's mother caught sight of my barely touched plate, she paused and then turned back into the kitchen. Carrying her own breakfast plate, she crossed the room and positioned herself in an armchair, next to the servant girl, Lakshmi, who sat on the floor plucking coriander leaves from their stems and placing them into a silver bowl.

"Mama, come join us," Ajay said, moving his newspaper aside.

"No thank you," she said. "There's not enough room at the table."

Mr. Singh sat across the dining table from Ajay and me, wordlessly munching on his *parathas*.

"So, Mr. Singh, do you like visiting Delhi or do you prefer being at the haveli?" I spoke very slowly in my *Mary Poppins* accent and tried hard to make eye contact.

"Both are okay . . ." He looked up. His eyebrows were impressively long and bushy, like a kindly old terrier's.

A few minutes later I tried again. "So, Mr. Singh, what's your favorite newspaper?"

He shrugged noncommittally. "I like all the papers." He wobbled his head and turned the page. He might simply have been tired after the late-night airport run, but after the third rebuff, I stopped with the small talk. I was desperate not to make any more missteps, in my platforms or otherwise.

As soon as breakfast was over, I dashed to my bedroom, ripped off my heels, and threw them across the room. So far, my arrival in India and my meeting with my new family had not brought the fusion of lost souls I had imagined. I sat down on the edge of the bed and put my head into my hands. "What's wrong?" Ajay said, as he entered my bedroom.

"Why is it that my newspaper column could charm half of Asia but I can't even get my own future in-laws to like me?" I shook my head. "Your father hardly spoke to me. Your mother doesn't understand a word I say and she thinks my favorite shoes are horrid. She barely faced me at breakfast. Things are not going very well."

"Give it time," Ajay replied. "Indian relationships take longer than American ones. We don't believe in instant noodles and we don't trust in five-minute friendships. There's a different rhythm to how we do things here." He sat down on the bed next to me and reached for my hand. "My mother and father are leaving for

Mokimpur early tomorrow morning," he said. "We'll spend a few days in Delhi. I'll show you my favorite places, and we can have lunch at the Foreign Correspondents Club. It'll give you a chance to get your sea legs back. But, Ali—you might want to leave the platforms at home."

The next morning, I glanced outside and saw that the Singhs' Maruti was gone. "Free to be me again!" I exclaimed to myself, and broke out into a little Bollywood dance. I slipped into a sheer blouse, jeans, and a pair of pointy-toe leopard-print flats and prepared for a beautiful day. At breakfast, I feasted on several bowls of delectably ripe mango and four of Lakshmi's *parathas*. "They're underspiced and overfried," Ajay huffed. "They're not a patch on my mother's."

The relief I felt at the sudden absence of Ajay's parentals didn't exactly bode well for my career as an Indian daughter-in-law. But at least for seventy-two hours or so, I didn't have to put on an act of propriety—and that made me feel as free and light as the beautiful nightingales that soared past my window. For the next few days, Ajay and I were on our own to enjoy India's capital.

I have always believed that a city deserves the buildings that line its streets. Beverly Hills, where so many actors, moviemakers, and other master illusionists have set up shop, is home to some of the most fantastical architecture on the planet—enormous faux Normandy châteaux and twenty-thousand-square-foot story-book houses that look as if they were airlifted straight out of a

Brothers Grimm fairy tale (and blown up to twenty times their normal size). Just around the corner from the Beverly Hilton, there's even a world-famous witch's house, replete with thatched roof and creepy sloping walls.

In Hong Kong, where commerce operates around the clock at a breakneck pace, skyscrapers seem to shoot up overnight. Too bad so many of them are unapologetically slapped together, pipes protruding at clumsy angles, live wires dangling from the ceilings. Most of the mass housing is depressingly basic, tiny characterless boxes that seem to say, "We're just here to make as much money as we can, so why should we care about the place we live in?"

Delhi, I discovered, was a land of extremes. Ajay drove me down Aurangzeb Road, where so many Western ambassadors and moguls reside. "Oh my God, they're like palaces that have dropped down from another planet," I said to Ajay. I felt my heart pounding uncontrollably as I gazed past ironwork gates at the mansions that lined the street. The houses were not only massive but also utterly stunning, with distinctive colonial and Mughal influences—scalloped arches, neo-Buddhist domes, cenotaphs, filigree stonework, and lush gardens. When I gazed at them, layers and layers of my past dreams came flooding to the fore of my mind.

During our city tour, we also passed slums, makeshift communities of the heartbreakingly poor. There, the homes were made of scavenged wood topped with corrugated metal, the doors fashioned from synthetic fabrics that whipped around in the winter wind. Families sat huddled around huge open fires. As we idled in front of the slums in the car with the windows tightly rolled up, I could see them making *chappatis* with their soiled hands, as dusty goats and dogs sniffed around them.

Ajay insisted on taking me to Gandhi's last home, the guest quarters next to the house of one of India's biggest industrialists. "This is one of the most special places in Delhi," Ajay said. "I come here whenever I'm feeling low." Gandhi, India's great spiritual leader, had lived here for 144 days before he was assassinated. But as we strolled through the grounds and then through Gandhi's house itself, I sensed nothing of his violent death, only feelings of his peaceful, balanced life.

Gandhi could have lived in the grandest mansion with the most lavish furnishings in India, so ardent and wealthy were his admirers. Instead, he kept his abode simple and spare. I stopped at his bedside: The Great Soul, as Gandhi was called, slept on a small mattress dressed in white cotton, on the floor. There were no photographs, mirrors, or paintings on the wall—and not just because Gandhi wasn't a Design Within Reach shopper. "His whole life was an experiment with truth," Ajay said. For Gandhi, Ajay told me, it was how you lived your life, not what you hung on your walls. That—and not the Armani Casa mirror—was the best reflection of your soul.

I thought about a Richard Neutra–designed house I once spent a few months in on Mulholland Drive in Los Angeles. One of the first magazines I worked for had set up a makeshift office there, and I loved running my fingers along the old wood panels and built-in cabinets, swiveling in the iconic Eames lounge chairs in the living room, and staring out at the city from the pool patio. The experience lulled me into an uncharacteristic calm, and I had vowed to myself to create a life like this for myself one day.

I looked around Gandhi's house one last time. Despite the tourists trampling through his quarters, the home felt spare, serene, pure, blessed. There was no million-dollar view, not an Eames chair in sight. It was something to think about.

⊷ 9 ⊶

So Close . . .

It was the night before our journey to Mokimpur, and I lay in bed staring at the ceiling, contemplating what I might find tomorrow. I wondered if Ajay had had a pointed reason for taking me to Gandhi's spare home. I still had not seen a single photograph of Mokimpur, although visions of what I imagined it to look like had flooded my brain. Not long after learning about the family palace, I hopped a minibus to a secondhand bookstore in Hong Kong and found a tattered old tome about Indian royals. One Sunday afternoon, Ajay and I flipped through the book together. "Look at the emeralds hanging around that elephant's neck!" I said, shaking my head, as I stared at a two-page photo spread of a maharaja and his favorite animals—including a pet cheetah, and a red macaw perched on his royal shoulder—parading in front of his Udaipur palace in West India. The king's abode was built of red sandstone and had cloudlike domes, delicate fretwork, and a pool-sized fountain lined with palm trees. The maharaja wore a white cloak, a gold jacket, a saffron turban, and eight pearl necklaces of varying lengths, each heavy with a diamond pendant.

"Wow," I said to Ajay. "If any other person were wearing this, he'd be the height of gaudiness. But this guy looks so intensely regal. And the palace—it's almost surreal."

"Well, don't expect pearls and diamonds at Mokimpur," Ajay said. "I mean, the haveli has its charms . . . it's beautiful in its own way, but . . ." He paused. Something dark crossed his face. He looked down. "We haven't really had the money to keep the place up. So many walls need to be painted. The balconies need rebuilding. Most of the gardens have gone to seed."

I glanced up at him suspiciously. Sure, we penny pinched in Hong Kong—had to make the rent and all. And yes, my parents owned two houses, two lives, when they could barely afford the one. Now I was hearing that Ajay's family lived in a palace but the paint was peeling. I sat there and blinked my eyes at him. Then I shut the cover of the maharaja book and got up to tidy up our small flat.

In Hong Kong, we now had a Filipina maid, Edith, to do the heavy cleaning in our flat twice a week—no more tub scrubbings for me. Still, almost every morning I caught the minibus or tram to work, and once even caught sight of Edith on the same bus. At the beginning of each month—also known as payday—I traipsed down to Central and bought myself something beautiful to wear. The rest of the month I compensated for that financial blowout by packing meager Swiss cheese sandwiches to eat at my desk and drinking the awful "death-by-caffeine" office coffee instead of spending three dollars on a barista-made cup.

When I studied my spending habits, a pattern emerged. *Feast or famine. Splurge and scrimp. We have each other but it isn't enough.* I started to realize that our financial status was largely a state of mind—my state of mind. My parents' unpredictable finances and their fire sale of the ranch house had clearly bruised my childhood psyche. Two decades later, I was discovering that I'd never really recovered from their fiscal anxiety. Indeed, along with an obsession for mansions and castles in the sky, I had inherited their complicated relationship with cash.

I am five years old and I have found my place in the world. Yet another Gee clan banquet in Chinatown. During my grandfather's years as mayor of Chinatown, we go to these fetes at least once a month. The bill of fare, much to my delight, is always the same: Ten courses served by white-jacketed waiters toting silver platters. Steaming bowls of shark fin soup. Plates heaped with shrimp in lobster sauce, Peking Duck, sliced char siu pork, long-life noodles. It's a monthly date for the Gee cousins to play together, to stick roasted duck heads onto their ivory chopsticks and chase each other around the Golden Dragon. "We just got back from Hong Kong last week," one aunt says, sizing up my mother. "Business-class flight on Cathay Pacific. We stayed at the Peninsula. My son-in-law paid for it all."

I wear a floral shift, with my mother's daisy brooch pinned at a diagonal on the Peter Pan collar. Before each banquet, I polish my Mary Janes, and as I run with my pack of cousins around the round banquet tables, I can't help but admire how my shoes gleam. At the

table, *I place the white linen napkin across my lap and wait my turn
as the lazy Susan delivers sweet and sour pork and steamed fish with
ginger right to my plate. When we empty the bottles of 7UP on our
table, we raise our hand and the waiter brings more, hustling out
from the kitchen.*

*On the ride home, I always ask my mother, "How many days
until the next banquet?" This time she's not in the mood. "We'll go as
long as Yeh Yeh is alive," she says, staring straight ahead. "Once he
dies, we won't go back. We won't be invited back." Silence fills the station wagon as we speed past the city lights of downtown. "Uncle George,
Aunt Faith, all your cousins—we are not part of them," she says. "If
you think it's any different, then you're fooling yourself." Looking
back now, I understand this: We are the foolish relations, the ones
who walked out on the family business. We are the unpleasant relations, with the six unruly kids, the hand-me-downs, and the noisy
old station wagon. We are the unfortunate relations, the ones with
the father who never quite figures out how to fly.*

✦

One day, many months after Ajay had moved to Hong
Kong and into my flat, I sat down and, just out of morbid curiosity, added up what he and I made together, translating our Hong
Kong–dollar salary into American dollars. The total: well into
six figures. "This can't be," I whispered, punching the numbers
into the calculator again. But it was. We were making a significant amount of money and by all accounts were doing well. Very
well. So why was I frying up tofu every night and choking on gas
fumes on the crosstown minibus? Why at the end of the month
was I always scraping up the change at the bottom of my purse

to pay for the tram? Maybe my salary wasn't the problem, but the way that I chose to spend it? Could that have to do with my family's knotty relationship with cash?

I remember driving with my parents to the Chart House in Malibu when I was a young girl, and feasting on filet mignon and lobster, as they fretted over how to pay the mortgage on our house—our *second* house. As my older college-going sister, Terry, put it later, "Steaks are nice, but I'd rather have the money for my books this semester." I looked at her and shrugged. "I'd rather have lobster."

Even though I had moved halfway across the world, I hadn't exactly escaped the past. My feast-or-famine childhood traveled with me, along with my favorite handbags and shoes. It hardly helped that Hong Kong was a land of material extremes, where custom-made pink Rolls-Royces glided past bamboo rickshaws, and women in silk cheongsams and Prada heels trotted past monks with begging bowls.

I was raised on extremes, and some part of me only felt truly comfortable when I was living at either end of the spectrum. Playing it safe? Taking the middle path? Just wasn't part of my psychological vocabulary. As soon as Ajay and I were finally on track to save some money, I would blow our extra cash on something wildly unnecessary. "I can't take this bloody parsimony anymore," I remember telling Ajay. "Lisa's birthday party is this weekend. I'm going to Queen's Road to buy those satin heels I wanted, okay?" On another occasion: "Oh, I don't think a weekend in Phuket would kill our budget, do you?" I somehow managed to convince myself (and Ajay) that we deserved to live like taipans on our just-enough journalists' salaries. Once, I showed Ajay the Polaroids of my lavish thirtieth-birthday party at the

China Club (a fete that Nigel had bankrolled), thinking he'd be charmed. Instead he said, "No wonder you're bankrupt."

Part of me wondered if a life in India would alter my fraught rapport with money, if once I witnessed the lives of the desperately poor I might reconsider my own dharma in a deep and meaningful way. Well beyond that, and in clear contrast, India would transform my place in the social hierarchy in concrete terms. This was solid ground for my castle in the sky, and the backdrop of my rebirth into a quasi-royal. In this next cycle of reinvention, of reincarnation, I was hell-bent on coming out on top, a Brahmin cow in a sparkling tiara, if you will.

So far, our trip had buoyed my visions of a grand resurrection. Our first few days in India were a dazzle of massive houses, beautiful gardens, wealthy family friends, and hot-and-cold running servants.

The next day, we would leave the Roop Nagar house early in the morning for Mokimpur, for my first glimpse of the palace I would one day call mine. I knew instinctively that there would be no need to set my travel clock that night. As soon as the first rays of morning sun passed through my window, I would rise from my bed, quickly pull on my clothes, click my suitcase shut, and head for the car. I'd been primed to start on this journey a long time ago.

High Spirits

Somewhere in my head, I had developed the fantasy that my first trip to the haveli would be, well, something special. A stately motorcade along tree-lined roads, perhaps. But we'd been driving eastward out of Delhi for more than three hours, and I'd quickly discovered that the road to Mokimpur was not exactly paved with gold. Rocks, oxen merde, and potholes the size of small craters was more like it. Crammed into a tiny gray Maruti Suzuki Zen that looked about as sturdy as a chickpea can on wheels, we bounced down the Grand Trunk Road, a blazing-bright highway that stretched thousands of miles, from Pakistan to Calcutta. Then we bumped along pockmarked dirt roads for what seemed like forever. After we swerved for the seventh time to avoid a wandering water buffalo, I was pushing a tolerance threshold. I rubbed my temples, turned to Ajay, and asked, "How much longer? Please—I need to know or I'm going to throw up."

"Uh, not long," he said, avoiding eye contact. "Maybe two more hours?"

"Two hours!" I shook my head. "I don't think I can take much more." I looked down at my dress. Lakshmi had packed us a tiffin of homemade *parathas* stuffed with potatoes, and now my clothes were covered with greasy crumbs. The queasiness rose to my throat.

"Why don't you check out for a while? Take a nap. I'll wake you when we get closer."

"Sure you don't mind?" I said, as the car bounced into yet another ditch, sending waves of nausea through my body. I closed my eyes, not waiting for Ajay to answer, and willed myself to sleep.

"Ali, Ali, wake up. We're here."

I was in deep slumber when I heard Ajay's voice and felt the tin heap bouncing slowly down a rough road. "What? We're here?" I asked, trying to shake myself awake. I gazed out the window at a row of huts made from mud and straw, a toddler boy and his older sister running barefoot around a small market square. Yet another cow sat at the edge of the road, her tail swishing at a dozen flies. Wild birds squawked in the distance. Nothing around suggested a palace. My eyes fell shut again.

A few minutes later, I felt the car roll to a stop. The engine sputtered, then died. "I think you might want to wake up now," Ajay said. And just as in the movies when unbearably bad actors do a clumsy double take, I glanced out the window, turned back toward Ajay—who was smiling smugly—and looked out again. Then I rolled it down and stuck my head out. There before me was a massive, whitewashed, three-story manor. Mokimpur! "Oh my God!" I whispered. Mango trees—I could smell the sweetness of their fruit—lined the front garden. A small reservoir shimmered under the cloudless bright blue sky. A circular driveway led to a main house, and that main house had two wings that looked like arms reaching out for an embrace. Bright pink bougainvillea hung from the rooftops, twisting down the face of the house like tendrils. It was early evening, and under a faint moon, the house looked otherworldly, utterly beautiful, like a porcelain deity levitating in the wheat fields.

I pushed the car door open and scrambled out. "Oh. My. God. This is *beyond* what I thought it would be," I said. "*Way* beyond!" I ran onto the grass, kicked my shoes off, and twirled around a few times. Ajay stood in front of the grass, his hands clasped in front of him, not saying a word. The palace spoke for him.

The door to the main house flew open. A small gray-haired man and a stocky woman with a long white braid, dressed in a yellow cotton sari, approached us. Both pressed their palms together and held them up. "Namaste, namaste," they said, baring their white teeth in a big smile.

"This is Hoti Lal and his wife, Phoola," Ajay explained. "They've been working with our family for—hmm, let's see— about four decades now." Hoti Lal said something to Ajay, and they both wobbled their heads. "Phoola has already planned our dinner," Ajay said. "Come."

As we walked toward the front door, I checked out the hand-painted tiles that lined the covered driveway, with its graceful arches. Clearly, Great-Grandpa Singh had a rare eye. The aesthetic was tasteful and spare, just the right balance of visual panache, color, and restraint—truly lovely. I placed my hand against one of the columns holding up the carport, maybe just to prove to myself that it was real. The column still held the heat from the winter day's sun. Or maybe, I mused to myself, the warmth was emanating from within, heat stored from a century of life. I was so thrilled to finally meet—so to speak—the haveli that it didn't strike me as odd when a small chunk of the palace crumbled under my touch. I looked at the pieces of whitewashed concrete in my hand, brushed them onto the ground, and wiped my hand on my dress.

Then I turned my gaze to the house's grand facade and took a deep breath. The frangipani trees were in full bloom. Their sweet, exotic fragrance filled my lungs.

"Holy cow," I uttered, no irony intended, before stepping through the main door's threshold. I had landed in nirvana.

Ajay and Hoti Lal gathered up our suitcases, and together we walked up two flights to the main rooms of the haveli. As we ascended the steps, I thought I heard some faint laughter. Maybe it was my imagination—which I've been told is vivid—but I felt the presence of dozens of people, through decades of time. It came to me as flashes of color and sound, but all of it was almost palpable.

"Ajay," I said, pulling on his arm. "I think I hear voices— what's going on? Are there lots of people upstairs?"

He looked at me and struggled for the right words. "My family . . . we've had hundreds of parties here throughout the past century. If you're hearing voices, well, I have heard them, too.

Everyone in my family has. It wouldn't surprise me if a few souls decided to stay on."

"You mean ghosts—this place is haunted?"

"That's not really how Indians perceive these things. We don't think about ghosts as those stereotypical spooks in white sheets that scare the knickers off everybody. We believe that we coexist with many, many spirits. They're all around us—because the soul never dies. The body withers away, but the essence of the person remains, watching over us." He pushed open a sizable wooden door, led me into a large light-filled room, and dropped my suitcases. "Speaking of which, this was my grandfather's room. Here's where you'll stay."

I looked around. The room was gigantic but spare, with only an old wing chair, a mirrored vanity, two wooden armoires, and a massive four-poster wooden bed. A wall of French doors led out to a balcony, overlooking the front yard. My cheeks flushed, betraying my excitement, and I squeaked out, "Well, I guess this will have to do."

Ajay grabbed my hand and led me onto the balcony, and we gazed out at the reservoir. Two buffaloes drank from the water's edge. Kingfishers glided past. Skinny cows grazed in the middle distance.

"This is some kind of amazing," I said. "Have you been coming here since you were born?"

"Three generations of my family have been born here. I was born in Kanpur, but my mother tells me I came to Mokimpur when I was three months old, just after the monsoon season. She tells me I bawled all the way here. But once I was taken into the house I didn't cry again—that is, until we packed up to leave. Genetic memory, I guess. I must have known this was home."

"What's your earliest memory of the haveli?" I asked him, as we watched a peacock and his harem of peahens jump into the reservoir.

Ajay thought for a moment. "When I was four or five my grandfather came out to the carport to meet us. He was dressed in a white kurta and wore a long garland of orange chrysanthemums, and when he pressed his hands together and bowed his head, I remember thinking he looked like a sadhu—a holy man. I jumped out of the car and he grabbed me, laughing. He carried me over his shoulders, up the stairs of the house, and on to the balcony of his bedroom—this room. Then he said, 'Look, Aju, look over there,' and he held me above this balcony's edge. He'd thrown a bucket of corn into the garden, and there were dozens of peacocks and peahens feasting on the cobs. Every once in a while they would look up at the sky and flap with happiness. They were in heaven."

I stood there looking at Ajay's face. In Hong Kong, his skin had taken on the dull gray cast of fatigue and stress. Now he glowed. His eyes danced with life.

"Well, this place is a bit of all right," I said, scanning the horizon past the reservoir. In the middle distance I could see a river and acres of yellow wheat fields. "Could we look around before dinner? Do we have time?"

"Put on your walking shoes," Ajay said, leading me back through the French doors. "I know just the place."

We bounded down the main hall steps and onto the fields. Soon we were striding along the river, where the villagers were out beating their laundry against the banks. When they caught sight of Ajay they put down their rags, broke into grins, and called out.

"What are they saying?" I asked Ajay.

"They're greeting me."

"Yeah, I gather. But what are they saying *exactly?*"

"Well, they're calling me *thakur* . . . there's no exact translation. But they're saying something like 'Good evening, Lord Singh. It's been so long since we've seen you.'"

"*Lord* Singh?" What's that about?"

"Well, that's my title here. It's not exactly lord, more like quasi-lord if that makes any sense. My grandfather was Rai Bahadur Thakur Shiam Singh, which roughly translates as count or lord. My father is Thakur Baldeo Singh, and now I'm a thakur of sorts, too."

The wheels turned in my head—so loudly, in fact, I wondered if the villagers would start looking up from their washing, wondering where the gearshift noise was coming from. Did that make me *Lady* Singh? I couldn't help but ponder. I decided that it did. "Oooh," I thought, "I can't wait to tell Lisa and Susan. Better yet, Arabella!"

I was spinning my big royal plans when my reverie was interrupted by a whiff of the most pungent, disgusting aroma. "Eeeeew! What is that smell!" I clasped my hand over my nose. I could practically see brown fumes rising from the fields.

"Oh, that's just the cow paddies. The villagers call them gold of the cow." The countryside before us was covered with twelve-inch earth-colored disks with handprints crisscrossed all over them. They looked like jumbo-sized, burnt peanut butter cookies but they smelled like, well, the devil.

"Cow poop? Why? What's with the disks?" Ajay explained that the villagers made cow paddies to burn for fuel. It's just one of the reasons cows are sacred in India, he said. "They're never eaten by Hindus. Never. Not in this day and age. There was a time, centuries ago, when Brahmins ate them, but then they realized—probably after a devastating famine—what cows meant to our society. Even in the worst of times they've given so much back—manure for fuel and milk for our food. That's why anything made from milk—*kheer, burfi, halwa*—is considered holy. We love our cows. Even McDonald's had to radically change its menu for Indians. The Big Mac would never have flown here. Beef burgers—American ones at that—would have been the height of sacrilege. Our Maharaja Macs are made of lamb."

I shook my head in amazement. I rarely thought about where my meat came from. I never gave much thought to what it looked like before it was plucked or chopped, ground into hamburger, or fancied up with sauces. I, canine lover, even knowingly devoured a stew made of dog meat in China's Sichuan Province, just because it smelled so good. In Hong Kong, while researching a story about ostrich farming, I scooped up every bite of the bird, thinly sliced and sautéed with black bean sauce. I had it over steaming hot white rice. It was sublime. During my idealistic college years, I fleetingly considered "going veg"—a resolve that lasted until the next evening, when the dining hall announced it was serving up beef lasagna, my favorite. And yet here was an entire society of people—one billion souls—that collectively understood the debt it owed to cows for the milk and excrement they provided. As I walked alongside Ajay, I thought about that profound act of gratitude and wondered if I could give up my filet mignon and carne asada tacos. Maybe buoyed by this understanding, I could.

We passed the family temple, a beautiful whitewashed structure with bright blue interiors. Inside, dozens of villagers sat on folded knees and chanted, filling the evening air with song. A few, catching sight of Ajay through the open temple door, held their hands up, palms pressed together. Ajay returned the gesture, nodding slowly.

We had ambled along the river for about another two miles, the sun sinking into the horizon, when we came across a small stone building.

"What's this?" I asked Ajay. I took a few steps toward the darkened entryway. Something was beckoning me into the little two-story house.

"It's my grandfather's prayer hut," Ajay said as we entered. It was cool and silent inside. "For two months every summer, he took refuge here, meditating and praying, not speaking to anyone, not even my grandmother, the entire time. The servants brought him meals on trays three times a day and left them right there." Ajay pointed out the door to a walkway paved with rocks.

"That's pretty extreme behavior, isn't it? I mean, only religious fanatics would do something like that in America."

"My grandfather wasn't a fanatic," said Ajay. "Not by any stretch of the imagination. But he was proud of being a Hindu. And he was to-the-core faithful to his favorite gods, Ram and Shiva. Like many Hindus, he spent his life trying to reach God." Ajay explained that most Indians believe there are three ways to attain spiritual enlightenment. The first is through the intellect; many Brahmins spend every free hour pouring over such sacred texts as the Vedas, the Upanishads, and the Gita.

Another is by praying and genuflecting to the deities—something that I found astonishing to witness. In Delhi, we'd paid a visit to Ajay's Aunt Booah, who was deeply religious. She woke up at four every morning, took a cold-water bath—even in the winter—and prayed until eight. "She spends just about every minute singing hymns and chanting mantras," said Ajay. "She'll stop for a veg *pakora* and chai, but then she'll get right back to it."

As soon as she moved into her luxury high-rise a few years ago, she transformed an entire bedroom into an altar. The walls of the room were covered with paintings of her chosen gods— Ganesh, the potbellied elephant god, and Hanuman, a burly monkey who guards Ram—and the floors were lined with statues, as well as carved wooden cows, bulls, horses, peacocks, and hydra-headed snakes. "In Hindu philosophy there are something like three hundred and thirty million gods," Ajay told me as we toured Booah's chapel.

"Well, they're all living right in Auntie Booah's pad, if you ask me," I said, as I picked my way past an elephant statue.

Once a week, she and her Nepali maids carried the idols, one by one, into a bathroom reserved specifically for the gods and gave them a warm bath in the sink. The servants lit dozens of candles to create a holy glow for the idols and blasted the space heater in the room if there was a winter chill. Booah would go to great lengths for her idols. Indeed, she had even taken one of her exquisite embroidered Kashmiri shawls and cut it up into small strips. She then made little cashmere wraps for each god. As it was winter when we visited, each of the statues was draped in a mini pashmina. "It looks like they're going to a cocktail party," I whispered to Ajay, completely charmed. "All they need is a pair of Manolo heels each, and they'd fit right in in Manhattan."

"Booah takes her religion seriously," Ajay said. "My other

aunts think that's why all her kids are now filthy rich—God's clearly taken care of them."

Ajay told me that yet another way to reach God is by developing your karma through good deeds. "Like what?" I asked Ajay.

"Say there's a famine sweeping the country," Ajay said. "The devout Hindu would take the rice and flour from his own cupboard and feed the poor before he fed his own children." He knew of one minor royal in Rajasthan who had even mortgaged his family's property and jewelry to build artificial lakes throughout his region—the only source of clean water for the surrounding villages. What's more, a proper Hindu would also never throw a family member out of the house. "And that's no matter what trouble he's caused," Ajay said. "It's just not done."

According to the Vedas, you also scored good karma points by strenuously guarding and maintaining your integrity, and that's what Ajay's grandfather did throughout his life.

"He was a police chief," Ajay explained. "In India, people always equate being in the police with being corrupt, as if every officer could be bought for a price. So every year at Diwali, he would get flooded with gifts—cashmere shawls, ivory boxes, Indian sweets. Everyone, from wealthy businessmen to landed gentry, wanted to get on his good side. They thought bribing him with gifts was the way. But these worldly trappings didn't mean anything to him. In fact, he'd pass the presents back, saying thank you, but he didn't want for anything. If somebody kept pressing the gifts on him, my grandfather insisted on paying for them. That's how pure he wanted to be."

Whenever he was visiting the village, Ajay's grandfather took long riverside walks just before dawn and right after the sun had set. "The villagers looked at him as if he were a god," Ajay said.

"They'd say, 'Ram, Ram, Sahib,' which in this social situation translates to something like, 'Good evening, my lord.' Instead of responding with some standard greeting, he'd say, 'Tell me how I can serve you.' He genuinely wanted to know. Once a villager begged him to release his son, who'd been charged with robbery, from jail. My grandfather went to the police station and had the boy freed."

"What? Wasn't that a major abuse of power?" I asked.

"You could see it that way. But consider the big Hindu picture of life and you'll understand that it wasn't. My grandfather had the boy promise he would never commit a crime again. And he didn't. Maybe justice wasn't served, but karma was."

My acts of daily goodness consisted of giving up my MTR seat for the elderly and nodding hello to strangers. Generally, I tried to carry myself without hostility—a tip I had taken from a Deepak Chopra book—although even that got tough to carry off on the mean, pushy streets of Hong Kong, especially when we were all racing for the last seat on the minibus. I was immeasurably kinder and more loving to Ajay than I had been to Nigel, but that could have been because Ajay was so much gentler and more adoring. I liked to think that most people would describe me as a nice girl. Coming to India, though, I was becoming aware of how much more work I had to do on the compassion front. These people were empathy machines!

Outside the prayer hut stood a hundred-year-old sandalwood tree, its lush branches arching over the grounds. Ajay spread out his jacket and we sat down together, gazing up at the moon. It was as bright and full as a child's birthday balloon. Ajay put his arm around me and laid his head on my shoulder. "I can imagine my grandfather looking up from here, at this very same moon."

They say that if you want to remember a day, you witness its sunrise or its sunset, or you gaze intently at its moon. As I sat there with Ajay, looking skyward, I thought about his family's ties to this village and to this earth. Their love for this place had endured so many years, so many crisp autumns as well as miserable summers and soggy monsoon seasons. The palace and its twenty-six acres, this was their core. Compared to Mokimpur, the American tract homes I had known, with their plywood bones and cramped plots of land, seemed as though they were built of cardboard. Mokimpur had gravitas—that much was palpable.

"Do you think the man in the moon is looking back down at us?" I asked Ajay. He squeezed my hand playfully but remained silent. In truth, I didn't expect an answer; I could sense that some spirit was hovering above us, taking note of the uncharacteristic bliss I had settled into. The spirit was reading my thoughts as I willed myself never to forget this moment, the happy silence between Ajay and me, the preternatural glow over the Indian night sky.

⊶ 11 ⊷

The Trophy Room

When we returned to the palace, Ajay took me through a different entrance, this one a series of white arched hallways. "Ah, I see Uncle Ram is here," he said, walking toward a room that glowed with lantern light. "Come, you must meet him."

Through the room's window, I saw a small man with a wiry frame sitting at a table, carefully polishing what looked like medals. "Well, there you are, my young man, I've been waiting for you to pay me a visit," he said. He had a tiny head, with a slick of silver hair combed back. His small black eyes darted back and forth, and gray hair spurted from his ears, as if he had sprung a leak. The whole visual effect was that of a monkey who had hijacked a human body—it was as if Uncle Ram were a human manifestation of Hanuman, the Indian monkey god. "Except unlike Hanuman," Ajay told me later, "Uncle Ram doesn't have any muscles!"

"And this must be Alison from the United States of America." Uncle Ram said, nodding his head courteously. "Fine country, fine country. Ajay has been writing letters home filled with stories about your life in Hong Kong. Very nice to meet you. You have some very interesting presidents in America—some of them real rascals." He cackled, flashing large tobacco-stained teeth.

"Whose are those, Uncle Ram?" Ajay asked.

"They're your grandfather's," he answered. "I clean them at least once a month." I noticed then that Uncle Ram was dressed in olive-green army fatigues and combat boots. Ajay had mentioned earlier that Uncle Ram had never quite accepted the end of his days in the Indian army, where he had retired as a major. "With his family background and his devotion to the job, he should have climbed much higher," he said. But Uncle Ram had clearly not studied his war strategy well enough. Midway in his career he discovered that one of his commanding officers was trying to steal expensive carpets from army headquarters. Like the upstanding citizen that he was, he questioned the officer. The colonel was not amused. Indeed, he retaliated by writing a scathing assessment for Uncle Ram's file, preventing him from moving any higher up in the army. "I think that's why he takes such pride in what my grandfather did during his life," Ajay said. "Because he was cheated out of the career he deserved, Uncle Ram basks in my grandfather's reflected glory."

"Alison, come with me," said Uncle Ram, grasping for my hand. His palms felt warm and leathery. "Let me show you the trophy room. Once you see it, perhaps you'll understand our family a little better."

We crossed Uncle Ram's courtyard and headed for a darkened hallway. There sat the trophy room, an immaculate, window-lined chamber with several wing chairs arranged to face each other. Glass cases held war medals and Thakur Singh's police uniform. Black-and-white photographs of the family lined every wall. There was one of Ajay's mother, lovely in a sweet eyelet sari. With her hair bobbed and her eyes exotically made up, she looked like a Bollywood star. There was another photograph of Mokimpur, its bougainvillea lush, its walls smooth and freshly whitewashed. "That was in the 1950s," Uncle Ram said, noticing my intense gaze. "Before the house started to crumble." I shot Ajay a look of surprise.

"Please sit down," Uncle Ram said, waving at a chair. "I must show you something very special."

He disappeared into a deep closet, and after several minutes emerged carrying an old leather book. "This has all my father's testimonials," he said, placing it gently on a wooden coffee table. He brushed the book jacket with his hand, sending the dust from the book's cover into the air, as if he were a warlock casting a spell. Then he read aloud letters from British officers detailing Grandpa's exploits chasing bands of "crafty dacoits" in the villages and investigating murders in the state's capital. But the letters also hinted at something darker from the India of that period—the colony's deep racial divide.

Throughout much of the British colonization of India, most Brits living here would not fraternize with "the natives," for fear they'd go "jungli." For the most part, they kept relationships cordial but decidedly superficial. Grandpa Singh, who was an expert hunter, a fiend on the tennis court, and a karma yogi, somehow transcended that unspoken barrier. Uncle Ram read a letter from a British colonel who had stayed at Mokimpur, recovering from malaria. As he did, his voice wavered.

The Trophy Room

March 21, 1945

Dear Shiam Singh,
  I am now completely cured thanks to your very, very kind nursing and to the skill of Dr. Mehta. There are no truer friends than Indian friends. I have had proof of it so very often. It is tragic to think of this thing called the colour bar or racial hatred. It need never exist and it never existed with me or with the old ones who know Indian virtues and Indian kindness so well. If I can ever do anything for you do not hesitate to ask.

  Yours very sincerely,
  Colonel G. Waddell

The room fell silent. It was like hearing a voice from fifty years ago float through the air. The voice told me that Ajay's kindness and humanity ran through several generations—maybe even through the entire culture.

Just as Uncle Ram closed the book, Hoti Lal's grandson, Laloo, a small pudgy-faced boy of about five, appeared in the doorway. He said something to Ajay in Hindi and looked skyward. "My mother is calling us upstairs," Ajay said. "It's time for dinner."

We walked up the main steps into a rectangular room set just off the terrace. The doors were open to the night sky, and a dozen pillar candles lit the room. Grandpa Singh's portrait hung on one wall, his eyes locking us in a benevolent gaze as we took our seats at a long wooden table. On another wall, a sumptuous piece of vintage red silk, hand-embroidered with gold paisleys, hung in an antique frame.

Mrs. Singh entered the room. "So you made it in one piece," she said, glancing at my linen dress and then down at my sneakered feet. "I see Ajay told you about the village. If you had worn your high heels here, you would have twisted your ankle and gone straight to the village doctor. These practical shoes are much better, even if they don't look as good." I could see her eyes shining in the candlelight. In Delhi, Mrs. Singh's movements were measured, her smiles rare. Here, at the palace, she was still frosty to me but her face was starting to open, like a frangipani about to bloom. "Come and sit down," she said. "Dinner is about to be served."

Phoola and Hoti Lal appeared, each carrying a silver tray, heavy with silver bowls heaped with *daal, aloo gobi,* and *saag paneer.* Phoola brought out freshly made *roti,* so hot they burned our fingers.

I glanced around the table at Mr. and Mrs. Singh, Uncle Ram, and Ajay—they would soon be my family. A week earlier in Hong Kong, I was sitting at Felix, the ultracool Philippe Starck restaurant at the top of the Peninsula Hotel. It was my friend Joanna's birthday, and she instructed the waiters to keep the Veuve Clicquot "flowing like the Li Jiang River." I remember gazing out the floor-to-ceiling windows at the sparkling harbor and thousands of city lights and thinking to myself, "Now this is living." In Mokimpur, as we scraped the last spoon of *daal* from the bowl, I thought about how this spare meal rivaled any I had ever had. The buttery lobster tail and the truffle salad at Felix were delectable, no question. But here, the quiet, the beauty of the house, and the simple handcrafted food—it satisfied me.

‹‹‹ 12 ›››

Gods and Water

The next morning I woke up with a headache that could cleave the Himalayas. It was as if a herd of elephants had charged my brain. I was rubbing my temples when Ajay pushed open the bedroom door. He was carrying a silver tray that held a tall glass of water and a small spray of bougainvillea in a vase. "Help me," I groaned.

"*Ah-ja,* you must drink this now," he commanded. "This is a dryness headache. You haven't been taking water, have you?"

He was right. Since we'd arrived at Mokimpur, I had barely drunk a few glasses, and that was despite the fact that he and his mother had toted along a case of Bisleri, India's premium brand of purified water, just for me. But I was worried the two dozen bottles wouldn't last our visit. And I'd be lying if I didn't say the Bisleri itself made me nervous. It might have been the country's finest, but its plastic bottles were so flimsy they lost their shape the moment the water drained, slumping like starved beggars. Who knew if the bottles actually held purified water or just amoeba-infected H_2O some vendor had gotten from a public fountain?

I was dutifully draining my glass when we heard a car roll into the carport below. Doors opened and the boom of a Bollywood soundtrack punctuated the quiet village air. A young child screamed. "Koi hai? Samaan lay jao!" *Anyone there? Take the luggage!* I heard a flock of birds flap swiftly through the sky as if trying to escape a descending storm.

"It's Anusha," Ajay said, referring to his three-year-old niece. "Karan and Kamala must be downstairs."

I had met Ajay's brother, his wife, and their daughter once before during a three-day visit they'd made to Hong Kong. They spent most of their time shopping Stanley Market for clothing bargains and trinkets and shopping Wing On department store for such must-haves of urban Indian life as electric razors, rice cookers, and Hong Kong Barbies.

Karan, a steward for Air India, charmed me with his appetite for chicken's feet and Shanghai dumplings. As for Kamala? She was one of a kind. In our first encounter, she looked me up and down and said, "You certainly looked a lot slimmer in the photographs Ajay sent." At two years old, Anusha could babble multisyllabic words in Hindi and ask questions about everything in sight. However, she was not exactly bliss to be around. Karan and Kamala hardly seemed to discipline her—no matter what she did. She gleefully kicked or punched whichever chair, bag, or toy came in her way. At one point, she threw a wooden block at my face. Their three-day visit felt like a month.

Sometimes people are completely different creatures when you meet them on their native soil. I know that no matter how wound up and stressed out I might have been in some foreign city, once I touch foot to L.A. ground, I transform into a breezy Angeleno again. So I was actually looking forward to meeting Karan, Anusha, and even Kamala in Mokimpur and seeing what might emerge this time. Rubbing my throbbing forehead, I got out of bed and bounded down the front stairs with Ajay.

Anusha was chasing one of the barefoot village girls in the front yard as Hoti Lal gathered up the family's suitcases. Ajay cried out, "Karan!" and caught his brother in an embrace.

"Kamala," I said, stepping forward and kissing my soon-to-be sister-in-law on the cheeks.

"I can't believe you made it to the village," she said, her large brown eyes shining with excitement—or was it mischief? She wore a salwar kameez and long scarf cut from crisp white eyelet; her thick black hair flowed down her back. She glanced at me. I had no makeup on and had not changed out of the kurta pajamas I'd slept in. "Thank goodness you didn't wear one of those skimpy sundresses you were wearing in Hong Kong," she said, laughing shrilly. "Ajay's mother would have had a heart attack!"

I looked at her, waiting for her to say, "Just kidding!" She adjusted her scarf instead.

Hoti Lal brought tea and biscuits down to the front garden, where the family—Uncle Ram, Mr. and Mrs. Singh, Karan and Kamala, Ajay and I—sat under the shade of a scholar tree. A dozen village children raced around the lawn as Anusha held court from within a plastic playhouse. "No, you cannot come in," she hollered at them in Hindi, slamming shut the house's flimsy door. "This is for princesses only."

Karan placed his teacup on a wooden stool and said, "You know, the villagers think of us as the 'Big Family.' We are the ones with the big house and the big name and influence. We've always taken care of the people here."

Mrs. Singh nodded. She joined the chatter in Hindi, raising her index finger to punctuate a thought, while everyone around her nodded slowly in agreement.

"What? What?" I whispered to Ajay, breaking out my Mokimpur mantra.

"My mother was saying that the grains of wheat our family has planted have fed the entire village—literally and metaphorically." Ajay then explained that because his family was landed gentry and descendants of a great man—his grandfather, whom everyone thought of as a karma yogi—the villagers saw them essentially as gods and goddesses. Along with that status, they held the Singhs to godly standards as well. Thus, whenever the Singhs celebrated anything, whether the wedding of a daughter or the birth of a grandchild, the whole village, now about a thousand people, expected to be included.

Throughout the decades, the Singhs held dazzling fetes. *Le tout* Delhi traveled with their luggage and servants in tow for a weekend in Mokimpur. A small army of servants set up luxury tents in the fields. Nights brought feasts on the terrace, with Scotch whisky and *pakora* served on silver trays. Women dressed in bejeweled saris, hair rolled into tight chignons, their diamond and ruby necklaces glimmering under the moonlight; men fancied themselves up in gold-embroidered kurtas, bright turbans, and pointed-toe shoes.

It was a spectacle right out of *The Arabian Nights*.

One glance over the side of the terrace revealed a different but equally festive scene. A line of villagers and their children snaked through the haveli's lawn and down the extended driveway. Each stood facing Mokimpur's kitchen. The aroma of fresh curries and cardamom-spiced desserts filled the garden. The townspeople were served a meal of curried potatoes, lentils, spinach, and *pooris* on freshly cut banana leaves. Servants offered not just seconds and thirds but fourths and fifths. Dessert—rice pudding or powdered jaggery soaked in clarified butter—brought rapturous looks from the villagers. When servants asked how much of the sweet stuff they would like, the townspeople would close their eyes and stand there holding out their hands, a sign to the household staff to just keep pouring until the pudding spilled off the side of the banana leaf. They picnicked on Mokimpur's grounds, and afterward the village children danced to the sitar and tabla music that floated from upstairs. Before they headed home to their huts, bellies full, the villagers said a short prayer: "May God protect the Singh family."

But since Grandpa Singh's death in 1969, the Singhs had stopped throwing these lavish bashes. They no longer had the influence, or the money, to draw the Delhi elite to Mokimpur. Grandpa Singh's five sons and daughters and their families moved away from the village and gradually stopped spending Diwali and Holi and the long summer holidays at the haveli. The Singhs not only left the palace echoing with absence, they left the villagers wondering what had had happened to their Big Family.

"Once Hoti Lal came by to find several villagers lounging on our chairs on the upstairs terrace," said Ajay. "That was the height of disrespect to our family. Their banana leaves were no longer heaving with our curries and puddings and they were angry."

Karan said something in Hindi, and his eyes flashed with annoyance. I tapped Ajay on his arm and whispered, "What? What?"

"He says the villagers expect us to carry them all their lives," Ajay explained, staring at the ground. "But we are not gods. We're human."

.✦.

That afternoon, Ajay and I read on the bedroom terrace. I put my book down and watched two peacocks drink out of the reservoir. "I'm getting a glass of water," I said to Ajay. "Want anything?"

"Maybe ask Phoola for some chai and cardamom biscuits. It must be time for afternoon tea by now."

I walked over to the kitchen and scanned the shelf where Ajay had carefully lined up my water bottles. Panic flashed through my body. There were only four bottles left. We were staying five more days at the haveli. I practically sprinted back to the bedroom.

"Ajay, come quick. My water's disappearing. Only four bottles are left."

"What? Phoola must have stored them someplace else."

He called for Phoola. As he asked her about the water she stood with her hands clasped and her head bowed. "Ka? Anusha?" Ajay said, his eyes bright with anger.

"What? What?" I asked.

Ajay shook his head. "Kamala has been 'borrowing' some of your Bisleri for Anusha. She says Anusha has a stomachache from all the village water. Phoola says that when she told Kamala that we'd brought the Bisleri from Delhi for you, she said, 'Anusha is a child. Alison is a grown woman. She can drink boiled tap.'"

142

I would sooner fly back to Hong Kong that afternoon than drink Indian tap; foreigners routinely got desperately ill from doing so. As it turned out, though, Phoola and Hoti Lal were innocently serving me boiled tap in the form of tea and in our curries. So far, so good. I just prayed my luck would hold.

When Ajay confronted Kamala later, she waved a manicured talon and said, "Anusha is feeling sick. I knew Alison would understand. Anusha is soon to be her niece, after all. Or have your marriage plans changed? I've known many foreigners who have boiled tap for drinking water. They've all been fine."

We brought my last remaining bottles into the bedroom and said nothing more.

The next morning, I awoke to yet another liquid challenge. The bath. A winter chill had descended on Mokimpur, and the daily cleanse with a plastic mug and a bucket of tepid water in a cold tiled room had not grown more comfortable, as I had hoped. When I told Ajay my concerns—"I just don't know how to take a bath here"—he laughed. "Okay," he said. "I'll show you how it's done."

We snuck into the bathroom together, me clutching the Hermès toiletries I had taken from my last stay at the Peninsula. We could hear Mrs. Singh and Phoola chatting in the kitchen as they pounded dough for breakfast *parathas*. Ajay shut the door behind us and held his index finger up to his lips. He opened up the geyser, an electric bucket that heated the bathwater. Topped to the brim, it was steaming hot. "You're going to have a fine bath today," he whispered. "Trust me."

He filled two-thirds of an empty plastic bucket with cold tap water and scooped the geyser's hot water in until the bucket was full. Grabbing another empty bucket, he repeated the steps. "Ah-ja," he called. I shed my robe, placed it on a wooden stool, and stood on the sunken tiled area near the drain. Lifting mug after mug above my head, Ajay poured the water—just hotter than body temperature—onto my scalp, shoulders, and back. "Ah-hhh," I said as the liquid ran down my body. Hot mist rose around us. The room's chill faded away. I flashed back to a press junket I had taken at the Mandarin Oriental's new spa in Bangkok. Four days of five-star bliss. Plush robes, petite women in sarongs, and sunlit halls fragrant with lemongrass. "This reminds me of hydrotherapy in Thailand," I said in hushed tones to Ajay. "These lovely therapists poured water on us for almost an hour. It was so purifying."

"Ha! Your three-hundred-dollar luxury treatment was probably based on some spa director's trip to an Indian village!" Ajay said. "Get ready for this." He lifted one bucket above my head and turned it over. A stream of hot liquid fell over my body, caressing my eyelids, my cheeks, my neck, my breasts.

"Now that," he said, handing me a towel, "is how it's done."

That morning we had chai, orchard chiku, and *parathas* on the terrace. I scanned the horizon and took in the verdant mango orchards and stark wheat fields. Birds streaked by in the silent sky. Villagers filed past clutching baskets, hoes, and shovels. I gazed at the haveli's whitewashed sprawl. I could have been watching a scene from the time of the British Raj or perhaps from Gandhi's era. I sighed. If the root of vacation was indeed "to vacate" one's life, I had done that. Here, I was not slave to my cell phone, my magazine deadlines, the relentless energy of a twenty-first-century city. Or was I?

Indian country life was a mixed bag. Long stretches of nothing gave me time to stroll, ponder, and idle. The day's familiar rhythm—sipping chai, eating, lounging, reading, and napping—soothed my jittery soul. But there were only so many Vikram Seth novels I wanted to read. By day six at the haveli, I began shaking my leg up and down. Unconsciously, I began tapping my index finger on the table. A growing part of me missed the buzz of city life. Surely there was something more to explore in the village. I turned to Ajay.

"So what are we doing today, cruise director?"

"Doing? You're looking at it."

I bit into a biscuit. "I'm having a good time—don't get me wrong—but I've had six days of this. You know, each of the family's teatimes lasts about two hours. And we have tea about three times a day. It'd be fun to explore a little more. Is there someplace we could go? Something we could do?"

"You like horses?" said Ajay.

"Sure," I replied, thinking of a hipster party I had attended in L.A. where the adult guests could ride horses around the grounds. I gamely climbed on the back of a black stallion—in a little black dress and high heels.

"We'll go to the stud farm," Ajay announced. As if reading my mind, he added, "Leave the platforms here, though. Jeans and sneakers, please."

We bundled into his mother's Maruti and drove about a mile out of the village to a large compound with six-foot-high brick walls. A guard in an olive-green uniform waved us in through an imposing iron gate beyond which lay a wide expanse of grassy land. On it were dozens of horses grazing, moving no muscles except for the ones in their mouths.

"Million-dollar racehorses," said Ajay. "They belong to one of my uncles, a first cousin of my father. He was a cavalry officer in the Indian army and on the national polo team. Dashing man. Played with Prince Charles."

"What! As in Princess Diana's husband?" I asked, my celebrity antennae abuzz.

"Yup, he's a personal friend of my uncle. I saw them play a polo match once in Delhi. My uncle and Charles were on the same side and my uncle scored the winning goal."

"Does your uncle still live here?" I asked.

"He spends the winters in Delhi and the summers in Sweden," said Ajay. "He's married to a former Swedish diplomat."

Just then, a tall turbaned man with a Salvador Dalí mustache walked toward us. He shook hands with Ajay and bowed gracefully in my direction.

"Raghubir Singh," he said, gently grabbing my hand. "Welcome to the stud farm, madam."

Raghubir was the horse farm's manager, a retired soldier who, like Ajay's uncle, had spent all his life with horses. Raghubir took us on a tour of the farm, introducing us to the choicest specimens housed in barns. The mares had names like Moonlight, Camilla, and Deccan Queen. One was named Red Chili.

"This one," said Raghubir, pointing to a sleek dark brown steed, "has been bought by the maharaja of Patiala." The maharaja's father, Ajay explained, was one of the richest royals during the British Raj. He said there was a famous story about his visit to London, where he was asked to leave a Rolls-Royce show-room because none of the salesmen believed a bearded Indian in a turban could possibly buy one of the world's most expensive cars. He was so furious, he bought all the cars on display and had them stuffed with garbage and then driven down the busiest boulevards of London the next day. Legend had it that the president of Rolls-Royce had to get down on his knees and personally apologize to the maharaja.

Ajay had grown up riding in Mokimpur. "A group of my cousins and I would gather here at dawn every morning in the summer and ride until our mothers dragged us off for breakfast," he said. His uncle, a cup of tea in hand, kept a close watch on them. He tolerated no mistakes and was strict about technique—things like proper posture and the importance of gripping the saddle with your thighs. "I don't want to see the slightest crack of sunlight between the saddle and your legs," he would shout at the children from across the field.

"We were good riders," said Ajay, "but we were kids—and the horses knew that."

"Horses knew what?" I asked, cocking my head to the side.

"Oh, they're very clever," said Ajay. "Horses don't really respect kids, especially if the horse is used to being ridden by bossy adults." Once, when Ajay was twelve, the mare he was riding deliberately took a wrong turn. He jerked the reins to the left, but she swung to the right so suddenly that he fell off. "Fractured my elbow," Ajay said, shaking his head. "I still remember how it bent out of shape like a boomerang. My uncle was furious. He actually punched the horse in the mouth."

I gazed at the beautiful animals grazing the fields. The family stud farm—it was all so charming. I laughed quietly to myself. My own experience as an equestrian was pretty limited. When I was a child, horseback riding wasn't much on the radar. Once my father had taken Brian and me to ride the ponies at Griffith Park. We stood in line with the teeming urban crowds for what seemed like hours. Finally, we reached the ponies—in hindsight I realize they were cranky old mares, their tails swishing at the iridescent flies that hovered above them.

Ba lifted us onto their backs and off we lurched, trotting along a short, fenced-in track that looped around the yard. As the animals bore down, the stench of their horse apples and sweat rose up into the air. At first, it was fun, especially when we started to canter. But after a couple of loops, I'd had enough. Being on that circular track bored me. I remember later we stopped on the park's main road to let riders from another stable cross to a steep mountain trail. As I watched them trot past, I asked my father, "Where does that trail lead?"

When we pulled into Mokimpur's carport, Karan was standing there, waiting for us. "Oh, I'm glad you people are back," he said. "The Singing Ladies asked if they could visit this afternoon. They heard you brought your bride to the haveli, and they want to welcome Alison to the village."

Indian Singing Ladies? The thought sent a blush to my cheeks. Ajay explained that in the evening, the town's mothers often sat outside their huts with their children, crooning traditional songs into the night sky.

"Oh, that sounds lovely!" I said, excusing myself to change into a salwar kameez. I imagined the dewy young beauties, their voices as sweet as the scent of the orchard air. Glancing into the vanity mirror, I checked my blush and lipstick and quickly neatened my hair.

When I reached the courtyard, Ajay, Karan, Kamala, and Mrs. Singh were sitting on wooden chairs under a shaded arcade. Anusha threw a ball against a wall. Hoti Lal brought out plates of *pakora* and freshly harvested pomegranates. Ajay waved to a chair. "*Ah-ja*, the Singing Ladies will be here any moment." Just then, I heard a din of voices and into the courtyard came the roughest group of women I had ever seen. They wore men's short-sleeved shirts over ankle-length skirts, dusty from the fields. Many had wiry gray hair covered with streaks of henna. Their children skipped around them, toenails crusted with dirt.

We perched on our chairs on the raised arcade floor, and they sat down on the courtyard floor. Then one wrinkled woman rose to her feet. "Radha Ramana Hari!" she cried out in Hindi, waving one hand toward heaven. Her voice flew out like a shriek. "*If you wish you can take my heart!*"

I blinked my eyes in surprise.

"What do you think?" Karan said, leaning toward me.

"Uh . . . gosh . . . I'm not, uh, quite . . . sure," I said, not knowing how to comment. One by one, the Singing Ladies got up and belted out village tunes. They were rough, no doubt, but what they may have lacked in vocal skill they certainly made up in devotion and joy. As I sat in the arcade, I thought for a moment about how different my life would be if I had been raised in this village (and no, not in the big house). The women held each other's hands and swayed to the singing, and the children danced and clapped. I looked at them—the dirty unfashionable clothes, the sun-weathered faces. They couldn't be any happier.

When they were done, Mrs. Singh brought out a silver platter heaped with cheap colorful candies. The children rushed forward, almost knocking her over. They grabbed sweets by the handful and stuffed them into their pockets.

"They're not exactly *ladoos*, but the villagers are thrilled to have anything from the big city," Ajay said. The women filed past us pressing their hands together and saying, "Namaste." I pressed my palms together and thanked them. The leader of the Singing Ladies pointedly stopped and grabbed my hand, locking my gaze in hers. She said something in Hindi and squeezed my fingers tightly—a little too tightly for comfort. I smiled and nodded and then glanced at my reddened palm.

"What did she say?" I asked Ajay, after the villagers filed out of the courtyard.

"I didn't really catch her words," he said. "But she probably said something customary about our marriage. Something like 'May you have a thousand sons.'"

That night I threw up three times. When Ajay tried to bring a dinner tray into my room, I groaned and waved him away. "No food. Not now, not ever," I mumbled. Then I passed out for the night.

The next morning, I heard a loud knock on the door. Before I could answer, the door flew open. It was Kamala. She dragged a chair to my bedside. "So, how are you feeling?" she asked.

"Not. Good. At. All." I cleared my throat and pulled the covers up to my chin.

"Well, I can see that. You look ghastly." She tapped one elegant finger against her lips.

"You know what I think? I think one of the village women didn't like the look of you."

"The *look* of me?"

"Yes, there was something about you she didn't like. She must have given you the evil eye."

"Is that so?" I let my eyes fall shut, willing her to disappear.

"Well, how else to explain it?" Kamala fanned herself with her hand. Then she got up, walked over to the balcony, and opened the doors. "You should get some fresh air. It smells awful in here. Feel better." With that, she turned and left.

I felt an intense heat rise to my cheeks. "Evil eye, my ass."

⤙ 13 ⤚

The Oiling

For a place that was built as an idyllic refuge, Mokimpur was certainly turning out to be a battlefield. If it wasn't the village women sending me questionable vibes (and the stomachache from hell), then it was Kamala, whose polished talons seemed to grow longer and sharper every time we spoke. I wasn't her favorite person on the planet—that much was clear. Whenever I walked into the dining room at mealtime, she narrowed her huge, clever eyes, as if to contain her latest thought. It never worked. I could practically read the imaginary thought bubble floating above her shiny raven head of hair: "Palace domination *will* be mine!" That followed by evil laughter, of course.

In her floral saris and gold bangles, and with a red bindi dot on her forehead, Kamala swanned around the haveli as if she were a goddess. One afternoon on the terrace, I mentioned her other-worldliness to Ajay. He snorted, "Well, if Kamala were a goddess it would have to be Kali."

When I asked which of the Hindu deities that was, Ajay started waving his arms around. "She's the one with the four arms and the black pointed tongue—the Goddess of Destruction."

I laughed and looked across the courtyard just in time to catch Anusha pushing a potted plant off a terrace wall. It fell and crashed onto the courtyard below. We jumped up from our chairs; Kamala raced out of the dining room and pulled her daughter away from the terrace's edge.

"No, no, no, no, Mama!" Anusha wailed as she grabbed at another potted plant.

Ajay and I glanced at each other with bemused smiles. "Let me guess," I said, raising my eyebrows. "That makes Anusha the Toddler of Destruction."

Kamala and Anusha weren't the only formidable female forces in Mokimpur. Mrs. Singh was Goddess in Residence, and she ruled the house with an iron skillet—and a stony face. Yes, she had initially welcomed me to the haveli with a promising expression, one that suggested a blossoming serenity and warmth between us. But in the days since—and with the stress of dealing with a foreigner—that flower seemed to have died on the vine. In fact, she smiled so infrequently it was as if she didn't have the facial muscles to support an upbeat expression. I also noticed that if I sat down at one end of the dining room table, she made sure to sit at the opposite end, even if it was only the two of us. After a few such snubs, I started to feel uncomfortable in her company without Ajay. I just tried to keep out of her way. The palace was her home, her universe, and I was a stranger stealing through her hallways in noisy high heels.

Before my first trip to the haveli, I spent more than a few minutes fantasizing about what my future mother-in-law would be like. Ajay had told me that as a newlywed she was a Delhi socialite, beautifully dressed, impeccably mannered, and always up for a party. "Sound familiar?" he asked, sending an adoring gaze at me, and I had to admit it did.

I guess that's one reason I had expected somebody, well, different. Somebody who was warm and embracing, full of life, and just a touch glamorous. I knew Mrs. Singh had never had daughters of her own. So I dreamed that we'd do all sorts of girly things together. You know, gab about Mira Nair movies over lunch at the Taj Hotel. Shop for exotic jewelry. Sneak in a decadent tea while decked out in our most beautiful salwar kameez. She'd teach me how to drape myself in a sari and how to rim my eyes with kohl. She'd tell me her favorite childhood stories about Ajay as we strolled together through the tree-lined Indian parks. She'd be the first to defend my decision to bring a dozen pairs of shoes for a two-week visit. Maybe she would even help me choose my wedding gown. My mother-in-law would be charming, gracious, and a phenomenal cook—I just knew it.

Well, she certainly could cook.

I should have paid attention to the first red flag. Before we left for India, Ajay warned me that until we were married, I should address his mother by this heartwarming moniker: Mrs. Singh.

As our days at the haveli unfolded, I grew not more comfortable but less. Before I left my bedroom each morning, I made sure to fold each piece of dirty laundry and tuck it all back into my suitcase. I lined my shoes up against one wall. My books stood in a perfectly aligned stack. I put on fresh foundation, blush, and a slick of lipstick every hour or so. I never ever did

The Oiling

this at home in Hong Kong, but somehow Mokimpur demanded such behavior. The palace was beautiful in its spareness, unearthly, fascinating. But, I had to ask myself, would this ever truly feel like home?

One afternoon, Ajay and I were stretched out on wooden daybeds on the main terrace. I flipped through an Indian fashion magazine—marveling at the size of the socialites' emeralds—while Ajay pored over *The Economist*. The patio door flew open and Mrs. Singh appeared, carrying a glass bowl of sage-colored fluid. I gazed up at her, a slight tremor coursing through my chest. She came toward us with the same humorless face—an expression that any future daughter-in-law would interpret as saying, "Why are you here and why did my son choose you?" But as she stood there in the midday light, I studied her carefully. She had delicate features—light olive skin, almond-shaped hazel eyes, long fringed eyelashes, and a heart-shaped face. They were all hints of an intriguing beauty. She was like the *Mona Lisa*, both in her striking coloring and the fact that her default expression—enigmatic—rarely revealed her emotions. Did she like me? Love me? Hate me? The answer changed every time I studied her face.

"Come," she called to Ajay, half-wobbling her head in the direction of the wooden patio table and chairs. Without a word, he got up out of his hammock and shuffled over. She ran her fingers through his tresses and shook her head.

"Ajay, what has happened? Your hair—it's falling off."

I looked up and felt my face grow hot. It was as if I had been caught carving my tag into the Taj Mahal. I knew what she was hinting at. In Hong Kong, the clock seems to tick at double time, and the crowds rush through the streets in a frantic mass, like a pack of cockroaches scrambling for their lives. I knew that the big move from Delhi—where Ajay had taken a two-hour nap every day, even workdays—to Hong Kong, where you were lucky if you slept two hours every night, had taken its toll on him. Big-city life, our sudden cohabitation, the tiny flat above the fish store, and the oh-so-tight budget—neither one of us escaped unscathed. Some mornings I would stand in front of our bathroom mirror surveying the new creases that coursed across my forehead. They were fine lines that no amount of Crème de la Mer could ease. I shrugged it off: This was the price we paid for seeking love in a hypermodern metropolis, across time zones and continents.

As for these DIY hair treatments, I can't say I hadn't been prepared for the ritual. In Ajay's version of crash dieting before a family reunion, the week before our trip to India, he appeared in our Hong Kong living room, carrying a bowl of warm mustard oil.

"Can you pour this in my hair?" he asked. I flashed back to my high-maintenance twenties, when I had tried to revitalize my own locks with Clairol Hot Oil treatment. I remember sticking the little tubes of honey-colored oil into hot water and then pouring the substance onto my hair. But this, what was Ajay carrying in his bowl? This oil didn't come out of a pristine package with instructions on the back. It came out of a cheap plastic bottle from the Indian store in Tsim Sha Tsui. Ajay sat in our dining room chair, and I wrapped a towel around his neck and poured the liquid. A moment passed. He looked up at me and held his hands out.

"Now massage it in," he instructed. I carefully stuck my fingers into the bowl and then into his tresses, trying to make sure the oil reached his scalp.

"There!" I said proudly, wiping my hands on his towel. "Even better than Le Salon Orient."

He sighed. The disappointment practically dripped off his head like the grooming gel. "That was the worst hair oiling I have ever had," he said, shaking his head. He stomped off to the shower, as if to wash away my deficiencies as a woman.

Now, in India, watching Mrs. Singh caress each strand on her son's head, I realized how things were done. I couldn't help but pout. Would my mother-in-law trust me with a houseplant, let alone her son? Ajay sat back as she applied a steady stream of mustard oil, warm as blood. As her hands moved through his hair, massaging his scalp, she clucked her tongue and whispered something to him in Hindi. They locked eyes. They wobbled their heads in unison. Ajay's face turned gray and serious.

"What? What?" I called from my daybed. I had the distinct feeling I was being dissed in Hindi.

Ajay turned to me. "My mother says that if my hair continues to fall like this, in one year I'll be bald."

After a thirty-minute head massage, he finally stood up, his hair slick with oil. Then Mrs. Singh motioned for me to sit in her chair.

"Ah-lee-son, your scalp is like the desert in Rajasthan," she said, straining to keep her tone neutral. "I noticed it the very moment you walked off the plane." She lifted the bowl and poured the remaining contents over my scalp.

In the winter chill, the oil had grown cold. But still she ran her strong, determined fingers through my hair, pulling clumps apart and—could it be?—surveying the richness of its color, measuring the heft of it, seemingly counting the strands.

"You're finished," she announced, wiping her hands on a towel and walking away from the table—and me.

Later that evening, we gathered for drinks in the den, a dark, handsome room that smelled of leather and cumin. Ajay, Mr. Singh, and Uncle Ram savored their evening medicine, whisky and soda, while Mrs. Singh and I sipped a truly bad Indian Chardonnay that could have stripped the polish from my nails. The discussion, about colonialism in India, suddenly turned heated.

"The British surely saved India from itself," declared Uncle Ram, pounding his fist on the table. Ajay shot me a look that said it was probably time to say good night. The room fell silent as the men picked up their golden drinks, the ice in their tumblers clinking against the glass. From the corner of my eye, I saw Mrs. Singh rise in her chair and turn her face to me.

"Ah-lee-son," she said to me. "What are you going to do about your dandruff?" Her eyes gleamed.

*

That night I lay in bed listening to the whup-whup-whup of the primeval ceiling fan that spun in awkward circles above us. Ajay lay next to me, his eyes open and his mind full as well. I turned toward him.

"Why do you think your mother said that about my dandruff?" I asked. "In front of everyone else, too."

He cleared his throat. "I was just thinking about that myself. I guess things with my mother aren't going the way we hoped.

Try not to take it personally. That's just the way she is." He stared at the ceiling.

"How can I take it as anything but personal?" I said, choking back my tears. "Why else would she say such things?"

"Honestly, I think my mom is shy, and she gets a little flustered whenever she has to speak in English," he said, placing his hands behind his head on the pillow. "Her English is good enough, but it's her third tongue after Hindi and Urdu. So there's a language barrier."

He paused, then after a moment said, "I think our relationship has been hard for her to accept—with me moving to Hong Kong and all. She knows my destiny may now take me far from India. I think she feels a lot of guilt."

"What does she have to feel guilty about?" I asked. There was so much about Ajay's childhood I simply did not know.

"Oh, so many things. Where do I begin?"

I reached for his hand.

By his own admission, Ajay had been a difficult child. Given the choice between a clear path and one strewn with cow paddies, he would instinctively follow the cows, gleefully arriving home with his shoes covered in dung. His mother had little patience for such antics, even when they were accidental. Once, when Ajay was a young boy, his father allowed him to ride on the family tractor as it putt-putted across the farm. Almost immediately he stuck his leg in the harrow, smashing his left foot. Ajay returned home screaming in agony on the shoulders of two sturdy farmhands. Mrs. Singh took one look at her son—he was sobbing, about to be carried up the main stairs to his bedroom—and said coolly, "Oh, let him be. He's always getting into trouble." Then she turned away and walked into the house.

Mrs. Singh had labored over her firstborn, feeding him an elaborate bone soup every evening. She still credits Ajay's robust, nearly six-foot-tall frame to the brew. But her methods were Draconian. If Ajay ever refused the soup, she had him locked up in a storeroom until he was ready to eat.

When Ajay was four, his mother gave birth to Karan. By then, her interest in child rearing had waned. After four years of tending to Ajay's minor (and not so minor) everyday accidents, she had had enough. Karan never got bone soup, nor did he get nightly lullabies in Hindi. As Karan grew older and more demanding, Mrs. Singh started to feel as though she could no longer handle two boys. "One of us had to be sent away," Ajay told me. "But I had no idea it was going to be me."

Early one morning, Ajay's mother appeared at his bedside. "Come, Aju." She used his childhood name. "Mummy and Aju are going on a trip." She wore her favorite sari, turquoise with white flowers, and dressed Ajay in pressed shorts and a short-sleeve shirt. The rest of his clothes she folded in a small brown suitcase. They took a taxi to the train station, where they settled into seats in a first-class compartment.

Through the gleaming picture windows, Ajay watched the Delhi buildings and the traffic pass by. He had never been so far from home before. Soon, the buildings and the cars gave way to wheat fields and mud huts and animals grazing in pastures. When evening came, Mrs. Singh spread out meals that Hoti Lal had prepared: *parathas,* mango pickle, and homemade yogurt with grated cucumber. After dinner, Ajay's mother made his bed on a berth in the carriage. Ajay was exhausted, but still he found it difficult to fall asleep. "I didn't know where we were going," he said. "My mother didn't tell me anything. But something was wrong—I sensed it."

Early the next morning, they arrived in Kathgodam, a hamlet in the Himalayas, from which they took a bus to their final destination, Nainital, a verdant valley with a mile-long, bean-shaped lake. For that day's journey, Mrs. Singh dressed Ajay in long pants and a long-sleeve shirt—"just like a grown-up boy," she explained. At one end of the lake she hired ponies, and they rode six miles uphill to Sherwood College, a British boarding school for boys. "Your dada-ji," said Mrs. Singh, referring to Ajay's grandfather Shiam, "is a great horse rider. He wants you to become one, too."

When they reached Sherwood College, Ajay's mother took him to a concrete bench overlooking the expansive campus. "Come, Aju, let's rest here," she said, and Ajay sat next to a leafy tree for what seemed like hours. She fed him enormous *ladoos*, the size of a baseball, and sang his favorite songs. But her efforts offered little comfort to Ajay. He watched as the sun behind them caused their shadows to shift, throwing the bodies of a boy and his mother into a slant onto a pebble-strewn courtyard. Their shadows mutated, growing longer and bigger, and less recognizable as human forms. Soon his mother's gray-black figure disappeared, merging with the shade of the tree. The boy's grew even bigger, until it looked like he was a giant, sitting on the bench alone.

"I'll be right back," said Mrs. Singh, gathering up her purse and tiffin. "Just going to the school store to get something." She ambled across a courtyard and then climbed a steep concrete path lined with chestnut trees. "Wait there for me," she called, and disappeared behind a building.

The sky grew dark. It was early evening now and his mother still hadn't returned. Ajay hummed a song that she had taught him to sing whenever he felt lonely. It was about a small village boy calling out to his mother, who worked in the field. "I thought the words would make my mother reappear," he said. But he sang for more than an hour and still there was no sign of her. Increasingly anxious, he began to run from one part of the court-yard to the other, searching the horizon for her.

A balding man with a leathery face and spectacles appeared. "Hello, Ajay, I am Mr. Samuel. Come with me." The man ush-ered Ajay into a stream of boys his age. The group made its way to a stucco building across the courtyard.

Ajay was deposited in Dormitory Number One, at the foot of a bed marked NUMBER TWO. He looked around him and saw the other boys pulling off their clothes and putting on their night suits. He tried to do the same, but being only four, he fum-bled with the buttons on his shirt. At home, his mother or a servant did that nightly. Somehow he managed to undo the front placket and pull the garment over his head. But he couldn't unbutton the sleeves. He was tugging on them as hard as he could when a tall, dark-skinned woman in a maroon sari suddenly appeared.

"Who do you think you are, a prince?" she shouted and slapped him hard across the cheek. "You think this is home, where a servant will take off your shirt?" The woman's voice was husky from chewing *paan*, betel leaf. She was the dormitory ayah, a combination den mother and maid. That night, Ajay curled into a ball under his covers. Hiding his face with a pillow, he cried until he fell asleep.

For several months, Ajay firmly believed that his mother simply lost her way that first afternoon. She would come back to get him—of course she would. "I returned to that bench every afternoon for four months to look for her," he told me. "But when I got there all I ever saw was shadows on the ground. When I was older, I asked my mother how she could have done something so heartless to her son. Do you know what she said?"

I shook my head slowly.

"She told me that for her to leave me there she had to summon every ounce of heart she had."

The next day I sat reading Vikram Seth's *A Suitable Boy* on the balcony of my bedroom. Earlier in the morning, Hoti Lal had brought in a breakfast tray of chai and *paneer dosas,* a crepe made from lentils and filled with Indian cheese. Ajay ate quickly and left to meet Uncle Ram for a country walk. I was looking forward to a few moments of solitude before lunch.

The morning spread across the sky like a swath of bright blue oil paint, with a perfect yellow sun poised at the top of the horizon as if I were sitting in a child's drawing. Just below the balcony, a pretty peahen, looking quietly chic in her beige and Godiva-brown feathers, foraged for insects among the poplar trees. A black ox, snorting happily, drank from the well. I could almost taste the sweetness of the frangipani blossoms. I flopped down on an old paisley wing chair, once the favorite of Ajay's grandfather, and propped my feet up on a leather ottoman. There were moments when Mokimpur outpaced the pool at the Four Seasons Bali as my favorite place in the world.

I heard the bedroom door creak open. "Ajay?" I called, turning to look.

It was Mrs. Singh. She was dressed in a flowing russet-colored salwar kameez, her hair freshly coiffed. I felt my body stiffen. "Good morning," I said, reluctantly closing my book.

"Look what I have for you," she said, with a cautious smile. Reaching into her pants pocket, she pulled out a shiny round brass box. She popped open the lid, and as she did, an image of Pandora's box, and the mischief that floated from it, flashed through my mind. The box held two intricately carved bracelets. They were cast from 24-karat gold.

"Wow, they're stunning," I said.

"They're for you," she said. She took hold of my left hand and slipped the bracelets on, one by one. "We want to welcome you to the family," she said, patting me on the hand. Then, without another word, she left the room.

I sat down and stared at the bracelets. There was clearly more to Mrs. Singh than last night's story let on.

Later, I tried to pull the bracelets off my wrist. I couldn't—they were too small to pull over my hands. "Oh my God," I muttered to myself. "Am I stuck wearing these forever?" I wore them to bed for three nights and they clanged together whenever I rolled over. They may have looked beautiful during the day, but by bedtime, the golden hoops felt like handcuffs.

On the fourth night, I let Ajay in on the dilemma. He grabbed my arm and marched me to the bathroom. "You have to rub soap on your hands and wrists," he said as he lathered up my skin. Then he pulled and pulled at the shiny circles.

"There!" he cried as they flew off.

I felt a flash of pain. I looked down at my hands, now covered with red streaks. The bracelets had left my skin ripped and bleeding.

And yet I put them on the next morning and the one after that. They were exquisite and given to me, if not out of love, then for an appreciation of destinies intertwined. Along with the pain of wearing those bracelets came their beauty. That much I understood.

A Wedding at the Palace

When I first broached the subject of our wedding with Ajay, he sighed and said, "Whatever we do, let's not make it an Indian one." He explained that for Indian families, no matter how wealthy or desperate, a daughter's wedding is the grandest party they will ever host. The nuptials of the country's elite traditionally last about seven days and often involve a spectacle worthy of a Broadway musical. Elephants decked out in emeralds, thousands of orange chrysanthemums strung into hundreds of garlands, dozens of exotic curries at every meal, tables covered with milk-and-sugar sweets and ice sculptures of the elephant god Ganesh that somehow stay alive in 112-degree heat. Nothing is too lavish a gesture.

For the poor, weddings are still a relatively ostentatious affair. Indeed, the bride's family often hocks its cows and all its gold bangles and earrings just to put on a good show. The whole clan slaves for days over the wedding feast, and every cousin and acquaintance within three thousand miles turns up for the meal. The groom, wearing a shiny turban and tunic with a sheathed sword dangling from his waist, arrives at the party on a white horse, followed by a cadre of relatives, friends, and local revelers. A large brass band swaggers behind the clan, belting out one Bollywood tune after the other while the groom's best chums dance drunkenly behind the band.

Of course, before I'd even arrived at Mokimpur, I half-wondered if Ajay and I might have our wedding at the palace. Now that I was actually here, I could see it was not possible. No way. Every guest would have to bring his or her own sleeping bag, foldout chair, table setting and wineglass, and if any friends wanted to bathe, they would have to stuff into their suitcases their own plastic mug, a bar of soap, and, oh yeah, some hot water. They would have to mind the crumbling balconies, duck under too-low doorways and arches, and occasionally run from irritated peacocks.

There had been a time when Mokimpur was the perfect place for such a celebration. This much I learned when visiting the Singhs' trophy room and caught sight of a black-and-white photograph of a dazzling young woman.

"Who is that girl?" I asked Uncle Ram.

It was Aunt Booah, he said, "all of sixteen." She was draped in a glittering red wedding sari with spun-gold embroidery and a veil draped over her head. Uncle Ram told me that Booah was married at Mokimpur in 1951 with five hundred guests. Whole extended families from the region's social elite traveled en masse to Mokimpur. Shiam Singh's servants pitched dozens of luxurious tents in the fields to house the visitors. Over the following two weeks, the family hosted nightly soirees by the light of a hundred kerosene lamps. The haveli servants, in starched kurta pajama suits, gold turbans, and leather slippers whose toes curled into a point, stood on every terrace, proffering *ladoos, jalebi* (sweet translucent pretzels), and *burfi* (luscious milk-based sweets) to the revelers. The women wore jewel-colored saris and heirloom emeralds and sapphires and chirped about their husbands and houses. The men, dressed in bright turbans and cummerbunds, nursed their drinks and traded tiger-hunting stories.

On the night of the wedding, Booah sat upright in her dressing room, tapping her foot. Her mother fussed with the kohl rimming the bride's eyes and laced fresh frangipani blossoms through her hair. Booah's delicate hands bore an elaborate lace pattern drawn with henna by Delhi's finest mehndi artist. She looked stunning.

In the great Indian tradition, Booah's groom, a handsome, rugged-looking boy from Delhi, kept the entire wedding party and their scores of guests waiting for him, his way of playing hard to get. He had been scheduled to arrive at 6 P.M. Four hours later, he finally showed up—on the back of an elephant. As the groom and the beast, bedecked with marigolds, lumbered through the village, the local children danced alongside, tossing blossoms into the air, ringing bells and crashing pot lids together.

Then a village elder ran into the path and shot several rounds from his rifle. The elephant reared in fear, tossing the groom into a low karonda bush. Shaken but unharmed, the groom stood up, smoothed out his wedding finery, and straightened his turban. One of Booah's aunts shouted from a palace window, "That is your karma for keeping us waiting, young man!"

After Uncle Ram told me that story, I lingered in the trophy room and gazed at the photograph until it was seared into my memory. Afterward, I shut the trophy room's door and wandered through the courtyard alone. I knew that with the haveli in its sorry state I could not get married there. But if we poured enough love and muscle into the house, maybe one day a daughter of mine could. I leaned against a courtyard wall and thought about a beautiful half-Indian, half–Chinese American girl in a flowing white gown crossing the wheat fields here, a bouquet of village flowers in her hands.

⤙⤙ 15 ⤚⤚

Christmas with Hindus

When I finally found a calendar at the haveli, I realized something essential: It was only a few days before Christmas. Not that the holiday meant much to the residents of Uttar Pradesh. Few in these parts had even heard of Jesus, much less Rudolph or Santa Claus. Ajay joked that with three million gods swirling about in the Hindu universe, Indians had plenty of religious figures to keep themselves occupied without worrying about Christian ones.

I, on the other hand, had always loved Christmas. As a Chinese American girl growing up in Los Angeles, I had grown used to celebrating this American holiday in a fashion that neatly reflected who we were and where we lived: The Gee family feasted on a glistening roasted turkey accompanied by Chinese sticky rice and dim sum, and we ate our dinner wearing shorts and flip-flops. Our glowing electric Santa sat below our antique ceramic Buddha. As my brother strummed his acoustic guitar in the living room, next to the Christmas tree (flocked tinsel in lean years, robust pine in fat ones), we were just as likely to croon "Silent Night" as we were to belt out "Grandma Got Run Over by a Reindeer." It was heaven for us quasi-Buddhists, quasi-atheists in Southern California. Even my unpredictable father gave it a rest for the holidays.

So when I realized that we would be spending the yuletide season in India, I knew we could not miss out. I decided to tote the holiday season in my suitcase and re-create a jolly Christmas for my soon-to-be family—even if that meant hanging gold and silver baubles from a mango tree and sticking a plucked peacock in the tandoor.

A few weeks before our trip, I started to hatch my plan: I would cook a traditional Christmas dinner for the entire Singh family. Never mind that I had few kitchen skills. My signature dish consisted of Contadina ready-made pesto over Contadina ready-made tortellini. Nonetheless, I was determined to give the Singhs a taste of this seasonal culinary extravagance. So before we left Hong Kong for Delhi, I trawled the aisles of a fancy gourmet supermarket for my favorite Christmas foods. Then I carefully packed the trove of brightly wrapped goods into our already bulging suitcases.

When Ajay announced my plans to his mother, Mrs. Singh smiled weakly and mumbled something in Hindi. Ajay shook his head and mumbled back.

"My mother says Hoti Lal could make a very good *seekh kabab* to go with your feast, but I told her not to bother. You'll be making the whole meal."

"What in the world is a *seekh kabab*?"

"It's like an Indian sausage. It's made of spicy, grilled meat."

My taste buds flared. If this crowd was looking forward to spicy, grilled meat prepared by the haveli's expert chef, then my simply roasted duck probably wouldn't cut it.

"Listen," I said, sighing, "if your mom prefers *seekh kabab*, Hoti Lal should cook those, too."

"Nonsense, that would mess with your theme," Ajay huffed. "They can have *seekh kabab* anytime. I think they'll be happy to try your Western spread. How often do they get to sample real American food anyway?"

"But—"

He held up his hand and said, "It's decided."

On Christmas morning, I woke up at seven, two hours earlier than usual. I had bags of imported walnuts to chop, fancy Japanese yams to boil and mash, village pears to slice. I had not yet figured out how I was going to roast the Christmas duck—Mokimpur had no working oven. I took some comfort in the fact that even if the bird didn't get cooked we would still have enough to eat. At most Western holiday dinners a showy offering of fowl, beef, or pork is the pièce de résistance, but more than half the Singhs were staunch vegetarians. They wanted nothing to do with a dead duck and would most likely gravitate to such delights as beet and goat cheese salad and rice pilaf.

Still, I reasoned, it would be lovely to have a beautifully roasted bird on the table as the meal's centerpiece. "God, who am I fooling? I don't know how to cook a duck," I said, my eyes darting back and forth. Then I caught sight of a photo of Gandhi in the living room. "I shall detach myself," I murmured, taking inspiration from the Great Soul, and serenely set about arranging the ingredients.

Even with my newly affected Mahatma-esque posture, things did not progress so seamlessly. I spent all morning sitting alone in the kitchen, in the semidark, perched on a metal stool, quartering walnuts. For every half nut I managed to cut, another half flew across the room and onto the floor under the pressure of the knife. I set a bowl of boiled yams onto the windowsill, only to hear a crash followed closely by a scream. (Turns out, my jittery hand had knocked the bowl off the ledge into the courtyard where Phoola was hanging clothes to dry.) A few minutes after that, I inadvertently set a kitchen towel on fire. Amid all this culinary stress I found some brief amusement in the juxtaposition of Pepperidge Farm Cornbread Stuffing boxes and the crude stone shelves of the kitchen. I wondered what Martha Stewart would look like in a sari.

Hoti Lal wandered by a few times, nodding with an amused smile. Once, he clasped his palms together and offered, "Namaste." Another time, I thought I heard him giggle.

"Hmmm," I said, drumming my fingers on the counter. "I wonder if the Iron Chef has an emergency hotline."

Midmorning, Karan came into the kitchen and ceremoniously placed a toaster oven down on the counter, adding that he'd already asked Uncle Ram to fire up the generator. "And don't worry," he said, catching sight of my furrowed brow. "We'll have your goose cooked in no time."

I took the aluminum foil off the bird, which I had marinated in fresh chopped garlic and my own secret ingredient, Paul Newman's Italian Dressing. Once the generator was on, I placed the duck in the oven. By late afternoon, the fowl had turned an impressive shade of brown. It smelled divine. Phoola, who had rescued the remaining yams off the courtyard floor, rinsed them off for me in the kitchen sink. After I folded sautéed pears, nectar, and walnuts into the mashed yams, the mixture firmed up into a luscious pie. The stuffing plumped up in a fragrant pile in its serving bowl. After so many hours of hard, hot labor, I was seeing results.

"Ah, Christmas!" I said, shut the kitchen door behind me, and headed to my bedroom to change for dinner.

From my suitcase, I pulled the outfit I had brought just for this night—a black cashmere turtleneck and a floor-length skirt I'd had made in Hong Kong out of bright pink sari fabric. As I was dressing, I heard the door creak open. It was Kamala. She looked cheerless in baggy jeans and a worn-out gray sweater. Her eyes widened. "Well, you certainly did yourself up." She placed her hands on her slim hips. "What a pretty getup. I can't believe you bothered to drag your best clothes out to the village."

I was about to make a surly remark, but then I paused. What Would Gandhi Do? "Oh, I know it's too much," I said, smiling and batting my eyelashes. "But in America, Christmas is an excuse to have a little fun."

"Ah, I see," she said, tapping her index finger on pursed lips. She reached into her pocket and pulled out a black velvet pouch. "Open your hands," she said, wobbling her head. She loosened the pouch's strings and tipped the pouch upside down. Into my hands slithered a beautiful silver necklace with a heart-shaped pendant.

"Oh, my God," I said. I searched her face for some meaning. "This is too much."

"Well, what kind of sister-in-law would I be if I didn't share my jewelry," she said. "Here, let me put it on you." She carefully pulled my hair away from my neck and fastened the necklace's clasp. I walked over to the old wooden vanity and looked into its tarnished mirror.

"Wow," I said, gazing at my reflection. I couldn't help myself.

"Welcome to our world," Kamala said. She pushed up her sleeves and left the room.

✦

Dinnertime was soon upon us—it was showtime! When I entered the dining room, Uncle Ram and Mr. and Mrs. Singh were sitting at the big wooden table, nursing tumblers of whisky and soda. Anusha sat on a miniature chair, trying to pull the head off an Indian Barbie. Phoola had set the table with house silver and frangipani flowers, and she had placed the Chinese cake I had brought from a Hong Kong bakery—a decorative brown-crust pastry filled with bean paste—on a gleaming silver platter.

"Very nice," Mrs. Singh said, clapping her hands together as she took in my Indian skirt and new necklace. Her eyes darted past me and she cried, "Aju!" In walked her firstborn, dressed head to toe in regional finery. He wore a bloodred kurta embellished with gold thread, silk pajama pants, and pointed red leather shoes. On his head he donned a bright yellow turban. "Hoti Lal made this out of an old scarf," Ajay said, beaming.

Suddenly, all heads turned again. Anusha let out a gasp. "Mummy!" she cried, dropping her headless doll on the floor. Kamala had shed her ill-fitting "cricket mom" jeans and draped herself in her wedding sari, a dazzling length of red cloth with an elaborate floral embroidery. A dozen gold bangles shimmered on each wrist. Her gold earrings were shaped like the elephant god Ganesh and hung low from her lobes. "Thought I'd join in the celebration," she said, tossing her hair back. "Americans wear red at Christmas, don't they?"

For once I didn't mind being upstaged. After all, it was turning into a real party here in the middle of Mokimpur's wheat fields. Hoti Lal and Phoola brought out my meal in silver bowls, steam rising from every dish. Ajay and I piled our plates with yams, stuffing, and sautéed cauliflower. I helped myself to several slices of duck. I hadn't eaten anything since breakfast, and my stomach rumbled with a painful hunger. I tore into a sliver of duck. "Ack!" I said, spitting it out. Using my fork, I rolled the chewed meat over on my plate. Beneath its beautiful golden skin my Christmas duck was almost completely raw.

The other meat eaters among us—Mr. Singh, Karan, and Anusha—obviously noticed it, too. I heard quiet gagging sounds throughout the room, and half-chewed pieces of fowl appeared on the edge of people's plates. Anusha pointed at the duck and shouted something in Hindi. "Shhhh!" Karan hushed, and slapped her on the wrist. My beloved cornbread stuffing hardly dazzled anyone's palate. I half-wondered if it was too late to dump some *garam masala* into it. The only good news was the yams. They were an Indian staple during the winter, and mine, even in their American form, were deemed acceptable. Karan and Kamala pointed at the pie and nodded their heads as if to reassure the others. I saw Mrs. Singh hesitate as she bit into a spoonful. Her face burst into a look of wonder, as if discovering hamburgers weren't actually poisonous, and she surreptitiously offered Kamala a thumbs-up. She shoveled more onto her plate and then sprinkled some chopped chilies into it.

Halfway through dinner, everyone lifted their heads and sniffed, their eyes widening. A cooking smell—earthy, spicy, delectable—wafted in from the servants' kitchen. Hoti Lal was making dinner for Phoola and himself. *Seekh kababs!* I caught Kamala and Mrs. Singh exchanging frozen smiles. Anusha's face grew gray and sullen, and she smacked the pile of stuffing on her plate with her spoon. At the end of the meal, most of my American delicacies remained in pathetic heaps in their silver bowls. Other than the yam pie, Mrs. Singh's only form of sustenance was the Hong Kong bakery cake. She ate two slices of that.

Later, I sized up the leftovers and covered them with dishcloths. They would be placed on the terrace overnight, Mokimpur's only reliable form of refrigeration. Kamala sidled up to me and waved a manicured hand at the table. "It was a little—um, what's the word?—'bland.' Yes, it was bland for our tastes," she explained.

"Oh, I realize that now," I said, shaking my head. "Poor Mrs. Singh, she must be starving. She hardly ate a bite all night."

"Cheer up," she said. "She liked that Chinese cake you baked."

Thank goodness for Christmas presents, which I quickly learned was a universally appreciated tradition—even if Pepperidge Farm stuffing wasn't. Before leaving Hong Kong, Ajay and I spent hours drawing up a list of gifts we needed to bring. We searched the musty floors of China Products, a sort of Walmart with Chinese characteristics, and Stanley Market, an open-air flea market, for distinguished goodies at meager prices. We snapped up carved rosewood boxes, calligraphy brushes, a brass gong, and lots of counterfeit Burberry and stuffed it all into our suitcases.

We stumbled through the crowded streets of Hong Kong

with bulging plastic shopping bags, our ankles a mess of cuts and bruises. Just when I thought we had bought our last present, Ajay shouted out, "Oh God! I almost forgot. We need to bring something for Hoti Lal's son's best friend." Another time, as we rode in a taxi home with more bags, Ajay tapped the side of his head and cried, "Oh, no! Rajinder, my friend Sanjay's servant, asked me for a camera." I looked at him without blinking. "A camera . . . for Sanjay's butler. Are you kidding? We are going to be bankrupt by the time we board Air India." Two seconds later, we got out of the taxi and headed for the camera store.

In the end, I was grateful for every half-price T-shirt and box of White Rabbit Creamy Candy we had toted to Mokimpur. The look of sheer happiness on everyone's faces was so worth it—even if we'd be paying off our Visa bill for the next three months.

The morning following our yuletide dinner, all the Singhs appeared on the terrace looking suitably merry in their bargain China Products Christmas gifts. Uncle Ram turned up in his new Ralph Lauren–esque argyle vest. Mr. Singh proudly wrapped his faux Burberry scarf around his neck. As Mrs. Singh set the table for lunch, her cloisonné bracelets—not gold as she had first believed, but brass—slid down her wrists and clinked. Anusha clapped her hands and her battery-operated panda flashed its tacky fluorescent green eyes and slowly crawled toward her. Hoti Lal emerged from the kitchen in his cut-price navy blue Banana Republic T-shirt, wearing the biggest grin.

Even last night's leftover duck made a happy return appearance. Hoti Lal, clever man, had deftly fried it with diced onions, garlic, and cumin. He glanced at me as he placed a big dish of chopped chilies by the side of the duck.

I swear I saw him wink.

✦ 16 ✦

Servants and Masters

With my Christmas deemed a merry success by all, I was riding high. "I think I'm getting the hang of this India business," I told Ajay, tossing my hair back. The two of us were lazing around on the sunny front lawn, as Hoti Lal's grandchildren threw around a ball made from cloth and twine.

"The trick to surviving life with an Indian family—it's really kind of simple. You just have to accept that India is the center of its own universe. Nothing and nobody else makes any impact on this place at all, does it? Not a dent."

"That's right," Ajay said. He turned the pages of a two-month-old issue of *India Today* that he'd scavenged from Uncle Ram's quarters. "Well done for figuring that out. It's the kind of attitude that will get you far in these parts. There's just no stopping India. It seeps into your mind, your pores—like the fumes of fried onion. The only way to understand India is to surrender unconditionally."

I handed him a *ladoo* from a plate piled high with tea treats and then grabbed one for myself. I held it in front of me and considered the bubbles of cellulite one ball of butter, sugar, and cardamom would inspire in my thighs. If I had been in Hong Kong or L.A. I would have scoffed at ingesting such a diet-sabotaging sphere. "But we're in India," I thought to myself. "So what the hell." I popped all four hundred calories of pure saturated fat into my mouth and licked the remaining spice off my fingers.

✦

Ajay was right. To resist India was futile. With that thought, I decided to hand myself over to the most famous icon around: the Taj Mahal. I loved the Taj. I had loved it for as long as I could remember. When I was a child, some neighbors gave me a little glass snow globe of the mausoleum—a memory of their honeymoon trip to India in the 1950s. I would spend hours shaking the globe, watching the plastic snow fall on the mini Taj's cloudlike domes, dreaming of maharajas and elephants. I took that little tchotchke with me to college, to grad school in London, and finally to Hong Kong. It was a tiny watery world that encapsulated my past, my present, and, now, my future.

During his first visit to my Hong Kong apartment, Ajay came across the Taj snow globe sitting on my bedside table. He picked it up and shook it.

"Do you like it?" I asked, smiling.

"Ah, it's a pretty little toy." He held it up to the light. "But you'll despise the real thing. The Taj is full of clueless tourists, beggars, and scoundrels. It's hell on earth."

I grabbed my precious bauble out of his hand. "Every famous place in the world attracts beggars," I said, as my ears grew hot.

"I don't care if the place is surrounded by Ali Baba and his forty thieves. I'm going."

Ajay eventually capitulated to my Taj Mahal plans. This was not a battle he would win. The snow globe next to my bed had said it all.

We planned to leave a couple of days after Christmas. I was so excited I had already put aside my wardrobe—a new gold-colored salwar kameez from Anokhi (India's answer to Anthropologie), a white cashmere sweater coat, and a red shahtoosh. Ajay and I were poring over a train schedule one night before the trip when Kamala appeared. "Anusha, Karan, and I would like to accompany you," she announced, chin up, one hand on her hip.

"Oh . . . how, uh, lovely," I said. This time it was my turn to put on a frozen smile. Ajay nudged me under the table.

"That'll be good fun, Kamala," he said, filling in the silence. "We'll all watch the sunrise over the Taj. All of us."

Fate had different plans. On the morning we were scheduled to leave, I lay in bed, trying to rouse myself from under the covers. Suddenly, I heard a high-pitched shriek. Then came a tirade in Hindi, the sound of a door slamming, and footsteps scurrying down the hall. I jumped out of bed, wrapped a shawl around my kurta, and ran to the kitchen.

Kamala was standing there, eyes blazing. Catching sight of me, she picked up a tray of neatly stacked sandwiches, whose crusts had been carefully removed, and threw the whole thing on the floor. Triangles of bread flew in every direction. "That man!" she screamed. "Hoti Lal spread butter in Anusha's sandwiches for the trip. Can you imagine? Bloody fool! The butter would go bad by the end of the trip and Anusha would get sick. The stupidity of these people!"

I knew what my future sister-in-law meant to say when she spat out the phrase "these people." I'd been in India only two weeks, but that was long enough to figure out an essential truth: Indians were obsessed with social standing.

Whenever Ajay and I went out in Hong Kong and he caught sight of another Indian man, Ajay would completely ignore him. I found this curious because I tended to do just the opposite: Whenever I saw another person of Chinese descent anywhere in the world, I would make eye contact and give a little wave.

"Don't you find other Indians interesting?" I once asked Ajay. "Oh, yes," he replied, "But only the Indians in India, the 'real' India, that is, the India in the villages."

Indians abroad, he opined, were the worst advertisement for India—"They're so ugly," he said. He also deemed them uncouth. Or horrid. Or obnoxious. Of course, since relocating to Hong Kong, Ajay himself was an Indian abroad. But he seemed to be his own exception. I never said anything, but I wondered if his caste-conscious upbringing was what was driving these condemnations.

It's not as if I didn't have my own class issues. Having grown up with five siblings, each of us scrambling for more, I knew we were the so-called poor relations of a moneyed Chinese American clan. But most of my brothers and sisters went to fancy private colleges (generously funded by merit scholarships, of course), and we lived like suburban bohemians who had passion, education, and culture. We convinced ourselves that being intellectual and iconoclastic elevated us in caste, even above our wealthy cousins. We all have our notions of what constitutes class, and our brainy oddness was it for me.

During one of my first stints as a magazine journalist, I remember one scrappy editor asking me point-blank, "What class are you?" I looked at him, perplexed. He asked me again, this time more insistent: "What class are you?"

"Gosh, I don't know," I said. "Middle?" Not satisfied with my own answer, I stood in his office doorway and recounted for him a family story about my Chinatown-mayor grandfather. My mother had often told me that, at least once a month, he would drive down to skid row and look for homeless men—during that era they were just called "bums." So he would look for bums who seemed the hungriest. He drove them a few miles to his general store and put them to work unpacking canned lychees and dragon fruit. At the end of the day, he'd sit them down to a meal, hand them each twenty dollars, and drive them back. "I guess I've always been intrigued by his noblesse oblige and if anyone represents my family for me, he's it," I said, raising my palms in the air and turning to escape the editor, his office, and his very strange question.

Kamala was from the Brahmin caste—the highest social category in Hindu culture (but not necessarily the economic one). Her parents, who are Kashmiri, had little money and lived in a rented apartment cluttered with worn books and newspapers in Old Delhi. Even so, because they were Brahmins, they thought of themselves in lofty terms. On one of my first days in Mokimpur, Kamala had taken me aside and told me that she and her family "didn't think much of the Singhs."

I puzzled over her admission for a few days. It felt somehow intimate and yet overly familiar at the same time. Just what was she up to in making a statement like that to me, someone she barely knew? During my two weeks at Mokimpur, I'd heard her shout at Hoti Lal many times. An unmade bed, tepid water in the geyser, Anusha's shoes left unpolished—it didn't take much to work Kamala into an ugly froth. But this morning's rant reached a whole new level.

"You people carry on with your program," she said, throwing her hand into the air and kicking aside a cucumber sandwich with her slippered foot. "Go to the Taj if you want. We won't be joining you."

✦

When I reported the morning's drama to Ajay, he scratched his cheek and calmly explained that we would have to cancel our trip. To carry on to the Taj after Kamala's big outburst would be deeply insulting to her. "It's Kamala versus Hoti Lal. And we need to be here in solidarity."

"Us against Hoti Lal? Isn't that a bit over the top?" I shook my head.

"I know it sounds a little cruel," said Ajay, "especially to someone who's not from India, but now that she's had this big showdown we'll need to take a stand. The Taj will have to wait. I'm sorry."

I fought back tears. But the sadness wasn't just due to the canceled trip. There was something else that was tugging at me.

For the next few hours, the Singhs sat around flipping through old copies of the *Times of India* and avoiding eye contact with each other. Whenever Hoti Lal walked into the room, they would all lift their papers and books up to their faces. Kamala crossed her arms and stared straight across the room. As Hoti

Lal placed a platter of vegetable *pakora* on the coffee table, I stole a glance at him. He was small and wiry, and his hair had faded to gray and white. His blue cotton kurta was clean but frayed at the edges, and his canvas shoes had holes that exposed yellowing toenails. The backs of his hands were a motley pattern of age spots and what looked like cooking burns. He backed out of the room, bowing his head. Ajay had told me that Hoti Lal had been serving the family since he was in his early twenties. He was now in his midsixties.

Later, I pulled Ajay into the bedroom and closed the door. Now it was I who crossed my arms against my chest. "What in the world is this about?" I asked, shaking my head. "The way everyone's freezing out Hoti Lal is obscene."

"Don't worry," he said, holding up a hand. "This is all just a part of the relationship in Indian households—you know, servants and masters. It will pass."

Suddenly, tears streamed down my face. Ajay looked startled and then quickly fished his handkerchief from his pants pocket and dabbed at my eyes. Guiding me to his grandfather's old wing chair, he sat down on the ottoman and held my hand until my sobbing died down.

"I know being at the haveli hasn't been easy," he said. "This place must feel like the end of the earth for you. We do things differently here. But there is a method to what must seem like our madness. I promise you that."

It was then that Ajay and I talked about what must be one of the most baffling aspects of Indian society—the relationship between servants and their bosses. In certain situations, he explained, the arrangement is like one between employee and employer; in others, it's like close relatives who share years—sometimes decades—of emotional baggage. In yet other circumstances the tie is more like that of slave and master.

While doing research for our trip I had come across a *New York Times* story on servants in India. I learned that most middle-class households typically employed about three domestic helpers who worked a 24/7 schedule. Each was paid less than fifty cents a day. Of course, a half dollar went a lot farther in India than it would in America, but it was still a pittance by any measure.

Ajay grew up with servants, but he said his first lessons about dealing with domestics came from his Aunt Booah, the eldest of his father's five siblings. Booah's golden rule was that servants should always be treated politely and respectfully. So, whenever Ajay wrote letters home from his boarding school, he always asked after the health of Hoti Lal and his children.

But Ajay also learned that they should always be kept at a distance. Becoming overly familiar was just not done. Servants were never to be sat with, dined with, or joked with. Never.

"At all times, they needed to be made aware of their place in the social order," Ajay said.

"Does that bother you?" I asked.

"Not really. You see, there's a logic to the caste system," he said, shrugging. According to Hindu beliefs, he explained, the life you are born into—that of a servant, merchant, warrior, or intellectual—depends on the karma you cultivated during past lives.

"In our society, everyone has his place," he said. At the highest level are the Brahmins, who historically were priests. They acted as spiritual counselors to the maharajas. At the lowest level are the Untouchables. Even their shadows are considered polluting. Ajay told me about an elderly great-uncle of his who would throw away fresh milk if an Untouchable so much as walked past its container—a statement that left me clutching my chest and gasping. Until the early 1900s, Untouchables were forced to wear brooms that hung off the back of their belts and grazed the ground. The broom swept away their footprints so that people of higher castes who walked on the same path wouldn't be contaminated. In order for society to function properly, all trace of the Untouchable needed to be wiped away.

Of course, I knew that since Mahatma Gandhi crusaded to reform the caste system, the position of the Untouchables had become less rigid, less inhuman. And Ajay pointed out that Indian president K. R. Narayanan, elected in 1997, was from that lowest of castes.

"An Untouchable as the leader of India?" I asked Ajay. "How did that happen?"

"Well, it proved to the world that India had broadened its thinking, that we were progressing as a society on the human front," Ajay explained. "It was supposed to show the world that Untouchables were no longer, well, untouchable. But to be perfectly honest, everyone in India knew the election was purely political. India is a democracy—every person gets a vote. So Narayanan's party wanted to kiss up to the masses by placing one of theirs in office."

"So do you think it worked? I mean, would you ever eat a *ladoo* that an Untouchable made?"

"Yes," Ajay said slowly. "I would."

"Do you have any Untouchable friends?"

Ajay was silent for a while. "No, I don't."

"Why not?"

"Well, I guess we just wouldn't have a lot in common. I know of lots of Untouchables in the village. They're weavers and leather tanners and the like. I just wouldn't have anything to say to them." Ajay explained that he still believed there was a beauty to the caste system. "Almost everyone has somebody to feel superior to," he said. "In India, there isn't this mad, all-consuming struggle to climb up a social hierarchy, like there is in the West. You can't really transform your place in society that much."

"Fascinating," I said. "But completely appalling. I mean, you treat holy cows better than Kamala treats Hoti Lal." I recalled something Mark Twain had once written about Hindus, after his late-nineteenth-century visit to the Subcontinent: "Indians seem to worship all forms of life except human life."

During one of our first nights in India, when we were staying in Mrs. Singh's big family home in Old Delhi, I walked downstairs to find Hoti Lal curled up on a stained mat in the garage. His clothes and a small hand towel were rolled up into a tight ball beside him. He was emitting the deep, atavistic snores that only come from those who do hard physical labor. I headed back upstairs. "How can you let him sleep there like that?" I asked Ajay. I could feel my cheeks flush with heat. "With all the rooms in this big house, why can't he have one to rest in?"

Ajay put his arm around me. "It's okay. Trust me. He doesn't want a room. He knows where servants are supposed to sleep— in the garage or on the kitchen floor. This is his place. If we offered him anything else, he would feel uncomfortable."

In his own small way, Hoti Lal tried to alter the fate of his caste. He was born in a small village in Bihar, an East Indian state that was considered desperately poor and lawless. Poverty is so dire in Bihar that many people roast rats for dinner. Hoti Lal had eaten his share of rodents before setting out for Kanpur, a highly industrialized and cosmopolitan city, in the 1950s. Even though he was illiterate, he hoped to get a job. The best work he could find was cleaning dishes at the home of Ajay's parents. At the time, Mr. Singh was an executive with a British sugar company based in Kanpur. Hoti Lal could have ended up like millions of poor villagers who migrate to the city every year—rootless, bouncing from job to job in a state of anomie. He had left his family behind, and while he washed the Singhs' cups and plates, he sang mournful tunes about the loneliness of his life. One day, Ajay's mother heard him singing in his native Bhojpuri. She was so moved that she asked Hoti Lal to return to Bihar and bring his family back to Kanpur to live with him. This he did, and the Lal family has been serving the Singhs ever since.

For a peasant like Hoti Lal, landing a place in the Singh household was like striking gold. After thirty-five years of his toil, the Singhs gifted Hoti Lal and his wife, Phoola, a residential compound in Mokimpur. "By all measures Indian, Hoti Lal and his clan have fared extremely well," said Ajay. "My mother treated his sons almost as equals to us—well, almost. If Karan and I got a mango to eat, they did, too." Yet even as much as the Lal boys fraternized with the Singhs, Ajay says that he and his brother were always conscious that they were the servants' sons. "If we were out playing cricket together in the courtyard, the boys could never sit down on chairs that were on the same level as ours," he sad. "They either had to crouch or sit on the floor."

"What!"

"Yes, it's the same with Hoti Lal and the rest of his family. That's why he's always sitting on the ground."

My stomach dropped. What the hell was I getting myself into? I had to ask myself that much. Not only was I marrying into a family that made comments about my dandruff at the dinner table and "borrowed" my precious drinking water, I was aligning myself with a culture whose deeply held customs I simply couldn't fathom—or, frankly, respect.

That evening I passed Hoti Lal. He was sitting cross-legged on the kitchen floor, chopping bell peppers and onions for the night's meal. I peered into the kitchen and saw a slab of meat, still coated in fresh blood. Ajay would tell me later that Hoti Lal had slaughtered a lamb to make a conciliatory meal for Kamala. He would serve it with *baigan bharta* (eggplant curry), a rich chicken *korma*, and freshly harvested farm vegetables. No doubt he was thinking that a small feast would coax the family into a better mood. I moved into the kitchen and my shadow fell across him. "Uh, namaste," I said, breaking the family embargo against the man. Hoti Lal nodded but didn't look up. He knew his place. And just because I made a friendly gesture did not mean we were friends. This was the life he was born into. The life his karma had determined. Neither he nor anyone else was going to argue with that.

During that maiden visit to India, we never made it to the Taj. For once, I didn't whine about my bad luck.

↤ 17 ↦

Haveli Rich, Cash Poor

We had been at Mokimpur for more than a week—a few days longer than initially planned—and the Northern Indian winter had definitely taken hold. Mornings were so frosty that the bathwater would inevitably go lukewarm, making for a mug shower so bracing that I dreaded my daily ritual. In the evening, the family sat around the dinner table wearing blankets wrapped around our shoulders and torsos—we all looked like mummies slurping down curry. But there was no way to make winter more comfortable at the haveli. The Singhs simply couldn't afford to run the generator more than a couple of hours a day, and they couldn't buy more kerosene to heat the stoves or to keep the lamps blazing longer. They may have been living in a hundred-room palace, but the Singhs seemed grateful just to get simple meals on the table every night.

During one of our early-evening walks, I finally felt brave enough to ask Ajay about his family's financial state. "My father left his job at the sugar plantations to make a go of farming at Mokimpur," said Ajay, as we walked through the garden picking up fallen peacock feathers, so beautiful and yet so lonely as they glimmered in the last moments of sunlight. "But things have not worked out so well. The land has not really produced the crops we counted on, and my father says the farmers who rent land from us are scoundrels and cheats. All this has taken its toll over the years. Our bank accounts are almost empty now." He held a feather up to the light and looked at it, as if its loveliness could redeem the situation. "Our family used to rank fourth in the state," he said. He let the feather drift through the air and fall to the ground. "Then all the nouveaux riches started coming up and our family was cast aside."

Ajay floated off onto a dreamy tangent, telling me his beloved memories of Mokimpur. One of his favorite recollections was the winter he spent alone there, save for the company of his black Labrador, Doma. While his parents stayed in Delhi for the season, Ajay took on the farm, having come up with his wild scheme to farm eucalyptus trees on the grounds. He stayed in one cavernous room in the haveli that had two twin beds placed at either end of the chamber. Every night, he slept in one bed, and Doma slept in the other. "One night the winter storms were so loud they woke both of us up," said Ajay. "Then we heard a huge thud on the roof, as if some animal were trying to get into the house. I looked over at Doma, and she looked over at me, as if to say, 'Do something about it!'

"I wasn't going to get up to look around, and neither was she. So we both just peered at each other through the darkness, cowering in our own beds, with the sheets pulled up under our chins until dawn."

By the end of the winter, Ajay's foray into eucalyptus farming had ended disastrously. He had planted the trees on land that was vulnerable to termite attacks, and the ravenous insects had feasted on their tender roots. Ajay found his infant trees toppled, like tiny fallen soldiers, beyond the point of resuscitation. "Do you know, it was my mother who had given me the money for that particular folly? And when the trees died she didn't say a word."

He stopped in his tracks and grabbed my hand. "Do you know what my biggest dream is? My biggest dream is to give Mokimpur its life back. Can you imagine the entire house with walls that aren't covered in mold? With well-tended flowering gardens instead of the neglected dirt patches you see everywhere now? With couches that aren't frayed at every corner and faded by the sun? With a pool where our children can learn to swim? Mokimpur is my mother's all-consuming passion, and coming here with you, I'm starting to feel the same way about the house. This is our future. It's the future of our children."

I considered a life here—with no Internet, no bookstores, no restaurants, no cinemas, no boutiques, no electricity, no telephone, no television, and no stereo. This place was just so vastly different from the world I was used to. What would I do without the gadgets on which my life depended?

But I also knew that this magical place was where Ajay would choose to live the last few years of his life, that Mokimpur—not Delhi, not Hong Kong, not Los Angeles—would be the realm in which our lives intersected those of the Singhs.

Our trip was coming to an end. We were scheduled to fly back to Hong Kong the next morning. It was time to return to our jobs and our lives in the big city. As I packed my newly acquired Indian saris and salwar kameezes next to Donna Karan dresses (which remained folded in my suitcase), I heard Ajay and his mother talking outside in the courtyard below. I stepped out onto the balcony and sensed that they were deep in heavy conversation. Hiding behind a potted palm tree, I saw Mrs. Singh grasp her son's hand and stare into his eyes. "I know you have a new life with Alison far away from Mokimpur," I could hear her saying, "but you know, we could really use some money." For the first time since meeting Ajay's mother, I saw vulnerability in her eyes. She suddenly looked older to me. I couldn't help but wonder how long it had taken her to summon the courage to say those words to her son.

That night, after everyone had gone to bed, I stood alone on the balcony. The winds had risen and now whipped around me, creating such a noise—as if a hundred souls were howling. I tried to sleep, but the voices were speaking much too loudly.

Part III

18

Hong Kong Luxury, Indian Soul

Twenty-four hours later we landed in Hong Kong. It was close to midnight, but from the look of the streets in Tsim Sha Tsui—the apartment towers blaring with fluorescent lights, harried crowds pressed together at the intersections—nobody in this city was going to sleep. While in Mokimpur, Ajay and I had gotten used to keeping farmer's hours—in bed by nine and up again at six. Our eyes bleary from the five-hour flight across the South China Sea, we managed to resist the siren call of a taxi ride. Instead, we toted our suitcases onto a double-decker bus, and then onto the cross-harbor Star Ferry. We'd be sixty dollars richer for taking the harder road, and we both knew we needed the money.

Once on the boat, I laid my head against Ajay's shoulder—he still smelled of cumin and cardamom, his mother's home cooking. We gazed out at Victoria Harbour. It was holiday season, and the skyscrapers that lined the shore were strewn with bright, colorful lights. The first time I saw them, they looked like whisky gift boxes wrapped in shiny holiday paper. Tonight the buildings seemed cold and garish, blinking like battery-operated gadgets in a tacky toy store. I glanced at Ajay. In the neon glow, his eyes looked hollow. He had barely said a word since we landed. I reached out and placed my hand on top of his.

"Welcome home," I said, but the whir of the ferry engine drowned my voice out. We rode across the water, both of us surrounded by the clamor of the city, and the din of our own silence.

Two days later I met my *Asiaweek* friends Susan and Lisa for a long-promised tea in the Peninsula Hotel lobby. Since I moved to Hong Kong, the Peninsula had become my Tiffany store window—the place to which I ran whenever I was feeling low. I adored the hotel's ridiculous opulence—the doormen in their white pillbox hats, the monogrammed teacups, the currant scones and tiny crusted sandwiches arranged just so on top of tiered plates, the string quartet playing from the balcony. It was the epitome of Hong Kong luxury, and even the jaded *tai tais* lingered here. We had scheduled tea for the middle of the day, but I put on a little black dress and taupe sandals anyway. I couldn't help myself. Susan and Lisa were Americans, as smart as they were glamorous and vivacious. They had known Ajay a few years longer than I had, and watched, mouths agape, as our romance blossomed over e-mail. They didn't say much about the relationship—well, at least not lately—but I knew that some part of them couldn't believe that the magazine's rough-and-tumble Delhi correspondent had captured the heart of the entertainment editor, a woman who had Michelle Yeoh and Jackie Chan on her speed dial.

After we talked about the latest journalistic coup at *Asiaweek*, Susan turned to me and said, "So cut to the chase. What was it like being an Indian princess?"

"A lot tougher than you'd think," I said, gently shaking my head.

"You mean, like learning just the right words in Hindi to say, 'Please iron this sari and bring my chai'?" Lisa asked, lifting a cup of Earl Grey to her lips.

"Ha! There wasn't even an outlet to plug an iron in to, so no, I wasn't asking anyone to iron anything. Actually, I take that back. At one point I did ask Mrs. Singh if her servant, Hoti Lal, could iron my skirt. They ended up sending it to the nearest town to have it pressed. But otherwise, the palace—and, girls, I use that term loosely—had no telephone, no hot water, no television, and yes, forget about cable. We ate by candlelight most nights. And don't think that was for ambiance, à la the Mondrian or something. You couldn't turn anything on without the generator blasting away."

I told them about the frigid mug baths and the village women. I showed them the mosquito bites on my legs, glowing red in a curved formation like a question mark. I recounted for them all the highlights from my dicey Christmas dinner. Then I confided about Mrs. Singh and Kamala, the way they scrutinized me. "It was worse than sorority hazing. Try dealing with that and no hot baths for three weeks."

"So, I guess a royal wedding at the palace is off," Susan said. "But . . . is the marriage still on?"

I raised my hands in the air. "Tell you the truth, I'm just not sure. Not sure about the Singhs, not sure about India, not sure about . . ."

They both leaned in, their brows furrowed in concern.

"Not sure about . . . much of anything anymore," I said, just as the string quartet above us ended its set and the waiter brought the bill.

Truth be told, now that we were back in Hong Kong, on my home turf, Ajay was starting to get on my nerves. Most of the things that bothered me were little. At the same time, though, they reflected bigger issues, things that could explode in the future. Like why did I have to tell him how to get home every time we went as far as the gourmet supermarket in Central? I mean, how many times did I have to repeat, "Take the Number 1A minibus from Stanley Street and ask them to stop at Dai Sam Gai, Third Street"?

And was it my imagination or did Ajay not know how to do the simplest of household tasks? Once, when I went on a weeklong reporting trip and left Ajay alone in Hong Kong, three large boxes from the States arrived at our flat. Ajay shoved the cartons into the center of the living room and maneuvered around them for the next seven days. Even when a couple of friends dropped by, he kept the boxes smack in the middle of our ruined Tibetan carpet. Then he sat our friends on opposite sides of the box, so whenever the three of them wanted to converse, someone had to stand up or crane his neck to peer around the box just to make eye contact.

"It wasn't the most comfortable visit," Ajay told me once I returned home.

"Why didn't you just push the boxes into the spare bedroom?" I asked.

Ajay shrugged. "I have never had to deal with such things before."

Add to all this the Indian love of chaos, which seemed to take over every room of our house like a swarm of tenacious flies. Whenever Ajay couldn't find a pillowcase (linen closet, top shelf, left side), he would stick his pillow into an old T-shirt. Old socks became coasters; an unwanted length of fabric turned into a sleeping mask. A wooden hanger, one end stuck into a night-stand drawer, transformed into a toilet-paper dispenser (which now did double duty as low-rent Kleenex). Ajay collected tiny bits of leftover bath soap, placed them in a mug, lathered them up with hot water and a spoon—*et voilà!*—we had a new source of dish soap.

When our refrigerator (a secondhand leftover from the previous renter) finally gasped its last breath, I asked Ajay to find a new (but used) one in the city classifieds. He dutifully marked the ads and called each number, but when it came to actually sealing the deal, he just couldn't.

"There was one on offer in Jut-Ye-Chong, or someplace like that," he said, waving a dismissive hand in the air. "But I couldn't figure out how to get there, so I just let it pass." To keep our milk and butter cool, Ajay ran up to the Park 'n' Shop at the top of the hill every morning and brought back a bag of ice. He put our perishables in the kitchen sink, poured the ice on top, and suddenly—a low-tech fridge *est arrivée!* I would have considered that cute, not irritating, if this time-consuming early-morning process hadn't dragged on for a month. Yes, I could have stepped in, given him step-by-step instructions on how to buy a used fridge, but I decided to let him tough it out. That tough-love strategy didn't get us anywhere, however, except one step closer to food poisoning. Finally, Susan's boyfriend Kaushik took pity on him and gave us his old refrigerator.

✦

About a month after our Delhi visit, Ajay scored a professional coup: He snagged a private interview with the Dalai Lama. To see the spiritual leader, he'd have to fly back to Delhi and board a small plane to Jammu, the winter capital of the state of Jammu and Kashmir, at the top of the Subcontinent. Then he'd have to take a five-hour taxi ride 4,400 feet up the Himalayas to the Dalai Lama's palace in Dharamsala. Ajay got *Asiaweek's* travel coordinator to book his flight and taxi. So that just left the hard part: packing for himself.

To that end our spare bedroom became a disaster zone, an ever-growing heap of heavy wool sweaters, underwear, and hiking boots. "Why don't you fold the stuff up and put it in a suitcase?" I asked Ajay the night before the trip.

"I don't know how," he said in a voice dripping with self-pity. "That's the thing about having a wife in India. They do the packing for you." I rolled my eyes and headed to the couch, where I tried to read a novel. After a few pages I snapped the book shut, threw it on the couch, headed to the spare bedroom, and arranged Ajay's gear in his suitcase in ten minutes flat.

After Ajay jumped into the cab and left for his Dharamsala trip, I looked around the apartment. His things were packed up and gone, and the place looked suddenly sparer and more organized. The sun streamed in through the terrace doors, and a cool winter breeze coursed through the flat. I switched on the CD player and blasted Sheryl Crow's "All I Wanna Do Is Have

Some Fun." Then I changed into my denim cutoffs and danced around the living room. Seven days all to myself. One hundred sixty-eight hours to reclaim my life.

I woke up early the next morning and headed to the kitchen. For the first time since Ajay moved in, I had to make chai for myself. Thank goodness for the handful of times I stood by his side in the kitchen, witnessing the laborious steps of this daily ritual. Nothing, declared Ajay, but homemade tea would do.

"Starbucks' powdered chai is for Westerners," Ajay sniffed, as he read the label of a Tazo Chai Latte at a store in Central one afternoon. "Dehydrated ginger? Powdered cardamom? This is an insult to centuries of tradition! If you want the real stuff, you have to put in the time."

I won't lie. That morning, staring at an empty tea pan, part of me considered heading to Central and picking up a Chai Latte to go. But then I thought, no, I've learned enough from Ajay to make this happen. I could do this. So I pulled the ginger from our refrigerator drawer and broke off a thumb-sized piece. Then I began paring it with a tiny knife that Ajay had brought from Delhi.

When Ajay pulled the wrinkled skin from a piece of ginger, he almost always found a fantastical shape inside. Once it was a little blue bird, complete with a spur for an eye. Another time it was a rose. Still another piece was a tiny turtle. My favorite shape uncovered by Ajay: Gandhi's nose.

With the introduction of this spiced and caffeinated beverage to my life, my mornings took on a different rhythm—they slowed to an Indian pace. What's more, Ajay had taught me his secret recipe. The mystery lay in layer after layer of flavors.

After I grated the ginger, I dumped a handful into a pot of

boiling water. I loved placing my face over the steaming concoction, letting the mist settle onto my skin, and inhaling the earthy aroma. "Ahhh, better than an Oriental Bangkok facial," I said aloud. Once the water turned a cloudy chartreuse, I poured in a capful of loose Ceylon tea. The mixture bubbled joyfully, turning jet black. After a few minutes of steeping, I poured in a cupful of skimmed milk. (All the while I heard Ajay's voice admonishing, "Never skim, always whole. That's the way we do it, calories be damned." I took the whole out and poured a splash in.) While that returned to a boil, I placed a heavy stone mortar on the kitchen counter. First came the whole white peppercorns, which I rolled around and around under a heavy granite pestle until they cracked open. Then I brought out the bag of cardamom pods. On more leisurely mornings, Ajay would take out the seeds in whole form and grind them in the mortar. It made the tea process longer, but I decided fresh cardamom was necessary—my way of marking the week as my own.

I pulled the green pods off the seeds and breathed in. Mokimpur mornings all over again. This was the first time I had ever touched cardamom in its natural state, I realized. I ground the spice and the pepper together, rolling the stone pestle over the pods until they turned to dust. I had once read in a spa magazine that contact with natural elements—wood, stone, grass, ocean water—was a deeply satisfying experience for most big-city folk. It allowed us to recall inherited memories of our ancestors foraging in the wild, sending echoes through our bodies of when we return to our natural state.

Into my favorite cup—an oversized Muji mug with a Japanese cartoon bunny on it—I spooned two tablespoons of lavender honey. Then I poured the boiling chai into the cup and sprinkled the white pepper and cardamom into the mix.

"Not half bad," I purred appreciatively as I idled over the chai on our terrace. "Not as good as Ajay's, of course. But it'll do for a fix." I didn't really expect my concoction to compare. How could it match the taste of Ajay's chai—its richness, its depth, its mystery? "It can't," I said aloud. "It would never be as good without Ajay." I put the mug down and gazed down at the city streets as the streams of frazzled Hong Kongers dashed to work.

A week later, I looked up at the digital clock in my *Asiaweek* office—it was 7:30 P.M. Ajay's plane home from India would have landed by now and perhaps he was already back at our flat. I switched off my laptop, shoved it into my bag, and headed for the minibus queue.

The week alone had been strange. Ajay and I were completely incommunicado—there wasn't much wireless service in the Himalayas. I had gone out for cocktails or dinner every night, making the rounds with friends I hadn't seen since my Indian suitor had moved to Hong Kong. I pulled my shimmering cocktail dresses and beaded purses from the depths of my closet and popped into a few of the hot new bars and restaurants that lined Lan Kwai Fong. And yet my mind seemed to have disengaged from my body and floated off to a different world. At night, I tossed in bed. I awoke from dreams in which I was strolling through the village, plucking heavy mangoes from the grove, inhaling the fragrance of jasmine and frangipani.

During one night out in Kowloon, I passed by the Chungking Mansions, an infamous broken-down boardinghouse for Pakistanis, Indians, Bangladeshis, and Sri Lankans, on the Chinese side of the colony. I caught a whiff of *garam masala* and cumin—Indian home cooking!—and I felt my face brighten; all my senses suddenly came alive.

Back at the flat, I pulled the iron gate open. It was unlocked—Ajay had made it home. "Ajay?" I called into the dark.

"I'm here," called a sleepy voice. "In the bedroom." Ajay had a length of silk fabric wrapped around his eyes, and he reached out from the bed, signaling for me to join him.

I kicked off my heels and snuggled under the covers next to him. "Close your eyes!" he said, looking a little ridiculous with his DIY eye mask on. I closed my eyes and could hear him rustling around. "Open your eyes!"

I turned toward him and looked. Ajay held up the biggest teddy bear I had ever seen. It was black, with raggedy fur, a pointed nose, and felt eyes. It was sheathed in a hand-embroidered raw-silk vest with a little pouch for Tibetan coins.

"Oh! He's adorable," I said, hugging the bear.

"It's a she-bear named Norlinga," Ajay said, "made by Tibetan refugees in Dharamsala. And here." He pulled a lustrous ivory-colored shahtoosh from under his pillow. "To keep you warm the next time I'm away."

"I'm so glad you're back," I said, planting a kiss on his lips. At the sight of Ajay, glowing from his trip, all of my questioning drained away.

✴

During his reporting trip, Ajay had stopped in Delhi for a couple of days, staying with his parents in the Roop Nagar house. "How was everything at home?" I asked him over dinner on the terrace that night.

"Okay . . ." He grimaced and clasped his hands together. "Okay, but not great."

I turned away and stared out to the street, not wanting to hear the rest but somehow knowing I would anyway.

Both in their sixties, Ajay's parents were retired and lived off rent from the family farmland. The proceeds barely covered Delhi expenses, not to mention the upkeep of Mokimpur. The rapidly dwindling rupees were a constant source of anxiety for the couple.

"My mother told me she might have to sell the haveli cow."

I sighed. "Oh, God, not the cow." I grabbed our cloth napkins off the table and carefully refolded them. "Look, I'd like to help," I said finally. "But we're barely making ends meet here." I lifted my hand, and my nails gleamed from the manicure I'd gotten while he was away. Part of me knew that what I was saying was my PR spin, and not the hardscrabble truth. We could have pared the budget of every morsel of fat—a maneuver that would have meant no eating out, no cocktails with friends, no weekend jaunts to Macau (the Portuguese colony across the bay)—and squeezed out three hundred dollars a month to send them—but what about our quality of life? What would be our reward for working our asses off in corporate Hong Kong? Ajay had no real understanding of household input and output, so what I said stood as the gospel truth. If I said there wasn't any money left, he believed me. "We don't have the cash for this," I said, shaking my head and hiding my nails under the tablecloth.

"I know. I know," he said quietly, gathering up the dinner dishes and heading inside.

Ever since Ajay and I had the last big blowout about money, I had tried hard to follow his Hindu advice: Never look up and compare your life to those above you. Instead, look down and consider your blessings. Every once in a while, though, I could not help but revert to my old aspirational ways. I thought about a college friend, a beautiful Newport Beach–raised WASP who had heeded the siren call of her destiny and married the scion of a family who owned a department-store empire. At thirty-one, her life consisted of riding her horse around the Napa Valley hills (they owned a sizable estate there), scheduling meetings for her sons' private-school board (of which she was a trustee), and dabbling in interior design.

Another journalist friend had married a husband who was an international magazine photo editor. She planned to spend her fertile motherhood years freelancing and taking a stab at novel writing. When I told her that my hope, too, was to quit my big magazine job and freelance for a while, she patted my hand and said, "If it's viable to live on Ajay's salary, then do it. If it's not, don't torture yourself with false dreams." I knew she wanted to be helpful, but I actually considered punching her. I was back to my old unsettled state of mind: When would compromise morph into its ugly cousin, sacrifice? And when would sacrifice feel like hardship?

I wasn't the only one in the house who was experiencing a bit of mental turbulence. Ajay, too, returned from India a changed man. Instead of shorts and polo shirts, he now threw on his cotton kurtas after work. He often shunned the minibus and even our occasional taxi splurge in favor of walking home—three miles along the harbor front. I sensed his yearning for home.

One day I went down to Swindon Books in Central and picked up Madhur Jaffrey's *Quick & Easy Indian Cooking* and Camellia Panjabi's *50 Great Curries of India*. Then I walked over to the Chinese market and bought a heavy skillet and about five pounds of onions and three pounds of tomatoes. The next Saturday I sent Ajay off to play field hockey with his *Asiaweek* friends. Four hours later, he came flying up our apartment stairs and flung open the door. "I could smell *chunnas* cooking from down the street—I just knew that aroma was coming from our flat!" I lifted the pot lids and showed him the feast I was cooking—*kabuli chana* (white chickpea curry), *paneer tikka* (the grilled Indian cheese that I was turning over the stove's flame), and basmati rice. He grabbed hold of me and smacked my cheek with his lips. "It smells like Hoti Lal's kitchen!"

A few days later, a letter from India arrived. It was Mrs. Singh writing from the palace. "Daddy and I have missed you terribly since you left, Aju," she penned on thin blue airmail paper in her precise Hindi that looked like caterpillars crawling across the page. "We want to let you know of the repairs required at the haveli."

As Mrs. Singh told it, Mokimpur was in dire need of a new bathroom (no surprise), mosquito netting on all the windows, a sturdy terrace wall (which would keep Anusha from falling off the second floor and into an abyss of peacock nests and basil bushes), and floor-to-ceiling whitewash. "If there is extra money," she continued, "we could certainly use another cow. Aju, your daddy and I are desperate."

After Ajay read me the letter, I rubbed my temples. I stood

up, stretched my arms, and paced a few circles in our minuscule living room, wishing Mr. and Mrs. Singh's problems would go away.

"So what do you want to do?" I asked.

"I don't know. What can we do?"

I turned my attention to straightening up the living room, stacking all my tattered copies of *Elle Decoration* and *Metropolitan Home* in neat piles, as if that would make all the difference in our lives. I was in the midst of packing for yet another reporting trip—this time to cover two luxurious spas in Thailand for *In-Style*. I wanted to laugh. Once I lived for such treats as lemongrass tea, Thai spa cuisine, and coconut-oil massages. At this very moment, however, it all felt more than a little self-indulgent, as if I were Marie Antoinette about to declare, "Let them eat cake."

That night, I awoke suddenly. The streetlight cast bars of illumination through our Venetian blinds. I glanced around the room and my eyes landed on one of the Vietnamese paintings I had bought during a trip a few years before. Just before my visit, the country had lifted its visa restrictions on Americans, and the Hong Kong expat crowd turned the once war-torn country into a veritable playground.

During that trip, my friends and I rode through Hanoi on Vespas and sailed through Ha Long Bay on motorized wooden boats. We supped on shockingly cheap French food and guzzled 333 beer. I could recall the intense ocean taste of grilled squid smothered in chili sauce. Even after years of adventure travel through Asia, this still stood as one of the best trips I had ever taken. From our last stop, Hanoi, I toted several oil-and-lacquer paintings back to Hong Kong.

Hong Kong Luxury, Indian Soul

As I lay in bed that night, I thought about how long it had taken me to find the right wall for each in our Sai Ying Poon apartment. Despite my decision not to invest too much in this temporary place, I had worked hard to make this tiny flat into a home. These paintings—a Modigliani-esque portrait of a young girl, a richly textured abstract done up in the colors of straw and wood and pomegranates, another abstract that recalled the work of Philip Guston—were beautiful, and now they were worth quite a lot. Ajay lay next to me, in heavy sleep, unaware of my visions of ruined palaces and precious paintings. I willed my eyes to shut and my brain to think of nothing.

A few nights later, as I packed for my early-morning flight to Bangkok, I noticed Ajay wander out to the terrace. I could see through the bedroom window that he was smoking, even though he had "quit" several months before. He stood at the terrace's edge, puffing away and staring out into the street below. Thinking that perhaps he was unsettled about my upcoming trip, I walked outside to join him.

"Hey there, what's wrong?" I touched him on the shoulder. He had wrapped my Dharamsala shahtoosh around his neck. His eyes were downcast, his lips pulled tight. He breathed in deeply and let out a sigh.

"It's Mokimpur. Since I was born, the haveli has been the soul of our family. My parents have no one to turn to. Nobody seems to care. We are letting the house crumble. In time it will be little more than dust."

Was Ajay being overly dramatic? It was hard for me to judge. After my parents had lost their ranch house, some part of me tried to avoid attachment to the places I lived in. On the surface, I convinced myself that the four walls that made up any dwelling were mostly about shelter and convenience. If you became attached, then you became contained, beholden, vulnerable. And yet I knew that for Ajay Mokimpur was much more than four walls, a roof, and a spray of bougainvillea.

"This is where all the souls of my family have come to rest," he once told me when visiting his grandfather's prayer hut—even though his ancestors had all been cremated, their ashes thrown into the holy Ganges. Upstairs in the prayer hut, a marble sculpture of his grandfather's feet and a plaque commemorating his time on earth sat on a wooden altar. From the black-and-white portraits that hung all over the trophy room, the Singh ancestors' eyes appraised us, keeping watch.

I recalled a passage I had read in Paramahansa Yogananda's seminal (and, yes, slightly freaky) book, *Autobiography of a Yogi*: "Places are forever permeated with the vibrations left there by the divine souls who walked those grounds. Their vibrations will remain until this earth is dissolved."

At Mokimpur, some part of me knew that Ajay was right—I could sense the presence and almost hear the laughter of so many Singh clan members. To let Mokimpur crumble would be to cast his family to the wind.

"Okay." I rubbed my hands over my face. "Let's figure this out."

When I returned from Thailand, we put a listing in the *HK Magazine* classifieds and offered three of my paintings for sale. Our friends spread the word, and then we hosted a small viewing party, serving *samosas* and white wine from a box. The artwork sold quickly—all to expats in the Mid-Levels. As they toted the canvases off, I made a mental note to avoid dinner parties at any of the buyers' flats.

From the sale, we made a few thousand—enough at least for the palace whitewash and a bathroom remodel. A few days later we headed to the bank to wire the money to the Singhs. A bespectacled clerk hawked over us as I filled out the forms, my hand shaking ever so slightly. I signed my name and pushed the forms toward the clerk, and as I did, Ajay caught my eye.

"It's okay," I said, and sighed, not knowing if it was in despair or relief. My mind flashed to the bare walls of our flat.

"We'll find other paintings when we have some money," I said. We headed out the bank's doors, into the hot, bright Hong Kong afternoon, and made our way home.

19

Resurrection

Ten months later, I stood in the heart of Mokimpur—the palace's central courtyard. My fingernails and hands bore a thick crust of earth, while my legs carried an impressive collection of cuts and scrapes that looked like hatch marks, as if somebody up there were keeping score. I was wearing a T-shirt that bore the message "There's no place like 'OM'" above a sequined drawing of Ganesh in lotus position, a pair of cutoff Levi's, and vintage Adidas trainers. As I poured soil into big terra-cotta pots and moved sapling scholar trees and poinsettia plants around, I caught sight of myself in the trophy room windows. Not bad, I thought, pulling my hair out of a ponytail and shaking it loose. A few minutes later, Ajay poked his head out of the house. He looked me up and down and then broke out in laughter.

"What's so funny?" I said, placing an unruly potted palm down with a thud, and crossing my arms.

"One of Hoti Lal's workers saw you in your work outfit. He asked me, 'If she's a rich American why can't she afford a full pair of pants?'"

I rolled my eyes, picked up the palm, and pushed it against the courtyard wall. In Los Angeles cutoff shorts were de rigueur; here they were a bank statement. "How about putting on your own shorts and pitching in here? Your mom wants this place ready by tonight." I surveyed my handiwork. Earlier that morning I had whitewashed the courtyard walls (how half of the paint ended up splattered on my shirt, I'll never know). Now, with the newly potted trees and flowers almost in place, the courtyard was starting to look quite civilized.

Almost a year had passed since our last visit, and I was starting to wonder why. On the surface we blamed our absence on the weather. During the spring and summer months, Delhi transforms into the tenth circle of hell. The heat practically blows the mercury out of the thermometer; the cities become a toxic soup of car fumes, air-con exhaust, and sun-baked, muck-covered beggars—and, believe me, the sight is soul-shattering. Most upper-crust families don't even step out of their houses until nine at night, when the angry sun of the day has finally faded away. Being confined to the inside of a house with the Singhs for ten out of twelve of our waking hours didn't exactly sound relaxing to me.

Actually, I knew the real reason for our long absence. After we had wired the money from the sale of my paintings, I felt drained and blank, as empty and colorless as my living room walls now looked. The problem? I had given up a piece of my own history, sold my keepsakes from a beloved trip, and the Singhs had not even bothered to send me a thank-you card.

Not one to stay silent, I finally asked Ajay about it. He just threw up his hands and said, "Indian families don't say thanks—not for something as simple as helping out. Sacrifice is woven into the fabric of our lives."

Yeah, and thank-you notes are part of the fabric of *my* life, I wanted to say. I had sacrificed an essential part of my own home, just so they could continue to live in their home. They could have spent a few rupees at a Hallmark shop and extended a simple "thank you."

But ten months later that wound had, if not closed, then scabbed over. And now that we were back at the haveli, I picked up on a vibe I hadn't expected: an atmosphere of hope, a feeling of transformation.

The Singhs had poured all of the wired money into the house, and it showed. They'd painted the entire haveli—the main house and the two wings occupied by cousins—added three new guest rooms that extended onto the patio, installed ceiling fans in the dining room and bedrooms, and built a terrace wall out of hundreds of decorative bricks. A black rotary dial telephone now gleamed in the hallway; dishes bought from a neighboring pottery-making town lined the kitchen hutch; and two shiny black cows grazed the front lawn. When we made our way out of the Singhs' Maruti, I inspected the entire house, my head whipping at every shiny new surface.

"What do you think?" said Mrs. Singh, when we walked into the dining room. A piece of an antique sari now hung in a gilt frame on the wall, and six matching wooden chairs surrounded the old family table. She placed retouched photos of Thakur Singh, his wife, and Booah in the silver Shanghai Tang frames we brought from Hong Kong and artfully arranged them on top of a handsome dark wood buffet.

Even Mrs. Singh had gone through a metamorphosis. The dark circles under her eyes had faded and a glow emanated from her face, as if she, like the haveli, had just been rewired for this century. "Mokimpur has come back to life," she said, as she grabbed Ajay's hands and wound his fingers in hers. I couldn't help but wonder what else had changed.

On our second morning, I heard Mrs. Singh and Ajay talking in front of my bedroom door—well, more like Mrs. Singh talking and Ajay listening. She rattled on for five minutes, with Ajay answering only, "Hahn, hahn." *Yes, yes.* I imagined Ajay standing there with his hands clasped in front of his body, dutifully nodding his head. Then came a knock at my door. I quickly tiptoed to the opposite side of the room and called out, "Uh, yes?"

It turned out Mrs. Singh had enlisted us for a day of duty. "The house looks different," said Ajay. "But there's still a shocking lot to do."

My face dropped in silent disappointment. I had taken ten vacation days off work. Being asked to engage in physical toil didn't exactly thrill me at first.

I thought about my first visit to the haveli. Mrs. Singh and Kamala shooed me out of the kitchen every time I so much as tried to chop an onion for the night's dinner. Instead, I usually spent the moments before dinner idling on the couch, reading a book or filing my nails, while the sound of their familiar laughter and whispered confidences floated through the air, dividing us even more concretely than the firmly shut kitchen door.

Clearly, I was now no longer a guest—more like a relative to be put to work. "I guess this means I'm really a Singh now," I said to Ajay, not knowing whether to blush with warm vibes or to grimace.

⋆

By the time I'd wrapped up my courtyard makeover, my shirt was covered in white paint and my hands were nicked and filthy from the plants. I stole into the bathroom, flipped on the geyser, and prepared my plastic mug bath. I examined my Om Girl tee and shook my head. Ah, vanity, I thought. What a fool I'd been to wear it. I might have looked cute doing manual labor, but now my top was soiled beyond repair, and I wished I'd put utility before fashion. I threw it in the trash bin and covered it with the lid.

Later, as I sat on the bedroom balcony with a steaming cup of chai in one hand and Arundhati Roy's *The God of Small Things* in the other, Ajay came in holding my discarded top aloft. "Did you accidentally drop this in the trash bin?" he asked.

"No, I put it there. Didn't you see the paint splattered all over it?"

"But it's a perfectly good shirt," he said, his eyebrows raised in puzzlement.

"Uh . . . not really. It's all covered with whitewash and dirt and sweat. I could never wear that thing again."

Ajay clutched the shirt to his stomach. I grabbed the armrests of my chair—I could sense a fit coming on.

"Maybe you think it's no longer nice enough to wear," he said, practically huffing steam out of his nose. "If that's the case, then it should move on to its next life. Phoola will wash it and then it will make a perfectly good kitchen rag." He raised the balled-up shirt and made a wiping motion.

"In India," he said, his eyes no longer meeting mine, "we think twice about what's rubbish and what's not. We don't throw away such things so easily." With the shirt balled up in his fist, he quietly left the room.

I sat there, puzzled. Had I really earned that dressing-down? I knew Americans were seen as wasteful, but I'd considered myself conscientious. I thought of Hoti Lal using my old Om Girl T-shirt to polish a pot or clean a window. Ajay was right. That shirt deserved more life.

Early that evening, we walked into the courtyard and found it completely altered. Candles blazed in hurricane lanterns throughout the house, making the haveli glow like a luxury cruise ship at midnight. Karan had even brought out a battery-operated boom box, and Nusrat Fateh Ali Khan wailed soul-stirring *qawallis* into the night.

Hoti Lal had set up the Singhs' one wooden patio table—our wired money could only go so far—in the center, and the new dishes were carefully arranged on top. Phoola emerged from the kitchen door, and the earthy smell of lamb curry wafted into the courtyard.

As it turned out, while I was toiling in the garden, Mrs. Singh and Hoti Lal had been whipping up a celebratory feast. The whole family would dine among the newly planted poinsettias and palms under the moonlight.

This—a mouthwatering barbecued wild boar, lamb *vindaloo* (a curry so spicy I decided the next morning to call it "vindictive *vindaloo*"), *saag paneer* (a homemade cheese cooked in a sumptuous spinach sauce), *saat daal* (seven kinds of lentils simmered overnight in a clay pot), *karela* (a deep-fried bitter gourd), and *kofta* (the most delightful potato dumplings in a ground cashew sauce)—was a maharaja's feast. We were celebrating, and big.

For the occasion, Mr. Singh even retrieved a bottle of Riviera Indian wine from a closet. With a huge grin on his face, he poured it into our glasses until it overflowed onto the table.

"Drink, please drink," he said, gesturing with his hand. I took a mouthful and almost spit it into a poinsettia. "There's a reason India isn't known for its wines," I whispered to Ajay. He laughed, then drained his glass.

"All this for fixing up the courtyard?" I said.

"Well, yes," said Ajay, laughing. "This is for your hard work and for Diwali—it's almost Indian New Year. We're celebrating a few days early."

Of course, I had read about Diwali in my tattered copy of *Fodor's India*. According to legend, thousands of years ago, the Hindu god Ram returned to his kingdom after rescuing his kidnapped wife from the clutches of the demon king Ravana. The glowing candles were meant to help Ram navigate the night and find his way home.

I didn't exactly get what the big deal was, but I knew that Diwali was by far the flashiest holiday in India. It was also the time of year Ajay hated the most. Like so many of the traditions in urban India, Diwali had devolved into a commercialized mess. Children set off hundreds of thousands of firecrackers— literally—and the smoke from them creates such a toxic cloud that hundreds of pigeons drop dead off the rooftops. "You can close all the windows of your house but you can't escape the fumes," Ajay said, shaking his head. "It seeps in under your door and into your body."

As I dug into wild boar and Ajay into his chickpeas, he turned to me and said, "Did you know that from the sixteenth to the nineteenth century, a few of the kitchen staff of India's Mughal rulers did nothing all day but tend to chickens that were fed only one food? They fed them pistachios! Nothing but pistachios! And the chickens were the offspring of generations of chickens that had eaten nothing but those nuts. That way, when the kings finally ate the chicken, the flesh would be buttery and nutty." I looked at Ajay, in his white kurta, a navy blue shawl thrown over his shoulders, and thought about my good luck in having found this man. I loved when Ajay went all Indian on me.

After dinner, I thanked Mrs. Singh, who was eating home-made Indian ice cream next to Kamala. "Everything was delicious," I said, pulling up a chair next to her. "Maybe one day you'll teach me some of your secrets." She smiled blankly, which I took as a positive sign. "You know, I've been making a few curries at home," I told her. "I got a Madhur Jaffrey cookbook. I've been practicing, and Ajay seems to like them. I could even make one for the family—maybe *baigan bharta* or *mattar paneer*." The roasted eggplant and the curry with peas and homemade cheese were becoming my specialties.

Mrs. Singh and Kamala smiled and exchanged knowing glances.

"What? What?" I said, breaking out my Mokimpur mantra once more.

"Alison, we were just saying that we'll make an Indian wife out of you yet," said Kamala, clapping her hands. Mrs. Singh gently touched my hair—without recoiling at my dandruff this time. I took that as a gesture of affection, if not yet love. Maybe, just maybe, our cold war was beginning to thaw.

Mr. Singh tapped me on the shoulder, his fingers bony and

insistent. "Mokimpur is looking so grand," he said, raising the wine to his lips. "I think even many American tourists would be enjoying it here." He clasped his hands and watched my face. I nodded, in a noncommittal way.

"We could build a swimming pool," he said, his eyes now dancing with visions. "I know those Westerners like to take the sun, even though that is very, very bad for the skin. We could take them sightseeing—to my cousin's stud farm and the pottery town." Holding one finger in the air, he said, "If we gave them a big room, served them all their meals and took them on such tours, we could charge them twenty dollars a day. Or do you think that would be too much?"

I imagined the scene: a group of chic adventure travelers lounging around the proposed Mokimpur pool; Hoti Lal in a ceremonial turban ferrying drinks from the kitchen, and collecting well-deserved tips in American dollars and euros; Mrs. Singh gaily stirring a cauldron of *saag paneer* for the haveli dinner on the terrace that night. Mokimpur as destination hotel would be filled with laughter and life once more. The manor and the Singhs might even make a comeback on the social scene. "Twenty dollars a day to stay at the Mokimpur Paradise Hotel?" I shot a quick smile his way and laid my hand on his shoulder. "I think that would be a brilliant price."

✦

I knew why Mr. Singh was thinking about Mokimpur's future as a five-star. He'd been eavesdropping on our big travel plans. Ajay and I were taking off the next morning for the Ananda, a former palace transformed into a swanky Mandarin Oriental resort three thousand feet above sea level in the Himalayas. No, we couldn't afford it. But I'd been invited there by my good friend Jill, who just happened to be the Mandarin's marketing director. She knew I wrote travel stories for *InStyle* and the *International Herald Tribune* and that Ajay penned a cooking feature or two for the *Los Angeles Times* (that Tokyo curry chef stint finally did come in handy for something besides his Sunday omelets).

I was looking forward to an Indian odyssey—yes, in addition to the adventure I'd been having at Mokimpur. A journey through these fabled Indian mountains, where Ajay had spent most of his boyhood in boarding school, climbing steep pine-strewn trails, would surely bring me closer to the heart of this country. What's more, I wanted to see how a real Indian palace—one that had running hot water—actually functioned.

At dawn, after our Choti Diwali (Little New Year's) feast, Ajay and I took a train to Dehra Dun, a small foothill town a five-hour drive from Mokimpur. It was a charming bohemian village where many artists, moneyed Delhi-ites, and retired bureaucrats set up vacation homes. Ajay's boyhood friend Sanjay had bought a modernist house set on six acres there. From Dehra Dun, we hired an Ambassador taxi, an old 1960s white sedan that looked like a cloud on wheels. After three hours of chugging up tree-lined mountain roads, we reached the Ananda. We pulled through the wrought-iron gates, and suddenly I felt my spirit rise through my body. It was as if I were returning to some place I'd wandered before.

A massive white mansion stood at the top of the hill like an aristocrat carved from stone. This was the summer palace originally built for the maharaja of Tehri Garhwal. The Mandarin leased the grounds in the late 1990s when the maharaja realized his family's purse was hemorrhaging its once grand fortune. Instead of letting his palace disintegrate into a moldering heap of stone (Singh family, take note), he struck a deal with the hotelier. The Mandarin took over a hundred acres of land, tamed the grounds for the upscale masses, and built a bland six-story housing complex. Sadly, compared to the maharaja's digs, it had all the exotic spice of a glass of tap water, but some of the original buildings were open to our wanderings. I loved the palace annex, with its library lined with the maharaja's rare books, the whitewashed yoga temple with its serene reflecting pool, and the stone fire pits, dancing with four-foot flames every evening. And I loved the food: Every meal was a buffet feast of creamy curries, roasted meats, and *galub jamon* (those decadent balled sweets bathed in syrup).

On our third morning, we headed over to the Ananda's ayurvedic clinic. I had read several books about the centuries-old Hindu system of holistic health care. Most people fell into one of three categories of body and mind types. In layman's terms, *vatas* were thin, frail, and nervous. *Pittas* were strong and emotionally explosive. *Kaphas* were heavy, slow, and good-natured. I found the ayurvedic connection between physical and mental types to be deeply considered; I'd certainly met enough social, X-ray-thin, neurotic New York girls (*vatas*) and jolly, sedentary fatties (*kaphas*) to support the system's core theories. But I could never figure out which I would be.

I had grown up a jangly-limbed kid who twitched at every loud sound and suffered from insomnia. Then I started hiking and rollerblading obsessively and developed muscles and a steadier disposition. But recently I noticed my regular curry dinners and chocolate desserts *à deux* with Ajay had left me a few pounds heavier than I'd ever been. (A few weeks earlier my friend who sometimes sewed dresses for me pointed at my newly flabby stomach and sniped, "You've never had *that* before." I took a cab straight home and did about two hundred sit-ups.) So my categorization was not exactly seamless.

My doctor at the clinic, a short, dark man in a white lab coat, didn't find it easy either. He asked me such questions as "Do your nails break easily?" and "Are you constipated?" Then he asked me to lift my hospital gown slightly so he could see my thighs; at the same time I was asked to turn around slowly. "Hmmm," he murmured as he took in my frame. "You are a *vata-pitta*, with a bit of *kapha*." That diagnosis confirmed what I already knew about myself: I was a skinny person who had developed some muscles but was now getting a little chubby. Ah, helpful . . . But the doctor had more to say: To ease my mental tensions and get my blood circulating and toxins exorcised, I needed to do a daily self-massage.

The next thing I knew I was in a whitewashed spa room, flat on my back on a terrycloth-covered table and coated with a slippery mixture of coconut and sesame oil. Two birdlike masseuses stood on either side of me, stroking my arms, legs, and stomach. After the rubdown, one woman placed me under a copper pot. "Uh, what is that?" I said, warily eyeing the huge vessel above my head. "Just relax, madam," she said, holding up one hand and wobbling her head. "Trust." She tipped the pot over and out rushed a stream of sage-colored liquid, which she aimed directly on my forehead.

I tried, but the trust didn't last very long. "Uh, what is this for?" I said, my voice rising.

"It is massage—for your third eye."

.⋆.

Three hours later, Ajay and I met in our room. Sprawled on the white couch with a magazine, he was blissed out and shiny. So was I. We both looked like slimy zombies.

I sighed, shook my head, and plopped down next to him. "So what was your prognosis?"

"I'm a *pitta*. Strong body, impatient mind." To ease his temperament, the doctor ordered two male masseurs from Southern India to walk on his back. They held on to cables strung from one wall to the opposite one to control their weight as they took step after step across Ajay's body. Rather than appreciating the rare situation he was in, Ajay grew angry. "I asked one of the guys if he'd washed his feet before the massage. He just looked at me as if I was crazy. Kind of broke the spell, as you can imagine."

"Well, their feet might have been dirty, but did their footwork cure your impatience?"

"No, I don't think so. I couldn't wait to get back to the room, jump in the shower, and wash my back."

So much for the mystical healing of ayurveda. Indeed, my third eye had gotten such a pounding from all that mustard oil that I had a headache for the next two days.

.⋆.

At dusk, we strolled up the hill to the big house—the princely annex—and gazed out onto the Himalayas. I took in a lungful of the evening air: night-blooming jasmine, blue pines, and the scent of a kerosene fire from a nearby servants' camp. This would forever define the smell of India for me.

Ajay was often silent. One night he turned to me and said, "I grew up running up and down these mountains every day." I realized then that during these wordless hours, he had been recalling a decade of boyhood years spent on his own at boarding school. My mind flashed to my childhood: six kids bounding through a half-acre backyard with its cactus garden and mulberry trees. We played outside together almost every evening, until my mother called us in for a dinner of spaghetti and hot dogs, most often consumed in front of *The Brady Bunch* (or some other quintessentially American sitcom) blaring on our old gigantic TV.

What different lives Ajay and I had led. I glanced at him. He wore a loose collarless shirt with a green floral print, the ever-present white shahtoosh around his neck. During this trip, he had told me a story about boarding school that left me speechless. One afternoon when he was about eight, he managed to smuggle a cheese sandwich out of the dining hall. He stood on the soccer field and unwrapped it, imagining the delicious flavors soon to fill his mouth. Suddenly, a shadow crossed the field. It was an eagle. It swooped down, snatching the sandwich out of Ajay's grasp, leaving bloody streaks on the back of his hand. "I had no one to cry to, no one to soothe my fear," he told me. "And no cheese sandwich either."

I looked at him and saw the wounded little boy staring back at me. Maybe it was the emotional pain of our early years that bound us even more tightly. But I knew that my hardships, suffered in the comfort of a mostly loving if chaotic home, paled in comparison to his. My sadness and turmoil felt almost trivial compared to Ajay's childhood misadventures. Even as we stood at the edge of the Himalayas, the place where, as legend has it, the heaven meets the sky, I couldn't help but question if our love could ever bridge the many, many divides—class, culture, and worldview—between us.

That evening, we ate at Ananda's café. The mood was electric and fun; three elegant women in saris chatted loudly at the table next to us, a soulful couple in deep conversation sat across the room, and a group of French jet-setters sipped champagne next to them. All of a sudden, a hush descended on the restaurant. A slight-framed man wearing a Lacoste shirt, linen trousers, and a Rolex strolled in, his much younger wife in tow. "It's the maharaja," one of the bejeweled hens next to us whispered. The waitstaff quickly escorted him to a private booth, and he floated past.

"Poor man," Ajay sighed. "I hope we never fall into such dire straits that we have to hand Mokimpur over to the Holiday Inn."

It wasn't such an impossibility—and not just because Holiday Inn is now owned by an Indian family. In fact, failed royals all over India were capitulating and handing over the keys to their kingdoms.

The trouble for the maharajas and maharanis began in 1971, when Indira Gandhi decided to end the generous government stipends to noble families. Without the silk purse to maintain their kingdoms, many of these families found themselves contemplating something they considered beneath those of their station—getting a job. Some started up such businesses as running luxury tourism companies, heading up wild tiger hunts, or developing stallion stud farms. Others accepted a destiny of slow deterioration and social decline. Still others, like the savvy maharaja of Tehri Garhwal, opened the gilt doors of their palaces and turned their family digs into hotels, welcoming Brits hoping to play Raj for a week or two and Americans with designer yoga mats into their bedrooms and living rooms—just as the Singhs were now considering. After experiencing the princely comforts the Mandarin bestowed upon the Ananda, I began to think that sharing one's royal space wasn't such a deal with Kali after all.

✦

The next day we would head down the mountain and make the five-hour drive back to Mokimpur. I thought of the haveli and the tepid mug bath and moldy mosquito net that awaited us, and part of me (a little more than half) wished we *were* heading to the Holiday Inn instead.

As the Ananda's staff loaded our suitcases into the trunk of an Ambassador taxi, Ajay and I turned to take one last look at the Garhwal haveli. I gazed at the gold-leaf finish around the wooden doorways, glimpsed through the gleaming windows at the gilt portraits and antique books inside, and took in the 1920s fountain gurgling out on the circular drive.

Ajay gently grabbed my arm and led me away. "Well, that was a nice break," he said. "I wonder if we'll ever be able to afford to stay at this kind of place on our own."

"Oh, you never know." I looked off into the horizon. "I'm not ready to accept my fate as a fallen noble yet. Who knows what the future will hold."

.✦.

Five hours later, our car bumped and swerved violently as we drove down the village road that led to Mokimpur. The front drive was bare save for a lone buffalo grazing on the grass, so patchy it looked like a threadbare carpet. We got out of the Ambassador and puzzled at the silence. Hoti Lal and his crew did not bound out of the house to greet us. The village women and their earthenware jugs were curiously absent from the reservoir. There were no children wandering through the grounds or sitting on the stone walls and singing.

We had only been gone a few days, but the atmosphere at the Singh palace felt different, hushed and sullen. As we wandered through the halls toting our suitcases, I remarked to Ajay that not a single Singh was sipping tea on the patio or gathering blooms in the gardens.

We climbed the stairs to the terrace. "Mama?" Ajay called out. A few minutes later, we found the whole family huddled together in Thakur Shiam Singh's trophy room with the doors closed and the curtains drawn.

"What's the matter?" Ajay asked as we entered the room.

"There's been trouble," Karan replied. "Mummy's antique statue of Ganesh and grandfather's prized World War II rifle went missing while you were away."

"What!" cried Ajay.

"Cousin Chunnu and his wife heard they turned up at the street market in the pottery town," Kamala said. "Whoever took them from the house was trying to sell them—and not for very much, either. They obviously did not know the value of these precious things."

"Did you get them back?" Ajay's eyes were wide with anger.

They had, but barely. The Singhs sent Hoti Lal to retrieve the heirlooms from the pottery town. He had skillfully convinced the local police that the rifle and the statue belonged to Mokimpur and must be returned immediately.

But the damage had already been done. Someone had crept through the palace and betrayed the family.

Later that night, I wandered down to the trophy room. The day's events left me unsettled, and I thought that maybe looking at Booah's black-and-white wedding pictures would buoy me. When I opened the door, I heard a woman weeping. It was Mrs. Singh.

I considered sneaking away, but she looked up. Our eyes locked. "*Ah-ja,* come here," she said. I hesitated, my body frozen at the threshold. Why hadn't I stayed in bed and finished my novel? I asked myself. But she raised her hand and uttered, "Please."

I sat down next to her on the couch and slowly put my arm around her shuddering figure. Between sobs, she said, "We found out who had taken the statue and the rifle. It was one of Hoti Lal's distant relatives." The young man had just had his third baby, and feeling desperate for money, he took the treasures. Hoti Lal swore that he had had no idea what his relative had done. "We have trusted Hoti Lal and his family for four decades now," she said. "His family is our family. So, of course, we believe him."

Then she grabbed my hand, the touch of her fingers surprisingly soft and warm. "Promise me, Alison," she said, her eyes gazing into mine. "If anything should happen to me, promise me you and Ajay will help Karan and Kamala take care of Mokimpur." I reached in my pocket and fished out a Kleenex for her. But I could not bring myself to answer.

The time I'd spent at the haveli had been magical, almost sacred to me. Even so, the idea of committing to caring for the house overwhelmed me, as if I had just been informed that I now needed to feed and bathe an elderly aunt for the rest of her life.

When I returned to the bedroom wing, Ajay was already in bed, reading *India Today* by the glow of a kerosene lantern.

"I saw your mother downstairs," I said, slipping into his bed. "She told me what happened. She told me about Hoti Lal's cousin."

"Yep," said Ajay, not taking his eyes off the page.

"So what happens now? Are Hoti Lal and his family history?"

Ajay slowly folded the magazine and put it down on the stool beside the bed. "No," he said, gently grabbing my hand. "Things will continue as they always have around here. Hoti Lal has cared for me since the day I was born. His sons have been like brothers to me. His family may have made some mistakes, but now they know better. We cannot destroy our ties to each other over a statue and a rifle." He turned off the kerosene lantern and snuggled next to me under the covers. "It's like I told you," he said with a long, sad sigh. "We Indians don't just throw things away."

⤌ 20 ⤍

The Kitchen

The Singhs recovered their heirloom statue and rifle, but they had lost something irreplaceable—their trust. A trusted servant's cousin had stolen through the haveli and polluted the household.

Mrs. Singh sat on the terrace staring into the fields, a crumpled linen hankie in front of her on the table. Mr. Singh traipsed up and down the haveli stairs, toting a flashlight, poking his head into musty closets, whipping open cobweb-covered cupboard doors. Kamala, Karan, and Ajay had heated discussions in Hindi for hours, their faces gray.

"What was that powwow about?" I asked Ajay later.

"The future," he said quietly. "The next few decades and centuries for this crumbling old place."

Things were glum. I missed the old Mokimpur, the backdrop of three-hour teas and idle chatter and candlelit dinners. I kept puzzling over how I could break the bleak spell. Then it hit me. Another culinary extravaganza by yours truly—and this time it would be personal. I would whip up an Indian feast to end them all. Even if it weren't up to par, at the very least, my efforts would give the family something other than the burglary to talk about. Except that meant trying to measure up to the Singh women—and that would be a formidable feat.

Both Mrs. Singh and Kamala were legends in the kitchen. Each had done serious chopping and stirring duty since she was a young girl. "My mother is not just a good cook, she is a modern one," Ajay told me, throwing down the culinary gauntlet—or should I say, kitchen mitt? "Not only can she make any Indian dish tasty, she can do it without all the oil and *ghee* you find in the restaurants." (*Ghee* is butter that has been clarified by boiling.) Indeed, each of our visits to the Singh haveli was a blur of dazzling meals, each dish more delicious than the last.

Kamala had the domestic prowess of a Subcontinental Rachael Ray. The day after my Christmas feast debacle, she labored all day making dishes from her native Kashmir—lamb in yogurt, potato curry, lamb kebab.

Every day without fail, Mrs. Singh spent hours in the kitchen, wearing yet another gorgeous salwar kameez and orthopedic shoes. She and Hoti Lal stood in silence, side by side, chopping, grinding, stirring, As soon as we gobbled up one repast, they were back chopping, grinding, and stirring in preparation for the next astonishing spread or blowout teatime.

I was good at lots of things—traipsing through Chinese villages in my platform heels, making small talk with Hong Kong movie people, pairing the perfect sandal with a little black dress, leading a book discussion at the dinner-party table—but I just wasn't good at cooking. More to the point, I didn't have the patience for chopping onions into precise rectangular pieces or hovering over a steamy cauldron until a sauce reached its desired texture. Yes, transforming vegetables, meat, and spices into a truly great meal was an act of alchemy, no question, but that wasn't the kind of magic I was interested in making.

Yet I knew that in India, a woman's culinary skills contributed to her status. The better the cook, the better the wife, mother, and, yes, human being. According to *The Eternal Food*, by cultural anthropologist R. S. Khare, cooking was a reflection of one's ability to sustain and nurture life.

I was loath to admit that even Ajay left me in the dust as far as kitchen abilities. After his three months undercover as an Indian chef in Tokyo, he emerged an expert at concocting an impressive range of curries. (Yet another reason I wanted to marry him—the deal came with my own personal Indian chef.) Arranging sliced cucumbers into visually arresting patterns had become a kind of meditation for him, like creating a mandala. He could stay up all night stirring boiled milk, rice, and sugar until it formed the perfect *kheer*—no problem. I had many times caught him in the kitchen, stripped down to his shorts and flip-flops, chest covered with sweat, as he obsessed over a half-dozen king-sized eggplants roasting on the burners for the evening's *baigan bharta*. When I asked him why he cooked with such a religious-like zeal, he explained matter-of-factly: "The only food that is truly tasty is the kind you cook with love."

In Indian cuisine, particular dishes come with their own symbolism: Hindus hold anything made from milk in high esteem because they consider cows sacred. Thus, *kheer*, rice pudding made from gallons and gallons of milk, is a luxurious and holy treat. *Ladoos*, those giant sweet confections made from flour, sugar, and clarified butter, are traditionally placed at the feet of gurus. Mothers hand-feed *ladoos* to their toddlers as a way of demonstrating love and devotion. Many Hindus are strict vegetarians, as Indians see eating meat as a form of violence. After killing that village stork, Ajay gladly gave up meat. He only ever pined for wild boar, which his oldest friend, Sanjay, had roasted for him on an open spit at his farmhouse in Dehra Dun.

Indians in all parts of the expansive country have developed their own distinct and sophisticated cuisines. I especially loved the *dosas* (spicy crepes filled with potato) and fish curries from the south, and delectable lamb curries from the north. Ajay adored his native food. In Delhi, he would stuff himself silly with his mother's *parathas* and bitter gourd until he popped the buttons on his pants—his way of transporting the Subcontinent back to Hong Kong.

Funnily enough, though, many Hindus believe that one should only eat enough to live. The devout routinely fast, as they think the practice emphasizes the dominance of soul over body and intensifies one's own awareness of food and self.

Mrs. Singh and Kamala never openly said anything to this effect, but I could tell that they thought less of me not only because of my kitchen disasters but also because of my reluctance to join their culinary efforts. While they busied themselves in the kitchen, I often sat in the living room reading a book or sketching Indian fabric patterns. Once, as Kamala set dinner on the table, I caught her shooting a hostile glance at my supine self on the couch. Letting out an exasperated sigh, she marched back to the kitchen, nose in the air.

During that fateful moment at the haveli, when despair threatened to topple our lazy, joyful modus operandi, my taking on dinner could radically shift the mood. Not only that, but I could nourish my ties to my female relatives, too.

I just didn't want another Christmas disaster.

I'd been planning for such a moment. During our months away from Mokimpur, I had poured over my Madhur Jaffrey cookbook, practicing my chopping, perfecting my curries, growing stronger and more powerful as an Indian domestic goddess.

However, I knew full well that I should not perform too well if I wanted to stay in the women of Mokimpur's good graces. The kitchen was their domain, another realm in which they could assert their superiority over the American career girl with the swish wardrobe and impractical shoes. All that mattered was that I made an effort, didn't poison anyone, and produced a meal that was tasty but clearly failed to match anything they whipped up.

I needn't have worried.

On Monday morning, I woke up early and walked to the village market. As I breathed in the brisk morning air, scented with the smoke from household dung fires, I realized this was one of the first times I had ever been out alone in India. Whenever we were in Delhi, an entourage of in-laws, cousins, and nieces surrounded me everywhere I went, like a traveling band of familial suffocation anytime I wanted to dash to the drugstore to buy a tampon. Today, after stealthily slipping out the door, I actually managed to strike out on my own—and boy, did that feel liberating.

I strode past a family of five resting together on a single cot, past a huddle of women spinning wool into yarn, past a group of little girls practicing Bollywood movie songs and dances. I was wearing a very plain salwar kameez, my eyes rimmed with kohl, a decorative bindi painted on my forehead.

Earlier that morning, I had asked Ajay to teach me how to say, "Yeh kitna?" *How much for this?* After ten minutes of practice, I managed to master the phrase and deliver it with a decent Indian accent and slight head wobble. After all, I was buying groceries from locals and didn't want to get stuck with the foreigners' price—read: sucker's inflation. As far as my Chinese features were concerned, I was in luck. The northeastern states of India border China, so Indians there look like Confucian Asians. (Ajay and I had started referring to Asians from such northern countries as China, Japan, and Korea as "Chopsticks Asians," and those from southern countries such as Nepal, India, and Bangladesh as "Fingers Asians," for the way they handled their food at the dinner table.) The Singhs had even jokingly given me an appropriate northeastern name: Rina Dolma, a typical moniker in that region. I used that name whenever the village kids came over to the haveli to play.

It was Rina who triumphed at the market. Almost without a hitch, I trotted out my newly acquired Hindi—"Yeh kitna?" wobble, wobble—and bagged a freshly plucked chicken, a pound of jumbo cashews, saffron, ginger, a bag of chilies, and a pile of onions—all for less than two dollars. I practically swaggered back to the haveli.

I changed out of my salwar kameez and into a T-shirt that I'd had printed in Hong Kong. In big saffron-colored letters across the front, it read "Spice Girl." I headed for the cooking quarters.

The Singh family kitchen, like so many such rooms throughout India, was a temple to family sustenance. Shiny copper pans hung neatly from a ceiling rack. Dozens of aromatic spices, each boasting its own distinct color, were lovingly labeled in Hindi and arranged on two wooden shelves next to the cookers. Utensils, plates, and cups sat in pristine rows below the counter. Every surface shone under the sunlight streaming in through a small window.

My menu for the evening was chicken *korma* with *halwa* (carrot pudding) for dessert. Hoti Lal's *aloo gobi* and *rajma* (spicy brown beans) left over from lunch would round out the rest of the meal.

I shelled cardamom seeds, stopping to inhale their sweet fragrance—it was like being transported to every delectable, slightly exotic Christmas pudding I had ever had. I had grown to relish the tactile, sensual qualities of Indian cooking: grinding the cashew nuts with a stone mortar and pestle, sprinkling pumpkin-colored spices into yogurt made fresh from village cow milk, harvesting seeds from the trees and pulling them apart by hand. I chopped onions for the better part of an hour—the fumes sent me reeling and ducking into the loo to rinse my eyes—and a whole head of garlic cloves.

It was obvious why the Singhs employed the entire Hoti Lal family. The complexity of Indian cooking necessitates a servant culture. "Every bloody dish has twenty ingredients in it," Ajay once told me. "It's a wonder Indians get anything other than cooking and eating done." But there was no denying that all that labor produces a subtle layering of flavors and textures—something sorely lacking in a Domino's pizza. This I was learning—and actually loving—as I devoted myself to mastering the cuisine.

Mrs. Singh marched in, disturbing my cooking reverie. "Let

us see how it's coming along," she said, lifting the pot covers. First, she examined the chicken *korma*. "Smells very nice. You've done a good job with the curry..." She hesitated and then added, "But there is a problem. We worship Shiva, the god of creation—so we never eat meat on Monday. That is a sacrifice to him. We'll have to put this dish away until tomorrow." She took a clean spoon from the drawer and dipped into the sauce. "What did you use to thicken this?" Flour, I explained, the same substance we use to thicken so many sauces in the States.

"Well, it has left this dish tasting rather bland. We Indians only thicken sauces with things that add flavor—cashews, tomatoes, yogurt, seeds, and the like. This tastes more like an American dish."

She saw my face drop and hastily added, "But don't worry. We can give it to Sri Ram, who runs the family temple. He's not so very fussy."

"What else?" she commanded, lifting the lids off Hoti Lal's leftover *aloo gobi* and *rajma*. "Very nice." She wobbled her head. "These are perfect." When I explained that Hoti Lal had made them for lunch, she blushed and said quietly, "Oh, I see... No wonder they're so good."

Mrs. Singh had a raging sweet tooth, and I knew the *halwa* would impress her. When she looked into the pot, she shook her head. "We only make *halwa* for the cold winter months. Carrots heat the body up, which is not so comfortable in this mild weather. But we can make an exception and serve it tonight."

"Try it, Mrs. Singh," I said eagerly, grabbing the spoon she had dipped into the chicken korma and scooping up some pudding.

"No, no, stop," she cried, lunging at my hand. Her eyes grew wide. "Alison, we never dip a soiled spoon into a pot of food! We Hindus believe this contaminates the entire dish. We really shouldn't eat this now."

I stood in the kitchen, about to lose it. "What, then," I implored, "is the family going to eat?"

"Come, now," she said. "Let's prepare some *channas* and *daal*. They can be ready within the hour."

Chickpeas and lentils. Fine. I insisted on preparing them by myself, and Mrs. Singh raised her hand—as if to say, "okay, you win"—and left the room. I went back to the chopping board, diced two more onions, eight more tomatoes, and two branches of ginger.

Forty-five minutes later, Mrs. Singh poked her head in again. "It's smelling very nice in here," she said. She began placing dirty pans in the sink. "You know, my mother began my kitchen lessons when I was five. My sisters had other talents—Polly was extremely smart, and Usha was very beautiful. My mother told me I had no such outstanding traits to offer, so I'd better learn to cook. Of course, at the time that hurt me. But I am glad for it now."

"My mother said almost the exact opposite to me," I said. "She said, learn to cook and you'll be stuck in the kitchen, and you have too many talents to let that happen. That's why I'll never win *Top Chef*." We glanced at each other, a moment of empathy crossing our faces. I looked back down into the pots.

As I stirred the *channas*, she put her hand on my wrist. "You know, Alison. You have a good job. You have independence. You know the world. I understand why you can't cook."

"Thanks," I said. "But I am trying to learn. Maybe then Ajay won't miss India so much."

She lingered in the kitchen as I sprinkled a finishing touch of *garam masala* on top of the lentils.

"My brother, Krishna, loved to make his own lentils," she offered, a light shining in her eyes. "But he had a kitchen fear no one could tame. Whenever he saw a lump in the lentils, he always believed that a gecko had fallen from the ceiling into the pot. Without fail, he insisted on throwing out the entire dish and starting over. It didn't matter how hungry the family was. Out it went. Hindus believe geckos are poisonous, although Polly, who has studied science, swears that's just a wives' tale. But Krishna could not be swayed. A lump meant geckos, and geckos would be the death of you."

Geckos were one thing, but a brother? I had never heard of this brother before. I had met Polly and Usha, who were fascinating and distant creatures. Maybe it was from Uncle Krishna that Ajay had inherited his dark good looks. Perhaps this Uncle Krishna would finally prove the warm relation who would throw his arms around me and welcome me into the family.

"Will I meet Krishna when we return to Delhi?" I asked Mrs. Singh, putting down my spoon and fluffing up my hair, as if prepping for a blind date.

"Ajay didn't tell you?" Her face turned sullen. "Thirty years ago, we found Krishna lying in his bed. He had been poisoned—by his wife, we think. She set herself on fire a day later. My mother has not left the house since Krishna died. None of us has ever been the same."

Silence filled the kitchen and we stood there, both pretending to be engrossed by the bubbling curries. Then Mrs. Singh spoke quietly. "I have had a lot of sadness in my life—sadness that not even the grandest haveli in India can ever erase."

I stopped stirring and looked up at her. Mrs. Singh had entrusted me with such dark family secrets, and we both knew something had shifted between us. As if reading my mind, she said, "You must have a special talent about you, Alison. Few people can draw these stories out of me."

The lentils bubbled and the channas had finally turned tender. I poured each dish into a silver bowl.

And my heart sank.

The dishes looked a mess. In my haste to ready dinner, I had chopped the vegetables clumsily. Next to Hoti Lal's leftovers, my meal looked amateurish and careless.

"Well, it doesn't look so good, but it smells wonderful," Mrs. Singh said, and applauded.

"I guess I'm kind of the opposite," I said, grimacing. "I look good, but maybe I've not been the best thing for this family."

Mrs. Singh laughed softly and placed her hand on my back. "Come on," she said. "Khana lagao." *Let's put out the food.*

"Chalo khana kao," I replied, earning a look of pleasant surprise from my future mother-in-law. I had been studying key Hindi phrases for a moment just like this. *Let's go eat.*

⤎ 21 ⤏

Amusing the Singhs

I awoke at dawn one morning to the sound of creaking footsteps on the balcony and the whirring noise of something mechanical. Ajay had already gotten up, and he was wielding our new video camera. "Oh, sorry to wake you," he whispered. "I'm trying to capture that moment—you know, when the moon fades away and the sun rises. It's like the whole village turns violet for twenty seconds of time."

I had grown to love the dawn in Mokimpur. I happily rose from bed for a long, slow amble through the fields, and a little bird-watching thrown in for good measure. Mokimpur did indeed turn my world upside down. In Hong Kong and Los Angeles, I mostly moved from 0 to 60 mph in five seconds; at Mokimpur I felt my engine shift into idle. I was used to rushing from place to place, jumping into taxis, onto trains and hydrofoils and planes, and moving from assignment to assignment, country to country, at a manic pace. At the palace there was nowhere to rush to, and very little movement required of anyone.

I often spent mornings reading. Then I sat on a sun-warmed terrace slicking my toenails with not one but four coats of polish. I wandered through the front garden, picking frangipani blooms and holy basil stems for a bouquet, and then I would spend the better part of the afternoon arranging the stems. Sometimes, as I lay contentedly inert on a patio, I felt as if all the bones had been pulled from my body through some magical process. The same Hindi word means "yesterday" and "tomorrow," *kal*—something that made perfect sense at Mokimpur. Village time was elastic. Or could it be that here, there were simply more hours in the day?

I wasn't the only one who felt this way. Mr. Singh, usually a bundle of nerves in New Delhi, was practically comatose at the haveli. He and Uncle Ram would sit side by side in the courtyard, in their favorite decades-old army jackets. Uncle Ram's greatest joy was reading aloud the laudatory letters that British officers, heads of state, and important businessmen had sent to his father—reading them over and over again. His favorite missive was a banquet invitation from Queen Elizabeth to commemorate her 1953 coronation. During my first week at Mokimpur, I must have heard Uncle Ram recite that letter five times.

Ajay spent his boyhood at Mokimpur organizing cricket, field hockey, and traditional village games with Hoti Lal's sons and the strapping local boys—his grandfather called such sporting matches the Mokimpur Olympics. Shiam Singh also often orchestrated "sprinting" matches, gathering a dozen or so village lads and sending them off running as quickly as they could. Often they sprinted down the haveli's seemingly endless drive, lined with leafy scholar trees. Their younger brothers and sisters cheered them on with shouts of "Dau-do! Dau-do!" as they flew past in their village sandals. *Run! Run!* "The winner would get some small change," said Ajay. "Everyone else would get a snack—maybe some time-pass—to munch on."

The house, with its numerous wings and stairwells, became the perfect backdrop for an ambitious game of *chupam-chupai* (literally, "hiding-seeking"). Ajay remembers ducking into damp storerooms, where the family haphazardly stored stuffed tigers' heads, army uniforms, antelope horns, deerskins, and wooden trunks from the turn of the century, and standing silent for the better part of an hour. He had it easy compared to the kid who was "It." For him or her, finding all of his playmates could never be the point. In fact, the haveli's one hundred rooms invariably made being the seeker a losing proposition. "It was impossible! Impossible!" Ajay roared, when I asked him if he ever found everybody. "Most of the time we waited for hours until someone called out, 'Mein haar manta hoon!'—*I give up!* That was the only way the game could ever end."

I especially loved having the village kids over just after their 3 P.M. dinner and before dusk. They joined us in the den near the kitchen for *antakshri*, a simple indoor game of song singing. The little boys and girls with their lovely old-fashioned names—Shiva, Ganesh, Parvati, Chote Lal, Janaki—took turns singing the latest Bollywood songs and miming the elaborate dance moves, too. The first time I witnessed the *antakshri* I was amazed at the raw talent pent up in that village. Not only did so many of the children have beautiful voices, they could also re-create dance scenes move for move.

Every afternoon, the children's voices filled the house, until the swelling song of evening crickets signaled that it was time to go home. The children filed out one by one, the eldest holding a kerosene lantern as they traipsed down the long driveway, under the stars, toward home.

I wandered outside one morning to find Mr. and Mrs. Singh asleep on the terrace in side-by-side cots, draped in mosquito nets. "There's really nothing like sleeping under the moon," said Ajay, who grew up dreaming al fresco. I knew what he meant. At Mokimpur, the stars were my nightlight, the crickets my lullaby, and in the morning the nesting doves woke me up with their cooing. The greatest part about sleeping outside was that you moved with the rhythm of the earth.

I had not experienced a place in which I felt safe enough to sleep without walls. I grew up in Los Angeles, after all, where such legends as the Nightstalker, who sneaked into people's houses in the middle of the night, abounded. I'd never had the luxury of sleeping with the doors or windows flung wide open. Sleep, one's most vulnerable state, was something done under lock and key and a high-tech alarm system. But in Mokimpur, sleeping outdoors brought about a state of bliss in the Singhs, as if they'd become children again. They always woke up serene and rested.

Mostly, I loved waking up at dawn and going for a sunrise walk in the fields and alongside the river. The farming families were just arriving at the mango and guava groves. They sang morning songs, sometimes rising into harmony, as they stuffed sacks full of fruit, with the village birds perched in the trees, whistling alongside.

Had Ajay managed to capture that elusive moment, that shift from darkness to dawn, I wondered? And what about all the other moments of the past few weeks—the unveiling of my courtyard, Choti Diwali, my Indian feast, and yes, even the palace theft. I wanted to capture it all and keep it within me somehow.

We were leaving in a couple of days to return to Hong Kong, where we'd spend the next month packing up the flat—and our entire life—for a big, seven-thousand-mile relocation to Los Angeles. Yes, it was true. We had decided to move back to my hometown. As much as we loved living in Hong Kong, I think we both realized it would never be home for us. As we were planning the future, we decided we needed to be someplace where we could build our lives, not just enjoy the moment. Ajay and I were leaving *Asiaweek*. I had already accepted another job at Time Inc. as an entertainment correspondent for *People* magazine. Our days in Los Angeles would be as frenetic as our life in Hong Kong, a blur of Hollywood premiers, parties, and paparazzi. I felt excited about this new future in my hometown, but profoundly sad about leaving Asia, too. Yet Mokimpur would stay with us—not only in the form of the village pottery and antique paisley tablecloths Mrs. Singh had given us. As we settled into our new American life, I would try to hold on to the village's simplicity, its graceful pace and its stark beauty.

Yes, Mokimpur existed on the other side of the world. But the more time I spent here, the more I felt like it was the right side.

<+ 22 +>

The Garden of Truth

And then my whole world turned upside down.

It was July, and I had started the process of moving home. I was in New York meeting my soon-to-be bosses at *People* and staying with a friend whose parents owned an entire apartment block on the Upper West Side. She was away for the weekend, and I hung out in her sun-filled flat, thoroughly enjoying being back in America. Then the phone rang; it was Ajay, calling from Hong Kong, where he would stay for the next few weeks wrapping up our flat. His voice sounded thin and anxious.

"Your sister called from Los Angeles. She said it's an emergency. You need to call her right away."

I hung up and dialed my mother. My younger brother Brian, who lived thirty miles across town, answered. "Ali, you might want to sit down. Take a deep breath. Ba passed away." I sat there, silent. My father was dead. "It happened earlier this afternoon," Brian said. "Ba was sitting in front of the television, watching football." I shrieked and clutched my hands to my face. My Ba. He was gone.

At that moment, all I could think about was the sweet passages—the teddy bears he bought from a street-corner vendor and toted home for us, the weekend hikes up an Angeles Crest trail with all six kids following behind, the fresh summer corn he barbecued for us in the backyard. In that moment, all the crazed middle-of-the night family meetings, the taunts, the forgotten birthdays—they all faded away.

I had just been home two days ago and seen my father for the first time in eighteen months. In his worn pajamas, the flannel fabric stripes faded into mere suggestions of a pattern, he was mumbling about Disneyland, lower Baja, Temple City, and all the other places he believed he owned. Not much had changed since the last time I'd seen him. At least not to me. But at one point, he turned to me and said, "The doctor says my heart's not working properly. Soon you might not have a Ba anymore."

I said nothing. Nothing. Not knowing how to talk to someone who couldn't hear me, who had never really heard me, who often made me feel as though my words didn't matter. I turned and headed back to my childhood bedroom. He shuffled across the living room to his end of the house.

"You know, at least it happened this way," Brian said. He cleared his throat, and I could tell he was trying to hold himself together, too. "He died in peace. He died in his favorite chair. He died at home."

And so, just as I moved back to the States, we buried my father. At Rose Hills Memorial Park, we bought him a seven-by-four plot of land in the Garden of Truth. It had a sweeping view of the verdant valley below, and extraordinary feng shui, or so the cemetery salesman assured us.

As the writer of the family, I gave the eulogy. To an audience of black-suited and black-dressed Chinese relatives—including his brothers and sister—I spoke about my father's life: about the home he had labored to build in America for his wife and six kids, the places he loved and laid claim to throughout his life, and the castles in the sky he was now free to create, untethered as he was now from the earth.

For a while after the funeral, I thought about Ba and considered the life I had chosen. I had spent eight years away, only to come home to my father's death. Why hadn't I returned sooner and set up a home—a grand and beautiful house—that would have made him proud? When my father died, all he knew about my life was that I was moving back from Hong Kong and had signed a lease on an apartment—a lowly rental, even if it was in Beverly Hills. Why had I not told him about Ajay's family manor? Maybe that would have sent him off in peace, knowing at least one of his children had actually snagged a palace, after all.

Then my heart made a decision. For the time being, I was done with adventure and faraway places. I wanted to be in Los Angeles, where sunny skies and swaying palms graced my seamless days. Where I could meet my family for dim sum, Christmas, and birthdays. Where I could be with the brothers and sisters who knew me more thoroughly than anyone from Hong Kong society ever could. I wanted to be next to my mother, arranging bok choy and rice on her chipped plates, a dinner for one laid out carefully on our old Formica table. I wanted to be there to listen to her as she considered all the regrets she had heaped onto her life. I wanted to be home.

My father's new pied-à-terre was several feet underground.

But his new address was the whole of heaven, the greatest palace in the universe. For that moment, I let go of my dream of owning castles and manors.

Ajay asked me if I wanted to postpone our wedding, which we had finally scheduled for October of that year. I considered the idea but ultimately said no. The death of my father had brought to light for me what home meant—as did the joyful, quiet weeks I had spent with Ajay's family at Mokimpur. At that moment in my life, I did not need any fancy manors. What I wanted was to build myself a Memory Palace, a place to hold my happy recollections of a complicated past. What I needed was to surround myself with people who loved me, and with people I loved, people with whom I shared a vivid and never-ending history. My family, Ajay, and yes, even the Singhs—they had become my home, the one thing I needed. At least for now.

<+ 23 +>

The Singhs in America

After my father's death, we decided to stay Los Angeles-bound for a while. My mother, now alone after forty-eight years of marriage, needed us near. What's more, my job at *People* kept me tied to the city's studios, film industry fetes, and nightly red carpet blitzes. Mokimpur and India started to feel like an abstraction.

But soon Mokimpur would be coming to us, in a sense. Ajay and I had begun to plan our wedding in earnest; we set the date for October 2—Gandhi's birthday. Mr. and Mrs. Singh, Uncle Ram, Karan, Kamala, Anusha, and Ajay's good friends Sanjay and Shumita all told us that they would travel across the dozen or so time zones to witness our nuptials.

Knowing we could not hold our wedding at Mokimpur—tepid mug bath, anyone?—we struggled to find the right venue, Ba's obsession with grand houses forever echoing in my head. We stumbled upon a 1920s Moroccan-style hotel in the California desert, and Ajay and I knew we had found the place. Korakia, set at the foothills of the sculptural San Jacinto Mountains—a

Cubist landscape come to life—echoed Mokimpur's stark beauty. It also had a distinguished history: The villa, it was rumored, had once played host to Winston Churchill (who painted watercolors in the bougainvillea-strewn courtyard) and a stable of silent-screen stars. But unlike Mokimpur—and this was crucial to our hundred international guests—the villa had a lovely stone swimming pool, room service, Egyptian-cotton linens, and an air-conditioned Starbucks down the street.

Getting my friends and family there would be easy: Save for one Germany-based sister, the Gees lived around Los Angeles, and my friends happily agreed to fly in from Hong Kong, London, Paris, San Francisco, and New York. But how in the world would we transport the Singhs and Ajay's Indian friends halfway around the planet? I found out then that Mr. and Mrs. Singh had never stepped outside of India. They didn't even have passports.

For the next few months, Ajay in L.A. and his brother Karan in Delhi tussled with the thorny passport issue. Indian bureaucracy is a thousand-headed snake, and there was a good possibility that the Singhs' passports might not arrive until after the wedding—unless the family resorted to more aggressive measures. The good news: There were few bureaucratic Indians who didn't love a nice bribe. So Karan managed to procure the documents with a monetary "gift" and a dozen boxes of Indian sweets to a turbaned "fixer" who had an in with the officers at the consulate.

Then came the issue of money. Who was going to pay for Ajay's family and their friends? As I soon discovered, India custom dictates that the person who throws the wedding is the one who foots the bills, including transportation for out-of-town guests. Besides, the Singhs could hardly afford air passage, not even if they sold the farm's oxen and goats. We were already maxing out just paying for floral bouquets and wedding location fees. How could we also pay for so many thirteen-thousand-mile flights across the Pacific? We had no more art to sell. We had no more anything to sell. We did have one thing, though: During our two-year relationship, Ajay and I had managed to squirrel away a small nest egg, a cache I had hoped to use as a down payment on a house of our own.

When I talked to my mother about the predicament, she said, "Just think about it: How will you feel after the wedding if Ajay's parents don't come?" A huge sadness washed over me. I realized then that Mr. and Mrs. Singh were not just Ajay's parents; they had become my relatives as well.

I had grown fond of their austere, proud ways, which I now attributed to the failed aristocracy of India. Whenever Mrs. Singh shopped the dusty provincial villages that punctuated the fields around the haveli, she brought back the most beautiful finds: marble candlestick holders that had been carved by an eighty-year-old craftsman, pretty beads strung on a gold thread, the most exquisite filigreed silver jewelry—all for a meager collection of rupees. After displaying her treasures, she often asked Ajay if she could please, please give them to Alison. Even if he said no, that she should keep them for Mokimpur, I would find the pieces later in my suitcases, carefully wrapped for the long journey.

We would find a way to bring the Singhs to America. We simply had to.

Ajay and I decided to forgo the wedding photographer and videographer and enlisted a photojournalist friend and my brother

Brian and his Panasonic instead. I wired two thousand dollars to Karan's Delhi account, and he bought the Air India tickets for us. The Singhs were coming to America!

✦

While they were excited about their American adventure, Mr. and Mrs. Singh were hardly going to renounce their Indian citizenship for American passports. They were quintessentially Indian. They had no idea what cultural shock faced them on these shores.

First, there was the food. Imagine having eaten Indian food for every single meal, three times a day, for some sixty-five years, and suddenly being asked to dine on steak, cheese sandwiches, stuffed mushrooms, iceberg lettuce, and rice pilaf—staples that might sound good to an average American but were unbearably bland to any Indian.

I noticed early on that Mrs. Singh hardly ate when she was in America. At first, I thought she was dieting to look good for our wedding. But then I realized that whenever we sat down at a Western restaurant, she looked sullen and, well, hungry.

One night, she finally spoke up. I had managed to use my *People* muscle to book us a highly coveted patio table at the Ivy, where the paparazzi lined the sidewalk each night. She ordered a thirty-five-dollar plate of rustic fried chicken, took one bite, and shook her head. "It looks exactly like chicken *pakora*," she remarked as she inspected a drumstick, her voice a mere whisper, "but it is virtually tasteless." Luckily, we knew just the fix. For the rest of her two-week visit, we ran open tabs at India Sweets & Spices, Delhi Deli, and Chutney's.

Food was not the only issue. We also found our share of in-
trigue in matters sartorial. I had a feeling that the Singhs' im-
pression of America was formed in part by watching cable reruns
of *Dynasty*, because they brought only their most regal finery.
When my sister invited them to a casual barbecue in her backyard, Mrs. Singh turned up wearing a clattering armload of gold
jewelry and a sari so shiny it could blind a man at forty paces.
Picking their way across my sister's backyard, replete with three
pet cats, barbecue fumes, and a noisy Gee game of catch in progress, the Singhs truly looked like a god and goddess in ruins.

I admired their innate elegance—such a change from my
mother's nursery school teacher uniform of baggy jeans and college sweatshirts—but the next day I took them to Target to shop
for their own casual attire. Turned out they loved shopping for
the new duds but decided to "save" them instead for a debut in
India.

And how could we not take them to Disneyland? The Singhs
had heard stories about the Magic Kingdom for decades, and
when we announced we'd be spending the day there, they both
practically jumped up and down. Only what to wear? Those new
jeans and sweatshirts, perhaps? No, they were already neatly
packed away in their suitcases with other souvenirs of American
life.

Mr. Singh brought his elaborate forty-five-year-old kurta
from his own wedding to wear for our ceremony at Korakia. But
when he heard we were going to meet Mickey Mouse, he put it
on, exclaiming, "This is a very special occasion. It calls for a very
special outfit." Mrs. Singh donned another stunning sari, and
while wandering the park amid Docker-wearing families from
Iowa and Kansas, the couple looked like two peacocks amid a

field of pigeons. As the Singhs swanned past the line at It's a Small World, I heard one American man joke to his wife, "Debbie, take a look at those two. Is there some new India ride we haven't heard about?" Ajay and I exchanged glances and laughed quietly, our heads turned away from the Singhs. I felt proud of the beauty and dignity they brought to every landscape—even if it was Adventureland. Without saying a word, Ajay and I both realized we would never forget these moments.

For the Singhs, Disneyland was nothing less than a miracle of technology, a feast of creativity and riches—in short, a reflection of the West's greatness. As we cruised past ceramic hippos and felt-covered monkeys on the Jungle Cruise, Mrs. Singh leaned over to Ajay and gravely whispered, "They're real, aren't they?" When Ajay broke the news that they were indeed faux, she shuddered with disbelief.

We took them on Space Mountain—and instantly realized it was a serious error of judgment. As soon as the bobsled carts started moving along the track, Mr. Singh tried to stand up and escape. Straining his seat belt, he started shouting, "Slow, please! Slow!"

The two of them were like children again, gazing at the top of Sleeping Beauty's Castle, soaking up the mild autumn sun on the deck of Mark Twain's Riverboat, and marveling at a dozen exuberant Dumbos soaring through the sky. We wound up the day with a visit to the Mad Hatter's hat shop. Mrs. Singh put on Goofy's hat, Mr. Singh donned a wizard's cap, and Ajay a pair of Mouseketeer ears. I gathered the giddy trio together and took a few snaps, Mrs. Singh blushing crimson.

When I handed the developed pictures to Mrs. Singh the next day, she clapped in delight, her face lighting up in a state of bliss. "We will have to frame this and hang it in the trophy room," she said. She glanced at the Mad Hatter photo again. "But Alison," she said, shaking her head. "This won't do for Mokimpur." She handed the photo back to me. "We need one of the whole family. We need one with you."

◄◄ 24 ►►

The Wedding

A week before the wedding Karan called from Delhi to say that he and Kamala and Anusha would not be coming after all. Ajay slammed the phone down before he even heard an explanation. The telegram from Sanjay, Ajay's old friend from their hunting and bodybuilding days in Delhi, gave us the same sad news. America was just too far. Ajay had expected Sanjay to let loose a volley of rifle shots in the air at the exact moment we exchanged "I do's" at Korakia—a beloved Indian tradition (even though I told him that was illegal in America). Now there would be no rifle fire and precious few Indians. I was disappointed for Ajay. But what could we do?

On the morning of the wedding, my girlfriends Lisa, Susan, and Jane helped me lace up my dress, a beautiful butter yellow halter-necked gown cut from beaded Indian fabric. They pinned the veil in my hair and rouged my lips. My mother clasped around my neck the antique jade necklace Yeh Yeh had bestowed upon me the day I was born. As a finishing touch, I slipped

The Wedding

the heavy 24-karat gold bangles from Mrs. Singh onto my left wrist.

My mother, sheathed in a peacock-blue dress and wrapped in an elaborate silk shawl I had brought her from India, would walk with me down the aisle. After what seemed like hours of blow-drying, primping, and polishing, my brother Brian came up to me and said, "Okay, the crowds are getting restless. It's time to start the show."

Preparing for the wedding, I had visited Korakia many times. Still, I could not believe how luscious the bougainvillea-and-lily-strewn gardens were leading up to the altar. My elder brother, Peter, dressed in a royal blue kurta, held a framed portrait of my father. Ajay, dressed in an embroidered linen coat, a red turban, and a pair of curly-toed red shoes, caught sight of me and beamed across the garden.

He told me later that as I walked toward him I was giggling all the way down the aisle. "To see you in your dress, looking like a Chinese princess, laughing and so happy, it was just like a fairy tale."

Our reception took place in Korakia's courtyard, over which my friends Clive and Kevin strung hundreds of red silk lanterns that glowed from the light of votive candles. My best buddies from Hong Kong, Katherine and Luc, also journalists, got up to make a speech in tandem. They told the story—now Hong Kong legend—of how Ajay and Alison had chanced to meet, crossing continents and cultures to do so. Then, to my great surprise, they read from our first letters to each other. "I gave them to Katherine," said Ajay, squeezing my hand, which now sparkled with a ruby, sapphire, and diamond ring.

That night, after the wedding, as my family and my closest friends slept in the lovely little rooms at Korakia, I found myself replaying the day's events in my mind: Mrs. Singh merrily feasting on the Moroccan chicken and rice—not an Indian curry in sight. Mr. Singh disco dancing with my old friend Jeri, a vivacious blonde from San Francisco. Sanjay phoning Ajay from New Delhi, to fire ten rifle shots into the air above the Indian capital while Ajay listened from thirteen thousand miles away.

It must have been 3 A.M. when I slipped out of bed and snuck into the courtyard where our wedding dinner was held. The tables were empty, the courtyard silent, but I could still imagine the laughter and music from the evening's fete. Someone had forgotten to put the lanterns out and, miraculously, their votives stayed lit. The lanterns swayed in the light breeze, each one of them glowing like a small benevolent moon. As I sat there alone under the stars, I realized it all really had been like a fairy tale.

A few days later, we took the Singhs to the airport for their long journey home. Mrs. Singh—now officially "Mom"—and I sat in twin bubbles of silence in the backseat. Two weeks of All Wedding, All the Time had left me drained, blank. She, I realize now, was a swell of emotions. The adventure of America had filled her with happy, dazzling memories and a whole new universe of relatives—the Gees.

We said our good-byes at the immigration queue, and the stoic Mrs. Singh suddenly grabbed Ajay and me and started gushing hot tears.

"We've had a wonderful time, Alison, truly we did," she said, dabbing her eyes. "I have never been to a place like America. But now I realize it was our fate to come here, to be part of your family. Take good care of Aju. Always remember, he is very far from home. And never forget us. Never forget us and Mokimpur."

With that, they were gone.

⤙ 25 ⤚

At Last, the Taj

Two days after the Singhs left America, Ajay and I jetted off to Italy. No, we hadn't just won the lottery or cashed out our 401(k)s (all of which would have gotten us a nice trip to Sacramento and back). But by pooling wedding gift money and applying for a credit card with a three-thousand-dollar limit—I know, I know, not the way to start a marriage!—we were able to go on a honeymoon fit for a minor royal.

Of course, we were lured to Tuscany by the promise of amazing pasta, authentic gelatos, sultry evenings, and after-dinner walks along the shadows of the Coliseum. But something else made our Italian journey a requisite choice. My dear Hong Kong friend Anastasia had given us the most astounding gift: a weeklong stay in her father's rambling hundred-year-old villa near Pisa. The housekeeper, Mia Cappelli, was a neighbor who lived down the street, and she made the most delectable hand-formed gnocchi. Most intriguing about Mia was that during her younger years she had been the lady-in-waiting for an Italian princess.

Even though the delightful Tuscan villages beckoned us to come out and play, Ajay and I spent many afternoons lounging around the villa, wondering if we could ever manage a life like this, even though we knew that for one month a year in India we already had a quasi-royal life with a big rambling house and grounds that stretched out into the horizon. During the other eleven months of the year, we would be busting our rear ends at the MacBook churning out stories and scrambling to cover our car payments and the rent on our one-bedroom apartment.

When we got back to America, we settled in for a stretch of hard work (we had that three-thousand-dollar credit card bill to pay). When we finally looked up, two years had passed and we had not so much as seen a Bollywood film. It was then we decided it was time to head eastward—to Mokimpur and the Singhs.

During our long absence from India, we kept in touch with Ajay's family by sending them our published stories. When I began working at *People,* I changed my byline to Alison Singh Gee—and I wondered if the Singhs noticed this small but significant shift. As we traveled to Delhi on Cathay Pacific, I considered how my place in Ajay's family would evolve.

Mr. and Mrs. Singh picked us up at Indira Gandhi Airport and made it immediately clear our relationship had changed. First of all, they called me "Ali," my childhood nickname. I called them "Mom" and "Dad," even though I found myself blushing—and coughing awkwardly—for at least the first week of our trip.

The new labeling created a feeling that our destinies were now joined forever.

✦

There were other signs that things were shifting. First of all, I was no longer exempt from kitchen duty. Just like Kamala, I was expected to report to the counter an hour before lunch to share in the chopping, grinding, and stirring—the rhythm of domestic India. "Mom" then asked me along on a trip to the pottery village; she wanted my advice on which new platters she should buy for the haveli.

Kamala and I took long afternoon walks together under the scholar trees, chatting about the brothers we had married, our fathers, our siblings, and our career dreams. I still gave her a wide berth whenever she waved her laser-sharp talons. At least I no longer felt she was shooting me the evil eye every time I sat down at the dinner table.

Then came the real proof that that the cold war between the Singhs and me had melted. Practically the moment Ajay left me alone with Mom and Kamala, they cornered me.

"So," cooed Kamala, "when are we getting to work on this?" She made a rocking motion with her arms. I nearly spat out my chai, but the inquiry left me feeling that my contribution to the Singh gene pool was not such an unpalatable prospect, after all.

My official status as a clan member had another curious effect. I began to view Mokimpur with possessive eyes. I longed to paint our chambers—yes, Ajay and I now shared a bedroom—a vivid Indian-hued pink, a move I would not have dared entertain before marrying Ajay. I went to Fabindia, the country's answer to Pottery Barn, and bought beautiful Indian linens and bedcovers for our bedroom. I dragged Ajay out to Chandni Chowk, the famous bazaar in Old Delhi, where we scrounged for antiques and haggled with turbaned shopkeepers. They chewed betel leaf, their lips and fingertips stained a deep persimmon red, and looked me up and down for signs of foreignness. But clever me had borrowed a salwar kameez and a gold bindi from Kamala, and I let Ajay handle all the bargaining.

Still, I found these reconnaissance missions to be grand adventures in themselves. We found intricately carved wooden tables for twenty-three dollars each, wood-and-wicker planter's chairs like those from the days of the British Raj, and antique prints of finely garbed maharajas and maharanis parading through palace grounds on elephant back.

To bring a touch of my own world to Mokimpur, I commissioned a copy of a Le Corbusier chaise lounge in pony hair from an artisan in Delhi. We placed it in front of the bedroom's French windows, near the balcony. Once we arranged all our new treasures in our rooms, Mom came in for a look. "My dear Ali," she said, "you really do have an eye. Why don't you do the same for my bedroom?" I raised my eyebrows in disbelief and sputtered, "Uh, sure, anytime."

Once Ajay left the room, Mom pulled me onto the balcony and whispered, "You've done well, but don't you think you forgot something? Maybe you should go back to Chandni Chowk for a crib." Mom being Mrs. Singh, she just couldn't leave well enough alone.

It was during this visit to India that Ajay promised he would make my childhood dream come true: We would finally visit the Taj Mahal.

"Really?" I asked, my mouth agape. "We're actually going this time?"

"Our train tickets are booked for tomorrow afternoon. San-jay's butler also reserved us a suite at the Taj View Hotel."

That night, I packed my suitcases carefully, arranging my dresses and shoes just so. Tomorrow we would realize my decades-old fantasy, and there would be no end to the photo op-portunities. Problem was, all of my clothes looked somehow off—ill-fitting or something. I couldn't quite figure it out. Maybe it was the endless servings of Hoti Lal's irresistible curries or the lack of my daily Tae Bo on holiday, but all my little sundresses seemed to pucker at the waist. I finally settled on a spaghetti-strapped dress for our first glimpse of the Taj at dawn, and a pink salwar kameez for our second visit at dusk.

We arrived in Agra in the early evening, too late to catch a glimpse from the streets of the Taj's magical white domes. That was just fine by me. I wanted to be surprised by the sight of the monument during our first visit the next morning.

I awoke at dawn and looked at the date on Ajay's watch. I got out of bed and stood in the middle of the hotel room, pondering what to do next. I headed to the suitcase and pulled out a preg-nancy test—just in case. Two minutes later, I let out a yelp from the bathroom.

"What happened?" Ajay called, half-awake. I emerged from the bathroom, as radiant, I imagine, as a nuclear explosion. "Guess who's having a baby?" I said, shaking my head and rais-ing my hands to the sky.

With the news of a child now joining us, our lives shifted again—both of us felt it instantly. Ajay and I were both thrilled and terrified. As it turned out, our trip to the Taj would inspire the same extreme spectrum of feelings.

On the way to the mausoleum, my cheeks were flushed with optimism—today I was making two long-held dreams come true. But once our Ambassador taxi slowed near the monument, my enthusiasm began to wilt. The cab spat us out in front of a gravel road, several blocks away. "You must get out here," the driver said in Hindi to Ajay. "They don't allow gas vehicles too close to the Taj. You have to hire an electric vehicle or ride in a horse and buggy."

The streets were teeming with shoeless boys, each one holding aloft a flimsy trinket for sale. I suddenly saw ahead of us a showdown between first-world money and emerging-world need. Straightening our backs, we flung open the taxi doors and charged outside. We were, after all, in a tourist town in one of the poorest countries on earth. Before we could reach aesthetic nirvana at the Taj, we would have to battle the agents of tacky commercialism that crouched along its path.

"Madam! Madam! Postcard! Postcard!" cried a dozen touts. "Madam! Madam! Look!" Soiled hands shoved trinkets into my face.

"Stop it! I don't want any!" I cried.

We tried to scurry into an electric vehicle, but all were already hired, their passengers gazing at us smugly as they zipped past. The touts moved in closer, waving all manner of Taj Mahal detritus at us.

"Quick, let's ride in this!" Ajay grabbed my hand and hoisted me up into a horse-drawn buggy. I gave it a once-over. Its red plastic seats were covered in dust and Hindi newspapers. Its horse stank. I looked at its wizened old driver—he looked close to rigor mortis. But only the buggy could rescue us from this madding crowd and deliver us to the Taj. So we settled into the seats, collapsing with relief.

The horse began to clip-clop slowly down the road. Just at that moment, Ajay and I both looked up. There was the Taj's iconic dome glowing like a giant pearl in the middle distance. I gasped. I felt as though I had become Alice in Asian Wonderland and had somehow managed to wander into my childhood snow globe.

When we finally arrived at the Taj gates, yet another trial awaited us. Ajay had warned me about Indian tourist spots: They were forever angling to separate foreigners from their cash. Indeed, a sign at the ticket booth window made my heart sink: The ticket price for Indians citizens was twenty rupees (roughly fifty cents); the price for foreigners? Twenty dollars U.S.

"I am not paying that," I said to Ajay. "What a rip-off!"

"Don't worry," he said, holding up a hand and striking a Gandhi-esque pose. "I have a plan."

Ajay approached the man in the booth and said, "Two tickets, please."

The man looked at Ajay and then looked at me. He turned to another ticket seller and said, "Okay, one ticket for this man, who is an Indian. And one for his wife, who is a foreigner."

"My wife is not a foreigner," said Ajay.

"Yes, she is," said the ticket man.

"No, she's not. She's from Nepal."

The man looked at me. I was wearing a red gingham sundress—an almost comical declaration of Americanness—and aviator glasses. But, as I like to think about it now, maybe he sensed that after so many years traveling to India, visiting my

Indian clan and living in our dysfunctional family haveli, I was no mere clueless Western girl. I held my hands up in a *namaste* sign and slowly bowed my head.

"Nepal?" he said, narrowing his eyes and then, finally, nodding. "Well, okay, then. Two Indian tickets."

I could barely suppress a grin as we crossed through the tunnel, past the guards. We two Indians—Ajay and I—were on our way to the Taj.

When we finally stood before the monument, all luminous white marble, I could hardly believe how my life was unfolding—a prince, a palace, and now a baby. We sat on a wall just outside the mausoleum and, in silence, gazed at it, letting its silhouette imprint on our minds.

We spread a thick woven shawl out on the lawn, snacked on *samosas*, popped open a split of Perrier-Jouët, and toasted each other—well, I had a small sip—in the benevolent shadow of the Taj. Parakeets chirped in the trees around us. Children dressed in tiny kurtas chased each other across the grass.

Ajay read aloud from one of his favorite books about India: the American writer Jonah Blank's *Arrow of the Blue-Skinned God*, in which Blank tries to retrace the steps of the Indian god Ram. In an early chapter, when Blank arrives at the Taj, he meets an Indian man, the elderly Mr. Krishnan, who has visited the mausoleum at least once a week for the past seventy years. The man explains to the writer that he and his wife used to sit by a stone fountain in the shade, and the two would snack on *samosas* she had made especially for their afternoons together.

"She was always at her loveliest in the light reflected off the walls of the Taj," Mr. Krishnan told Blank. Even though his wife had been dead for two decades, he continued to visit the grounds by himself—at first every day, but once admission began to be charged he could afford to come only on Fridays, when the fee was waived for Indians. "When I sit by the fountain and shut my eyes," Mr. Krishnan sighed, "I can still taste the *samosas*."

Ajay closed the book and we looked at each other. Our *samosa* tiffin was now empty save for a few crumbs. "I'll always remember that story," I said, as we packed up our things and folded up the shawl. I reached for his hand, and we wandered closer to the mausoleum.

It was late afternoon now, and the winter light had softened the Taj's silhouette into a silver glow. "I know I sound like a Hallmark card," I said to Ajay, "but this place is even more beautiful than I imagined."

"Well, I guess I should thank you for forcing me back," Ajay said, suddenly shy. "It's true. It really is stunning. There's a magic here. I take back all the mean things I said about it." He raised the champagne split to his lips and took a swig. "Maybe it's the news that our baby is coming, but I don't think I've ever been to a more enchanting place." As he said it, he sounded just like a prince to me.

Months later, when I had thought deeply about our trip to the Taj, I realized that the journey was a mirror of my entire Indian experience. I had to deal with a whole lot of ugly stuff before I was able to see the beauty of the country.

✷

The next evening, we took a train back to Mokimpur. As the train clickety-clacked beneath us, both of us sat in a pregnant—so to speak—silence. Ajay was absorbed in his secondhand book on Taj semiotics; I was consumed with thoughts just as meaningful: those of the coming baby.

We arrived at the haveli close to midnight. The generator was quiet, and most of the rooms were dark. We tiptoed through the house and settled into bed. "I guess we'll share the good news tomorrow," I said to Ajay as we drifted off to sleep.

I awoke the next morning to find Ajay's side of the bed empty. He must have gone for a morning walk through the fields, I thought, as I noticed the sunlight streaming through the French doors. I reached for the shahtoosh on the nightstand, wrapped it around my neck, and stretched my arms out. It was going to be a glorious day.

And then came the knock on the door. "Ali?" called the voice. It was Mrs. Singh, I mean Mom. "Ah-ja," she said, waving her hand. "Come. Let's go to the garden."

I quickly threw on a robe and ran after her. "What is it, Mom?" I asked, concerned.

She brought me over to a wall on which sat a seedling sprouting in a large jar. "This is the beginning of a mango tree," she said. "I would like you to plant it in the garden—in honor of the baby." She stepped forward and wrapped her arms around me. She started to sob. "I am so happy for you and Aju."

She gently handed me the jar and allowed her hand to touch mine. Then she led me to a bare patch of land. "You and Ajay and the baby may live in America, but once you plant this, part of you will always be in Mokimpur. As the baby grows, so will this mango tree."

I knelt down with a rusty trowel in my hands, dug a deep hole, and planted the mango seedling into the ground. Then I poured a stream of water onto it and carefully patted the dirt around it, making sure that the seed would take firm root. By the time I was done, my fingers and hands were covered in a sticky, stubborn mud. But the sight didn't make me wince. To my great surprise, it made me smile. This was my family's earth, after all.

Epilogue

As soon as Anais was old enough to tell the difference between a peacock and a loaf of bread, we took her to Mokimpur. Even at fifteen months old, our daughter could sense that this was someplace special. Her eyes widened with surprise as we held a sweet frangipani blossom up to her nose. She cooed as the palace horses trotted past, their shiny black coats gleaming in the sun. She sat in the laps of village girls who tied bows in her hair, looped a purple scarf around her like a sari, and fed her *ladoos* and milk. The mango tree we had planted when we first found out I was pregnant was now a three-foot-tall treeling.

It was clear from the look of quiet contentment on Ajay's face that, after so many months in America, he was thrilled to be home. So was I. Something in my soul settled as soon as we walked through Mokimpur's gardens and into the house with our suitcases. I didn't even mind the winter rains.

It was December, and the skies were pouring out their souls. From the palace windows, we watched the rain fall in slanted sheets, trickling through the tree branches and on to the court-yard tiles, making a rhythmic music like that of a gamelan.

For me, rain in America always invoked the memory of some sort of urban misery—a bad commute, a ruined hairstyle, soiled shoes. In Mokimpur, the rain was like music, like diamonds, like white wine from the sky. With it came relief from a long year of sun, and a freshness that renewed the trees, the animals, and the aching, parched land itself. It also brought out the grate-ful peacocks and peahens, which danced wildly in the court-yards as the drops of rain fell onto their heads and cleansed their feathers.

I remembered the first time I saw peacocks in Mokimpur streaking the air as they glided from the trees. Back then I had no idea peacocks could fly. I thought about how much I had changed since I first visited the palace—how I'd gone from pam-pered city girl and clueless tourist in India to wife and mother who felt at peace singing lullabies in Hindi to her daughter.

"I love the rain," Ajay said, placing an arm around Anais and me. The baby cried out and pointed to the courtyard. Just for a moment, I carried her out under the pouring sky. We stretched out our hands and let the rain run down our arms and our faces. It was clear that, like the peacocks, we loved the rain, too.

Acknowledgments

I am deeply grateful to the people who helped to bring this book to life. To paraphrase Proust, you are the charming gardeners who made the soul of *Where the Peacocks Sing* blossom. Many of you appear in this book, and many of you are hovering just outside the pages—I have felt your presence throughout. For that, I offer my love and appreciation.

Eternal thanks to the Singh family, for allowing me to mine four generations of family history. Thank you for sitting through all those awkward interview sessions at the haveli, even when you wanted to turn around and say, "Enough!"

Gratitude to my mother, who spent many dinners in Los Angeles enduring endless probing about her early life with my father, and to my younger brother Brian and my other siblings, who gave me permission—and even shared my excitement—in telling my story.

To Brettne Bloom, who believed in me and Mokimpur from that very first e-mail. You took my just-forming ideas and fantastical images of an Indian palace and stood by me, brainstorming,

Acknowledgments

line editing, and sharing my dream, as I worked each anecdote and burning moment into a book. Without you as my champion, *Peacocks* would not exist. I am beyond fortunate to have found you.

To my phenomenal editor, Nichole Argyres, who graciously gave me the time (and we're talking years), trust, and love I needed to write this first opus, and then poured her brilliance and passion into transforming it into the finest book it could be. Heartfelt thanks also to Laura Chasen, who lavished each draft of my manuscript with attention and intelligence (and who put up with many blown deadlines).

To the Squaw Valley Community of Writers, the coolest, funniest group of scribes around. Brett Hall Jones, Lisa Alvarez, Alev Croutier, and James and Jeanne Houston, you've shown me what it means to be a writer through your wit, creativity, hard work, and generosity.

My special thanks to Amy Tan, who, from the first time I walked into her San Francisco apartment as a *People* reporter, showed me the writer's life I then always envisioned for myself. If anyone has represented for me what it means to be an artist and a truly admirable person, it's Amy.

To the UCLA Extension Writers Program—Linda Venis, Mae Respicio, and the wonderful staff who have supported my teaching throughout these many years. Further thanks to all my magical UCLA instructors, Samantha Dunn and Bruce Bauman and Dinah Lenney—you helped me write my book scene by scene.

To my treasured author friends Kavita Daswani, Kim Sunee, Joelle Fraser, and Meghan Ward, who have given me so much of their time and shared their artistry and perspective with me.

Acknowledgments

To my alma mater, Scripps College. President Lori Bettison-Varga, Professor Cheryl Walker, Adrienne Gibson, and all my Camp Scripps friends—thank you for your endless support of my work.

To all my Eastside Writers—each one of you gives me as much as I hope I give you. Write on, brave scribes!

And most of all, to Ajay and Anais, who endured five years of Saturday afternoons without me while I sat on the back patio at the Coffee Table, channeling the spirits and visions floating around a broken-down palace in the wheat fields.

Author's Note

To write this book I called upon my journals, letters, and e-mails, as well as relied on interviews with my family members, friends, the Singh family, and, most importantly, my husband, Ajay. Some of the events might be out of sequence or compressed, and I changed names and identifying details in the case of a number of characters.

I am certain that many people in my life would have told this story differently. But my desire was to recall the emotional truth of this period of my life—along with its drama, wonder, and humor. I believe my memories, however subjective and faulty, have their own story to tell.

Most of my friends who have heard my story say it's just like a fairy tale. I have to agree. And on good days, I tell them I still feel as though I'm living that fairy tale.